Plessy v. Ferguson

**Recent Titles in
Landmarks of the American Mosaic**

Plessy v. Ferguson

Thomas J. Davis

Landmarks of the American Mosaic

GREENWOOD

AN IMPRINT OF ABC-CLIO, LLC
Santa Barbara, California • Denver, Colorado • Oxford, England

Library of Congress Cataloging-in-Publication Data

Davis, Thomas J. (Thomas Joseph)
  Plessy v. Ferguson / Thomas J. Davis.
    p. cm. — (Landmarks of the American mosaic)
  Includes bibliographical references and index.
    ISBN 978–0–313–39187–3 (hardback) — ISBN 978–0–313–39188–0 (ebook)
1. Plessy, Homer Adolph—Trials, litigation, etc. 2. Segregation in transportation—
Law and legislation—Louisiana—History. 3. Segregation—Law and legislation—
United States—History. 4. United States—Race relations—History. I. Title. II. Title:
Plessy versus Ferguson.
KF223.P56D38   2012
342.7308′73—dc23   2012011735

ISBN: 978–0–313–39187–3
EISBN: 978–0–313–39188–0

16 15 14 13 12   1 2 3 4 5

This book is also available on the World Wide Web as an eBook.
Visit www.abc-clio.com for details.

Greenwood
An Imprint of ABC-CLIO, LLC

ABC-CLIO, LLC
130 Cremona Drive, P.O. Box 1911
Santa Barbara, California 93116-1911

This book is printed on acid-free paper ∞

Manufactured in the United States of America

To "Mag'alene"—there could be no better sister
and
To all my students over the years, who have taught me
more than they ever knew and more than I could
otherwise have ever known.

Contents

Series Foreword

THE LANDMARKS OF THE AMERICAN MOSAIC series comprises individual volumes devoted to exploring an event or development central to this country's multicultural heritage. The topics illuminate the struggles and triumphs of American Indians, African-Americans, Latinos, and Asian Americans, from European contact through the turbulent last half of the twentieth century. The series covers landmark court cases, laws, government programs, civil rights infringements, riots, battles, movements, and more. Written by historians especially for high school students, undergraduates, and general readers, these contents-rich references satisfy thorough research needs and provide a deeper understanding of material that students might only be exposed to in a short section of a textbook or a superficial explanation online.

Each book on a particular topic is a one-stop reference. This series format includes

- Introduction
- Chronology
- Narrative chapters that trace the evolution of the event or topic chronologically
- Biographical profiles of key figures
- Selection of crucial primary documents
- Glossary
- Bibliography
- Index

This landmark series promotes respect for cultural diversity and supports the social studies curriculum by helping students understand multicultural American history.

Preface

PLESSY V. FERGUSON lies as a ruined landmark in U.S. history. The decision of the Supreme Court of the United States on May 18, 1896, found no Constitutional violation in Louisiana's enforced separation of the races in its 1890 Separate Car Act. The decision set in law a rule known as the "separate but equal" doctrine. It let states mandate discrimination on the basis of race, and it let states make violating segregation a crime. The Court's ruling reached far beyond railway coaches, which were the immediate subject in *Plessy v. Ferguson*. The rule stretched from transportation to schools and other public services and facilities such as parks, pools, drinking fountains, and restrooms. The decision figured everywhere, extending tentacles deep inside public and private life throughout the United States. Its effects especially marked the South, where slavery long dominated society.

The Court majority rejected all reasoning that segregation extended slavery in violation of the Thirteenth Amendment. Writing for the 7-to-1 majority, Massachusetts-born Justice Henry Billings Brown professed to see no harm in racial segregation. Justice Brown and his concurring colleagues saw separate-but-equal segregation as treating nonwhites and whites the same. They saw race as a real and reasonable divider of people. They saw no way law could or should change or intervene in race relations. To them, racial segregation reflected what Justice Brown described as "the established usages, customs and traditions of the people." The majority saw its decision as confirming prevailing arrangements and attitudes. It represented no new development.

Plessy v. Ferguson became a symbol of resurgent white supremacy scrambling in the United States to reimpose the bulwarks of its domination breached with the outlawing of slavery in 1865. In many circles, the Supreme Court's decision reflected southern conservative whites' final reascendancy from the ordeal of federally imposed Reconstruction and civil rights enforcement. They had used the terror of vigilante violence with groups such as the Ku Klux Klan to rout and intimidate opposition. With the decision in *Plessy v. Ferguson*, the conservatives gained full legal sanction to segregate and suppress nonwhites.

No storm of protest met or immediately followed the Court decision. It disappointed those supporting Homer Plessy's challenge to Louisiana's law, yet segregation opponents understood they were battling against the tide. They understood also that the decision in *Plessy v. Ferguson* marked neither a beginning nor an ending. The battle against racialism had started long before the case of *Plessy v. Ferguson*, and it would continue long after.

The decision reached far beyond its day. In many ways, the case gained prominence with time. It grew ever more conspicuous as a symbol simultaneously cherished or detested. It became a banner for some and a target for others in continuing contention over state-enforced racial discrimination in the United States. The Court's lone dissenter in *Plessy v. Ferguson* predicted as much.

Justice John Marshall Harlan denounced the majority decision in *Plessy*. "In my opinion," he wrote in the case, "the judgment this day rendered will, in time, prove to be quite as pernicious as the decision made by this tribunal in the Dred Scott case." Chief Justice Roger Brooke Taney's 1857 decision in *Scott v. Sandford* declared that African Americans "whether emancipated or not . . . had no rights or privileges but such as those who held the power and the government might choose to grant them." They remained in perpetual subordination, according to Taney. Such conclusions earned the Dred Scott decision a title as one of the worst in U.S. history and law. It became roundly denounced. The Thirteenth, Fourteenth, and Fifteenth Amendments to the U.S. Constitution repudiated and reversed Taney's doctrine. Justice Harlan predicted *Plessy v. Ferguson* would suffer the same fate, joining the most disgraced ranks—and it did.

The U.S. Supreme Court's decision in *Brown v. Board of Education* on May 17, 1954, signaled the broad dismantling of the separate-but-equal rule *Plessy v. Ferguson* settled as the law of the land. A unanimous Court declared in *Brown* that "in the field of public education, the doctrine of 'separate but equal' has no place. Separate educational facilities are inherently unequal." The Civil Rights Act of 1964 further degraded the *Plessy* ruling. It re-acknowledged constitutional rights against discrimination in public accommodations, facilities, and education. In 1967, the U.S. Supreme Court fully repudiated the Plessy doctrine in *Loving v. Virginia*, when it "reject[ed] the notion that the mere 'equal application' of a statute containing racial classifications is enough to remove the classifications from the Fourteenth Amendment's proscription of all invidious racial discriminations."

But more than segregation lay the foundation for *Plessy v. Ferguson*. For Homer Plessy and the Creole people of color he represented, the case was about who they were. It was a last gasp of a people fighting to save their identity as neither black nor white, the final act in a centuries-long quest to be recognized fully for their multicultural ancestry.

The text that follows explores the case's origins, contents, and contexts. It unfolds the contemporary and historical background from which the case arose. It emphasizes that *Plessy v. Ferguson* arose from more than a historical moment. The issues sprouted over generations. The roots reached back to colonial Louisiana's first generations. The case presented more than a personal matter for Plessy; it presented the case of Plessy's people.

The text opens with a chronology identifying cultural and political events crucial to understanding the people and positions entwined in the case's development. The chapters start with events immediately leading to Homer Plessy's arrest and trial on charges of violating Louisiana's segregationist 1890 Separate Car Act. They then examine colonial Louisiana's racial configuration and trace the hardening racial divide American Negro slavery imposed. They treat generations of controversy over racial discrimination and describe the struggle on the ground surrounding what Louisiana law should be and who should make it. They note the developing constitutional issues of what the state had authority to do in regard to race. They analyze developments in law that produced the 1890 Separate Car Act and that produced the case that became *Plessy v. Ferguson*.

Six brief biographies profile the most prominent persons attached to the case and its outcome. A selection of primary documents allows readers to see for themselves the words of historical records leading to the arguments for and against the Separate Car Act. They describe the background in law and the constitutional arguments for and against Plessy's conviction. Also, they relate the Court's decision and the dissent in the case, as well as contemporary commentary on the result and its lasting significance. A brief glossary explains specialized or unfamiliar terms. The bibliography directs readers to key resources for further research.

I gratefully acknowledge the aid and assistance of the Arizona State University Libraries staff, particularly the Interlibrary Loan Services staff. I thank ABC-CLIO/Greenwood Press's team of editors and production personnel, especially copyeditor Jill Hobbs and Senior Project Manager

N. Magendra Varman at PreMediaGlobal, for their work. I am particularly grateful to editor Wendi Schnaufer for acquiring the work and to editor Kim Kennedy-White for her patience in shepherding the work to print. For their encouragement and support, I delight in recognizing Mary M. Staten, Sonja M. Kernahan, and Brenda M. Brock, who listened attentively and contributed expert research and reading services.

Chronology

1519 Spaniard Alonso Alvarez de Pineda maps the shores of the Gulf of Mexico.

1528 Panfilo de Narváez identifico the mouth of the Mississippi River.

1541 Hernando de Soto explores the Mississippi River.

1699 Pierre Le Moyne d'Iberville establishes Fort Maurepas on the Gulf of Mexico at what comes to be called Biloxi. It develops into France's first permanent settlement in what French explorer René-Robert Cavelier, Sieur de La Salle, in 1682 named "Louisiana" in honor of France's King Louis XIV (r. 1643–1715).

1718 Frenchmen found New Orleans, naming it for France's regent Philippe Duc d'Orelans (1674 1723)

1719 Louisiana colonists began to import increasing numbers of Africans as slaves.

1723 New Orleans (*La Nouvelle-Orléans*), built from 1718 to 1720, supersedes Biloxi, 90 miles to the northeast, as the capital of *La Louisiane française*.

1724 Louisiana imposes a *Code Noir* (Black Code) to restrict blacks' activities and to punish their "insubordinate behavior," whether or not they are slaves.

1751 Sugarcane cultivation begins in Louisiana.

1762–1763 France cedes to Spain all of Louisiana west of the Mississippi, which the Treaty of Paris confirms, while ceding to England lands east of the Mississippi.

1791–1804 A slave revolt in the French West Indies colony of Saint-Domingue sends thousands fleeing to Louisiana and elsewhere in mainland North America; the fighting spreads into a revolutionary war for independence that produces the Republic of Haiti.

1795 Slaves in Pointe Coupee Parish mount an uprising.

1800 Spain cedes Louisiana back to France in the Treaty of San Ildefonso.

1803 The United States completes the Louisiana Purchase from France for $15 million.

1811 Slaves in St. Charles and St. John the Baptist parishes mount the German Coast uprising.

1812 Louisiana becomes the eighteenth state; the steamboat *The New Orleans* becomes the first to navigate the Mississippi River, traveling from Pittsburgh, Pennsylvania, to New Orleans.

1815 U.S. forces under General Andrew Jackson defeat the British in the Battle of New Orleans.

1838 New Orleans hosts it first *Mardi Gras* parade.

1849 Racially segregated public schools are sanctioned in Massachusetts in Chief Justice Lemuel Shaw's decision in *Roberts v. City of Boston*, establishing what would become a precedent for legal segregation.

1861 Louisiana announces its secession from the United States of America.

1862 Homer Plessy is born on March 17 in New Orleans. At the end of April, U.S. Navy Capt. David Farragut captures New Orleans, the Confederacy's largest city. *L'Union* begins publishing as one of the first newspapers people of color produced in the South.

1863 President Abraham Lincoln's Emancipation Proclamation takes effect on January 1, declaring legally free any slave then held in rebel areas. The *New Orleans Tribune* begins publishing as one of the first daily newspapers people of color produced.

1864 Louisiana adopts a new constitution that abolishes slavery.

1865 The Thirteenth Amendment outlaws slavery and involuntary servitude. Congress establishes the Freedmen's Bureau to provide relief food, clothing, shelter, and medical care to refugees and ex-slaves. To extend the white rule in place under slavery, Mississippi in November enacts the post–Civil War era's first Black Code.

1866 Congress overrides President Andrew Johnson's veto to pass the first federal Civil Rights Act to recognize all persons born in the United States as citizens and to declare all such persons entitled to equal rights. A race riot in Tennessee called the Memphis Massacre kills 46 African

Americans and burns 4 churches, 12 schools, and 90 homes. Whites intent on terrorizing blacks form the Ku Klux Klan (KKK) in and around Memphis. In New Orleans, police attack a Republican party gathering of blacks and whites, leaving at least 38 persons dead and 146 wounded.

1867 Congress grants adult black men in the District of Columbia the right to vote. Congress takes over Reconstruction of the ex-Confederate states, directing the U.S. Army to maintain domestic law and order.

1868 The Fourteenth Amendment confirms birthright citizenship and guarantees all persons due process and equal protection of the law. Louisiana adopts a new constitution, providing universal adult male suffrage and declaring that "all persons shall enjoy equal rights and privileges upon any conveyance of a public character." A race riot in Opelousas, Louisiana (the Opelousas Massacre), leaves 200 to 300 blacks dead. The U.S. Congress re-admits Louisiana to representation.

1869 Ebenezer Don Carlos Bassett becomes the first black U.S. diplomat when President Ulysses S. Grant appoints him minister to Haiti.

1870 Republican Hiram R. Revels of Mississippi becomes the first black U.S. senator. The Fifteenth Amendment is ratified to protect the right to vote against discrimination on the basis of "race, color, or previous condition of servitude."

1871 Antiblack terrorism spearheaded by the Ku Klux Klan throughout South Carolina moves President Grant to dispatch U.S. Army units to restore law and order.

1873 On Easter Sunday, white vigilantes attack a black gathering in Colfax, 250 miles northwest of New Orleans, killing more than 100 blacks in what comes to be called the Colfax Massacre. The U.S. Supreme Court's 5–4 decision in *The Slaughterhouse Cases*, which arose in Louisiana, limits the reach of the Thirteenth and Fourteenth Amendments to protect personal rights.

1874 White Leaguers lynch five white Republican officeholders in the so-called Coushatta Massacre at the parish seat of Louisiana's Red River Parish, 300 miles northwest of New Orleans; it prompts more national outrage than the slaughter of blacks at Colfax a year earlier.

1875 Congress passes the Civil Rights Act of 1875 to guarantee all persons equal rights to public accommodations. Blanche Kelso Bruce of Mississippi begins serving what becomes the first and only full six-year term by an African American as a U.S. senator until the 1960s. A race riot in Clinton, Mississippi (the Clinton Massacre), leaves more than 20 blacks dead.

1876 The U.S. Supreme Court's 5–4 decision in *United States v. Cruikshank* allows members of the white militia who perpetrated the 1873 Colfax Massacre to go unprosecuted for their killings and generally weakens federal enforcement to protect blacks' civil rights.

1877 To settle the disputed election of 1876 and become U.S. president, Republican Rutherford B. Hayes makes a deal with southern Democrats to end federal protections of civil rights and withdrawing federal troops from the South.

1881 Tennessee's legislature mandates segregated railroad cars, and 13 states follow suit over the next 26 years: Florida (1887); Mississippi (1888); Texas (1889); Louisiana (1890); Alabama, Kentucky, Arkansas, and Georgia (1891); South Carolina (1898); North Carolina (1899); Virginia (1900); Maryland (1904); and Oklahoma (1907).

1882 Mobs lynch at least 49 blacks across the United States.

1883 The U.S. Supreme Court in the *Civil Rights Cases* declares the equal access to public accommodations provisions of the 1875 Civil Rights Act unconstitutional in restricting discrimination except by state action. A race riot in Danville, Virginia, kills four blacks and unseats the duly elected and racially integrated local government. Across the nation, mobs lynch at least 53 blacks.

1884 Mobs across the nation lynch at least 51 blacks.

1885 Mobs across the nation lynch at least 74 blacks.

1886 White vigilantes in Carrollton, Mississippi (the Carrollton Massacre), kill at least 20 blacks. Mobs across the nation lynch at least 74 blacks.

1887 Mobs across the nation lynch at least 70 blacks.

1888 Mobs across the nation lynch at least 69 blacks.

1889 Mobs across the nation lynch at least 94 blacks.

1890 The American Citizens' Equal Rights Association (ACERA) organizes at a national convention in Washington, D.C., to advocate for civil rights. Ex-slave Timothy Thomas Fortune and other African Americans found the militant National Afro-American League in Chicago, Illinois. Louisiana enacts its Separate Car Act to require racial segregation on railways. Mississippi adopts a new constitution with literacy and other provisions to disfranchise blacks; other states adopt similar measures, following what becomes known as "the Mississippi plan"—South Carolina (1895), Louisiana (1898), North Carolina (1900), Alabama (1901), Virginia (1901), Georgia (1908), and Oklahoma (1910). Mobs across the nation lynch at least 85 blacks.

1891 The Citizens' Committee to Test the Constitutionality of Louisiana's Separate Car Act organizes in New Orleans. A New Orleans mob lynches 11 of 19 Italians charged with murdering Police Chief David C. Hennessy. Mobs across the nation lynch at least 113 blacks.

1892 Louisiana's Supreme Court rules in *Abbott v. Hicks* that the state's 1890 Separate Car Act does not apply to interstate passengers. Homer Plessy gets arrested to further test the Separate Car Act's constitutionality, beginning the case *Ex parte Plessy*. Mobs across the nation lynch at least 161 blacks.

1893 Louisiana's Supreme Court rules in case *Ex parte Plessy* that the 1890 Separate Car Act is constitutional in applying to intrastate passengers such as Homer Plessy. A hurricane kills more than 2,000 persons in southern Louisiana and Mississippi. Mobs across the nation lynch at least 118 blacks.

1894 The Pullman Palace Car Company hires blacks as strike-breakers in Illinois. Louisiana's Edward Douglass White is appointed to the U.S. Supreme Court. Mobs across the nation lynch at least 134 blacks

1895 A race riot in New Orleans kills six blacks; mobs across the nation lynch at least 113 blacks.

1896 The U.S. Supreme Court in *Plessy v. Ferguson* affirms the legitimacy of state-imposed racial segregation in its 7–1 decision upholding Louisiana's 1890 Separate Car Act. Mary Church Terrell and other black women organize the National Association of Colored Women. Mobs across the nation lynch at least 68 blacks.

1898 Louisiana adopts a new constitution with a "Grandfather Clause," a poll tax, and literacy test to disfranchise nonwhites.

1925 Homer Plessy dies on March 1 in New Orleans.

1941 The U.S. Supreme Court decision in *Mitchell v. United States*, 313 U.S. 80 (1941), reverses the Interstate Commerce Commission's dismissal of a complaint against an interstate carrier and rules that compelling a non-white man to ride in a second-class car when he has paid a first-class fare for an interstate journey is illegal discrimination that violates the Interstate Commerce Act.

1946   The U.S. Supreme Court decision in *Morgan v. Virginia*, 328 U.S. 373 (1946), rules Virginia's laws requiring interstate buses in the state to separate white and nonwhite passengers an unconstitutional burden on interstate commerce.

1950   The U.S. Supreme Court decision in *Henderson v. United States*, 339 U.S. 816 (1950), outlaws segregation of reserved tables in railroad dining cars as a violation of the Interstate Commerce Act.

1954   The U.S. Supreme Court limits the reach of the *Plessy v. Ferguson* decision in ruling unanimously in *Brown v. Board of Education* that "in the field of public education, the doctrine of 'separate but equal' has no place. Separate educational facilities are inherently unequal."

1955   The Interstate Commerce Commission ruling in *Keys v. Carolina Coach Company* outlaws segregation on interstate buses.

1960   The U.S. Supreme Court decision in *Boynton v. Virginia*, 364 U.S. 454 (1960), upholds the Interstate Commerce Commission's ban on racial segregation in interstate transportation, including buses and terminals servicing such buses.

1964   The Civil Rights Act of 1964 outlaws racial segregation and many other forms of discrimination.

1967   The U.S. Supreme Court's unanimous decision in *Loving v. Virginia* invalidates the reasoning in the 1896 *Plessy v. Ferguson* decision, ruling "racial classifications . . . directly subversive of the principle of equality at the heart of the Fourteenth Amendment."

2009   Descendents of Homer A. Plessy and Judge John Ferguson join in New Orleans to create the Plessy and Ferguson Foundation for Education and Reconciliation to advance teaching of history and significance of civil rights.

ONE

The Arrest: Plessy's Ticket and Ride

HOMER PLESSY bought a train ticket on Tuesday, June 7, 1892. He paid first-class passage from New Orleans to Covington, Louisiana. The straight-line distance ran about 40 miles, but no route then took that path. Lake Pontchartrain blocked the way. Its 630 square miles lay as the second-largest U.S. saltwater lake, after Utah's Great Salt Lake.

Plessy's scheduled train route skirted the east end of the lake's uneven 40-mile length and 24-mile width. The track followed an arc moving east, then north, and west. It ran on a local 70-mile spur. Vacationers and weekend excursioners on bargain one-dollar trips made the route popular as they flocked seasonally along it to St. Tammany benches across the lake north of New Orleans.

Covington sat on Pontchartrain's north shore as a terminus for the East Louisiana Railroad (ELR). It was the St. Tammany Parish seat. Elsewhere in the United States, it would have been the county seat, but Louisiana had no counties. Its French and Spanish roots spread Louisiana into parishes, which served as the state's basic government units. They had nothing to do with churches. They were civil subdivisions. New Orleans sat in Orleans Parish. In fact, the city and parish became coterminous.

Plessy saw none of the Pontchartrain shore sights that trip. He had expected not to ride that far. He boarded a late-afternoon ELR coach at the Press Street Depot between North Peters and Chartres streets in the New Orleans district locals called the *Vieux Carré*. He was barely two city blocks from the old square outside historic St. Louis Cathedral that stood northwest overlooking the bending Mississippi River banks. The area sat at the center of what became popularly known as the French Quarter.

Plessy rode the train to only Press and Royal streets. The 30-year-old shoemaker could easily have walked it—but that was not the plan.

As the train had departed the Press Street Depot, Conductor John J. Dowling approached Plessy. He asked if Plessy were in the proper coach. Dowling's question was not about Plessy's ticket; he could easily see it was in order. His question was about something he could not so easily see. It asked about Plessy himself—the question was about Plessy's identity.

Louisiana law required the conductor to determine Plessy's identity and that of every other passenger who entered the train. It was not a question of examining or matching any paper identification. The question, and the law's command, ran deeper. It ran to the person's parents, lineage, and ultimate ancestry. It was a question of appearance and more—much more. The question reached to social place. It was about people knowing their place and staying where the social order directed by law.

Dowling accosted Plessy for being out of his proper place. He directed him to remove himself to another car.

Plessy refused.

When the train stopped at Press and Royal streets, Dowling enlisted Detective Chris. C. Cain's help. Cain also ordered Plessy to move. When Plessy continued to refuse, Cain arrested Plessy and removed him.

Plessy went gladly.

No fracas occurred. No one pulled or pushed. No voices rose. All were calm. It was all rather polite. Few immediately noticed the incident that delayed the train barely a minute or two. But people would hear about it ever after.

Cain delivered Plessy to New Orleans's Fifth Precinct station. He charged him with violating Louisiana's 1890 Separate Car Act. The statute's title in part read "An act to promote the comfort of passengers on railway trains." It required "all railway companies carrying passengers on their trains, in this State, to provide equal but separate accommodations for the white and colored races, by providing separate coaches or compartments so as to secure separate accommodations." The law's second section provided also that "any passenger insisting on going into a coach or compartment to which by race he does not belong shall be liable to a fine of $25, or in lieu thereof to imprisonment for a period of not more than twenty days in the parish prison" (Louisiana 1890, 152).

The morning after his arrest, Plessy appeared in New Orleans Second Recorder's Court. Judge A. R. Moulin arraigned him on the charge Detective Cain swore out in an affidavit. Local criminal attorney James C. Walker represented Plessy and waived any hearing there. Judge Moulin set a $500 bond for Plessy's appearance in Criminal District Court. Walker had the bond ready and waiting.

Plessy left with Walker for a later day in court. The toughest part was over for Plessy; he would have only a few more scenes before he finished his role in the unfolding production. Mostly, he was a walk-on. He had few lines to deliver. He stood more to be seen than to be heard. He was actually a bit player chosen for his looks and his lineage. His name would come to top the marquee in history, but his was hardly the actual leading role.

Plessy stood as the visible face of a larger body. He acted as a front man. He stood to serve others for principles dear to him and to generations long before him. He stood with and for his people, for what one of his fellows in their struggles described as "*Nos hommes et notre histoire*" (Desdunes 1911). The French meaning "our people and our history" signaled the heart of Plessy's identity. He represented first and foremost those who called themselves "*gens de couleur*" or "Creole people of color." Many called them simply *Creoles* or, later, Afro-Creoles. In its strict definition, the term *Creole* identified any "person of non-American ancestry, whether African or European, who was born in the Americas" (Hall 1992, 157). In early Louisiana the term applied to persons then considered of "mixed blood." Plessy exemplified them and their pride in their Creole heritage.

Plessy descended from a line of French men and Creole women of color. His paternal grandfather, François Germain Plessy, immigrated to the Americas from France. Born about 1777 in France's southwest city of Bordeaux, Germain as a teenager sailed out with his brother Dominique, seeking a better life. They landed in the French island colony of Saint-Domingue, the richest of the eighteenth-century Caribbean sugar islands. Mayhem met them. The revolution black ex-slave Toussaint L'Overture led to end slavery and establish independence roiled the two brothers' Caribbean destination in the 1790s. In 1804, it became the *République d'Haïti*, the second independent nation in the Americas. Along with thousands of other refugees, the brothers escaped 1,300 miles to France's mainland colony of Louisiana.

Germain prospered in New Orleans. He built Plessy & Co. into a family carpentry business operating in what in 1803 became a U.S. territory and in 1812 the State of Louisiana. He married Catherina Mathieu, the daughter of a Frenchman. Her mother also had a French father. Catherina bore Germain four sons and four daughters. The last of their sons and second-to-last child was Joseph Adolphe.

Born in 1822, Adolphe (as he was usually called) in time married Rosa Debergue. Her parents mirrored Adolphe's. Her father, too, was born in

France, as was her mother's father. Adolphe and Rosa's second of three children and only son was born on March 17, 1862. His birth certificate gave his name as Homère Patris Plessy. In time, he took Adolphe as his middle name to honor his father, who died in January 1869. Left with young Homère and his two sisters, Ida and Rosa, in May 1871 mother Rosa married Victor Martial Dupart. The recently widowed son of a shoemaker, Dupart carried his own father's middle name as his own middle name. That perhaps persuaded his young stepson to style himself later as Homère Adolphe Plessy; the Anglicized version dropped the final "e" from both the first and middle names.

Homer Plessy lived in riotous times. He was born in the Civil War's first full year. On April 12 and 13, 1861, rebels in South Carolina bombarded and then seized Fort Sumter in Charleston Harbor, 11 months before Homer Plessy's birth. On April 19, 1861, U.S. President Abraham Lincoln proclaimed insurrection had erupted.

Louisiana was chief among the places in rebellion. Secession had swept the state like a fever after the November 1860 presidential election. The Republican Lincoln's name had not even been on the Louisiana ballot. Nor had he appeared on the ballot in Alabama, Arkansas, Florida, Georgia, Mississippi, North Carolina, Tennessee, or Texas. At the polls, however, a majority of Louisiana's 50,510 voters rejected the fire-eaters campaigning for disunion. A clear majority (55.1 percent) backed pro-Union Democrats John Bell (40.0 percent) and Stephen A. Douglas (15.1 percent). The extremist pro-slavery John C. Breckenridge managed a slight plurality (44.9 percent), however. That seemed to feed the infection.

Louisiana's state legislature on December 10, 1860, approved a call for a convention to consider seceding. It set January 7, 1861, as the day to elect 130 delegates. At least 80 of the winners had pledged themselves to secession. On January 26, the delegates voted 113 to 17 to adopt a secession ordinance "to dissolve the union between the state of Louisiana and other states united with her under the compact entitled 'The Constitution of the United States of America'" (Louisiana 1861, 15–18).

Louisiana's secession painted a bull's-eye on New Orleans, and Union strategy early fixed the city for capture. It stood as the South's most populous metropolis. It was the South's first city to gain 100,000 residents. It stood near 175,000 in 1860, when it ranked as the sixth largest U.S. city. New Orleans was a premier commercial hub, handling the bulk of Mississippi River traffic to and from the Gulf of Mexico. The lower South depended on New Orleans for access to the world's markets and goods.

The port handled more than half of the South's cotton exports. It stood then as a major target in the war.

Homer Plessy was born, then, in the eye of a storm. U.S. Navy ships had begun on April 16, 1862, to bombard the lower Mississippi River forts guarding upriver entry to New Orleans. Twelve days later, as Plessy reached his first month of life, U.S. Navy Capt. David G. Farragut accepted the city's surrender without bombarding the city itself or fighting in its streets.

New Orleans found itself isolated, but not insulated, under Union occupation. It sat cut off from most of its ordinary supply chain, as much of Louisiana—even southern Louisiana—continued outside federal control. So the war was far from over for New Orleans in mid-1862. Moreover, long famous for its heated politics and social backbiting and bickering, the city replaced fighting off invasion with infighting. Much time would pass before it would be at peace.

Homer Plessy's people stood amid the uneven suffering war imposed on New Orleans. As a carpenter working with his father, Adolphe Plessy had a secure job, so baby Homer was better off than many. Yet the war produced various shortages, particularly food and cash. Many who had depended on cotton or domestic slave trading—for which the city had been the Deep South's center—found their livelihoods at least interrupted, if not halted.

New Orleans was more than the center of the domestic slave trade. More Louisiana slaveholders called it home than any other place. It was the official residence in 1860 for 4,169 (18.9 percent) of Louisiana's 22,033 slaveholders. That was more than four times second-place St. Landry Parish's 963 slaveholders. So the federal seizure of the city threatened a choke hold on slavery in Louisiana.

The war halted much old business in New Orleans, but it also opened new opportunities. Supplying goods and services to Union troops patrolling the city enriched some and paid the bills of others. Some scorned the federals as occupiers. U.S. Army Major General Benjamin Franklin Butler's heavy-handed command hardly soothed the already agitated. Detractors called Butler "the Beast." He rubbed so many so sore that he found himself soon out of command. Major General Nathaniel Prentice Banks replaced Butler in December 1862, which calmed some and provided the city a semblance of order even as the countryside suffered raids and worse.

Unrest tore at the city's fabric. Creole people of color were themselves torn. Like others, they feared for their homeland. Their lives seemed in less imminent danger after the city surrendered, yet some had to fear for their livelihoods and even their way of life. Losing home rule to federal control foreshadowed changes that promised to be radical. Not every Creole welcomed such changes.

Slaves might well cheer without question the coming of slavery's end. But most Creoles were not slaves. Some felt shackled akin to slaves; white supremacy subordinated them, too. Yet they were not chattel. Creoles formed an important part of Louisiana's unenslaved nonwhite population that numbered 18,547 in 1860. Of those, 10,939 (59.0 percent) lived in New Orleans. Most had never been chattel. For many Creoles, no one in their lineage had been a slave for generations. That was certainly true for the Plessys: No slaves or even unmixed Africans appeared in Homer Plessy's lineage for at least two generations.

Creoles of color like Homer Plessy's father and mother had liberties and opportunities in New Orleans that few other nonwhites in the antebellum South, or even outside the South, could match. Many did well. Creole men of color worked prominently as artisans. Some, like Adolphe Plessy, were carpenters, who led the list of skilled occupations in 1860 New Orleans with 257 practitioners. Others worked as barbers, bricklayers, cigarmakers, coopers, painters, shoemakers, and tailors. A few were physicians. A few were planters who also held slaves. Some were heavily invested in slavery's status quo (Blassingame 1973, 223; Schweninger 1990, 104, 111).

At least 3,000 Louisiana men of color had rallied in 1861 to muster for the Confederate cause. Some 1,400 in New Orleans organized in a state-sanctioned Louisiana Native Guard militia auxiliary. A letter to the editor of the New Orleans *Daily Delta* newspaper in December 1860 announced the loyalties of some. "The free colored population love their home, their property, their own slaves," the letter-writer stated. He and his fellows, he declared, "recognize no other country than Louisiana, and are ready to shed their blood for her defense. They have no sympathy for abolitionism; no love for the North, but they have plenty for Louisiana," he stressed. "They will fight for her in 1861 as they fought in 1814–15" (Sutherland 2004, 110).

Other Creoles of color stood among the foremost foes of the slavocracy. The white supremacist regime that imposed slavery rankled them. It subjugated all persons deemed not pure whites. So even as Louisiana law elevated free Creoles of color above slaves, it left them below citizens—a status restricted to whites only. It granted Creoles some economic rights: It entitled them to contract; it let them hold, buy, sell, and inherit land and other property. And it allowed them to testify in civil court cases. Yet it banned them from jury duty. It banned them from regular militia duty also.

It denied Creoles' political rights and limited their social privileges. The law segregated Creoles as its segregated slaves, although it recognized differences between the two.

Louisiana's Supreme Court in 1856 noted major distinctions in Creoles' status. State law sometimes treated nonwhites together in a broad category. The legislature's 1855 "Act relative to colored persons, whether bond or free" showed the common grouping (Louisiana 1855, 387). As a U.S. territory, Louisiana's first act on the subject had signaled the lumping, as it combined its first black code and first slave code. The title of its 1806 omnibus act clearly stated its purposes: "An Act Prescribing the Rules and Conduct to Be Observed with Respect to Negroes and Other Slaves of this Territory" (Louisiana 1806, 150). Yet sharp differences cut two classes among the nonwhites Louisiana law came to call "colored." The free colored and the slave stood as "two classes which it is impossible to confound in legal parlance," the state Supreme Court stated (Louisiana 1856, 722, 724).

"In the eye of the Louisiana law, there is . . . all the difference between a free man of color and a slave, that there is between a white man and a slave," the Louisiana Supreme Court explained (Louisiana 1856, 724). Free persons of color were not to be confused with slaves nor were they to be confused with whites. Simply put, Creoles of color had some recognized rights; slaves had none. Only whites had full rights. Creoles insistent on having full rights saw the need, then, to end slavery and the racial segregation that imposed it.

The federal capture of New Orleans offered Creoles of color an opportunity to press for full rights equal to those of whites. Leaders for the cause began to campaign boldly. They broadcast their call for what they cast as progressive reform, and they wanted a full public hearing. They appeared to believe the justice of their cause would persuade public opinion to their side. Getting their views out meant using the press, so they engaged in publishing what became a series of newspapers. The first was *L'Union*. Its initial issue appeared on Saturday, September 27, 1862.

"We inaugurate today a new era in the destiny of the South," *L'Union* declared on its first front page. Its title exposed its Creole roots and reach. It published in French—the preferred tongue of the Creole community, but its cause stretched beyond that community. It embraced an understanding of universal human rights. "We take for the base of our platform the Declaration of Independence of the United States," *L'Union*'s inaugural editorial declared. It persistently reiterated the principles that "all men are created equal, that they are endowed by their Creator with certain unalienable

Rights, that among these are Life, Liberty and the pursuit of Happiness" (Davis 1983, 152).

The semiweekly published on Saturdays and Wednesdays from offices at 195 Rue de Chartes in the French Quarter. It appeared in the immediate shadow of Abraham Lincoln's preliminary Emancipation Proclamation issued on September 22, 1862. The president presented the South another of his carrot-and-stick propositions to end the war. He hoped the Union repulse of Confederate General Robert E. Lee's advance northward at Antietam Creek in Maryland on September 17 would move the rebels to see they could not win the war.

President Lincoln prayed the carnage in the bloodiest single-day battle in U.S. history would sober the South. What Southerners called the Battle of Sharpsburg left 22,700 casualties. About 10,000 of them were rebels. The South could not long sustain such losses. Quitting the fight promised to save tens of thousands of southern lives. If they were sacrificed to save slavery, there was no point, Lincoln submitted as he offered to let rebels who laid down their arms keep their slaves. He gave them until New Year's Day 1863 to act. After that he promised to declare that "all persons held as slaves within any State or designated part of a State the people whereof shall then be in rebellion against the United States shall be then, thenceforward, and forever free" (United States 1863a, 1268).

L'Union hailed the proclamation. The newspaper was itself hailed in turn. Antislavery crusader Horace Greeley's *New York Tribune* lauded the fresh New Orleans entry "to fight for the cause of liberty and to aid the federal government in re-establishing the Union." Greeley tabbed *L'Union* as "proof" that "the Emancipation Proclamation has already begun to produce its effects in the rebel states" (Davis 1983, 154).

Greeley misjudged *L'Union* if he linked it with the Emancipation Proclamation as cause-and-effect. The publication was in the works before the proclamation appeared. Yet New Orleans did, indeed, provide ample proof of the proclamation's effect, as waves of slaves flowed into the city. The stream began almost as soon as federal troops had arrived in May 1862. It grew with news of federal provisions in July 1862 to free slaves of rebels. In its so-called Second Confiscation Act, the U.S. Congress declared that "all slaves of persons who shall hereafter be engaged in rebellion . . . shall be forever free of their servitude, and not again held as slaves," if they came within federal control (United States 1862, 589). A surge came with word of the proclamation.

Congress's July 1862 confiscation act cast many of the Crescent City's new arrivals as "forever free." That applied to slaves long resident in the city, too, if after the act's passage their holders had "engaged in rebellion" or acted "in any way [to] give aid or comfort" to rebels (United States 1862, 589). But the Emancipation Proclamation in January 1863 specifically exempted New Orleans from its reach. President Lincoln, in fact, exempted 13 of Louisiana's 64 parishes from the proclamation's operation. Slaves there had no claim to its provisions. But who was to distinguish which slaves belonged where or who had come within Union lines when? Who, indeed, was to identify who was a slave and who was not? In many eyes, color had long been the measure of subordination. The developing conflict of laws appeared to make the old standard unreliable, if not unworkable, or at least some wanted it so.

Slaveholders and others throughout New Orleans railed about what they viewed as slaves' increasingly impertinent behavior. They complained that under federal control slaves had forgotten their place. One holder complained that the force of 15,000 federal troops that entered the Crescent City on May 1, 1862, "operated as a general enticement to the slaves to abandon their master's service." Slaves simply walked off or refused to work, the holder recalled. "The master no longer knew when he could command his servant's labor, who might at any moment leave," the slaveholder grumbled in July 1862. He protested further that in the new circumstances he and other slaveholders stood "without the possibility of recovery." They had lost their cudgels, at least for the moment. The situation, he lamented, was "thus filling the master's mind with doubt, anxiety, disappointment and resentment" (Blassingame 1973, 26).

The scene in and around New Orleans in 1862 and 1863 was not quite as disgruntled slaveholders portrayed it. Slaves enjoyed no immediate or sure refuge under Union control. General Butler moved early to block blacks from rushing to the city. When commanding Fort Monroe in Virginia in May 1861, he had welcomed fugitive slaves. Classifying them as "contrabands," Butler refused to return slaves to slaveholders. Yet in May 1862 he barred slaves' entry into Union lines around New Orleans. His sympathies had not changed, but necessities of his command had. With the city cut off from its usual supply of food and other provisions, Butler found himself without the means to feed those already under his command. He had no way to support the surge of slaves seeking refuge in the city.

More than General Butler's tenuous position rebuffed slaves who sought shelter in New Orleans. Unsympathetic Union officers and troops sometimes abused fugitives. "Repeatedly they were knocked down, and brutally dragged away from under the folds of the 'Flag of the Free'," a Connecticut soldier reported in May 1862 on how some Union troops treated some slaves who managed to skirt Butler's ban and get into the city (Sprague 1867, 63). And get in they did: One count in midsummer 1862 put the number of fugitive slaves in the city at 10,000. By March 1863, an estimated one in four of all slaves on 15 plantations around Orleans Parish had run away.

By November 1862, General Butler had remanded his order to imprison fugitive slaves. They simply overburdened his resources. Instead, he set up camps for them, only to again find their numbers overwhelmed his wherewithal. Refugees soon overcrowded campsites, and sickening conditions developed. By December 1862, fugitives were entering Union lines at a rate of 200 per day. A few of the luckier refugees landed work for the Army: Some hauled supplies for the quartermaster; some built and repaired fortifications; and some simply chopped wood. Cleaning, cooking, and sewing occupied some. The pay helped them get by.

Seeing the distress of some of the fugitives sobered more than a few Union soldiers. "I used to think that the stories about cruel treatment of slaves were exaggerated," admitted one Connecticut captain in New Orleans. "But," he lamented, "the reality is fully equal to the worst description." The reported sights included slaves with "their backs shockingly lacerated by whipping; others had huge freshly-burned marks of the branding iron. Many had chains on their wrists, ankles and necks. A few wore great iron collars with long projecting prongs, like the spokes of a wheel." One affected soldier in the 13th Connecticut Infantry sadly noted that "it was hard to resist the piteous appeals of these slaves for protection" (Sprague 1867, 62–63).

Protecting slaves proved less a priority than maintaining order in the occupied city. To start, slaves throwing off their shackles scared whites. Used to black subservience, whites encountering fresh black attitudes worried about being safe. "I fear more from the negroes than Yankees and an insurrection is my continual horror," one young white woman in New Orleans wrote in her diary in early May 1862 (Solomon 1862, 199). She and others seemed to feel stranded without slavery's restraints.

Few white Louisianans knew blacks in any condition other than slavery. More knew Creoles, at least in New Orleans. Clear distinctions separated the usually free Creoles of color from the usually enslaved blacks. Color made a difference among nonwhites as it made a difference between whites and nonwhites. Even so, beyond New Orleans, few Creoles or blacks in Louisiana lived outside of slavery. Twenty-nine of the state's 64 parishes had 100 or fewer free blacks or Creoles in 1860. Six parishes recorded not a single free colored person. In only 10 parishes did free colored persons amount to 3 percent or more of the total population. The New Orleans population itself had only 6.3 percent free colored persons in 1860. St. Tammany alone topped it with 7.6 percent. In contrast, Orleans was the lone parish with less than 10 percent (8.3 percent) of its population enslaved. In every other parish, slaves accounted for at least 19.7 percent of all residents. In all but six parishes, slaves were at least one-third (33.3 percent) of all residents. They were more than half the population in 46 parishes, and they topped 90 percent in Concordia (90.9 percent) and Tensas (90.8 percent) parishes. Overall, 46.9 percent of Louisiana's total population in 1860 were slaves. Only 2.6 percent were free colored persons (University of Virginia 2004, 1860).

Images of unfettered blacks gave whites like the young New Orleans diarist nightmares. They feared being overrun and overwhelmed. Not just violence concerned such whites; livelihoods were at stake. Workingmen dreaded competing for jobs. "Thim [*sic*] d___d niggers will starve a poor white man out of house and home," one of the city's Irish workmen griped (Corsan 1863, 32). His fellow Sons of Eire and German immigrants were no fans of slavery. The pecking order often relegated them to common labor, with the docks being one of their preserves. They tended to work as stevedores, longshoremen, porters, and carmen. Much of their work shifted with the war, however, and they grumbled along with native white workingmen scratching for work.

U.S. Army projects offered the best employment for many. The early work put men on sanitation and repair details. They cleaned the city streets, sewers, and canals, and they patched the levees that kept the city from flooding, as its average elevation sat below sea level. Many muttered about the work and the pay. "What will a dollar and a half a day do toward keeping a man and his family?" one slime-covered white man complained (Corsan 1863, 32). Yet he and others were desperate for the work and pay. They stood determined, too, to keep the jobs for whites only.

So blacks who beat a path to the city came largely unwelcome. Their release from slavery cut adrift the foundation of Louisiana's old order. It portended problems for many, and it raised tensions almost everywhere. Indeed, it stirred a welter of conflicts. It pushed Creoles of color like Homer Plessy's family into growing social and political disorder. They found themselves lumped indiscriminately with untutored blacks fresh from the fields. They, too, for example, became caught in the pass system General Banks instituted soon after taking command in December 1862. Smacking of the slave system, it required all nonwhites to carry papers to prove they had permission to be wherever they were.

So while the slavocracy was clearly crumbling, Creoles and others had worries aplenty over visions of the shape of their present and their prospects. Federal sanctions and the rush of slaves into the city were shifting old lines of race relations. Statuses once clear now blurred. Ambivalence shadowed slaves, and uncertainty seeped through slavery's racial layers.

Many pronounced slavery dead. Plessy's people prayed for it to die. Creoles behind *L'Union* pushed to kill it. "The institution of slavery in modern societies is one of the most formidable obstacles which hinders the development of nations," the newspaper editors wrote in their issue of December 10, 1862. Creoles of color saw their own progress, and that of Louisiana broadly, tied to slavery's end.

The institution's death rattled with Union progress in the war. In October 1863, a state court in occupied Louisiana boldly declared slavery illegal. On December 26, 1863, as perhaps a belated Christmas gift, Union commander General Banks directed the removal throughout New Orleans of all public signs for slave trading or capture. On January 11, 1864, Banks suspended Louisiana's state constitutional provisions maintaining slavery, and a new state constitution was soon in the making.

Starting on April, 6, 1864, a convention met in New Orleans to comply with President Lincoln's directions for reestablishing the state in the Union. Lincoln hoped for Louisiana to help pioneer the rapid restoration detailed in his December 1863 Proclamation of Amnesty and Reconstruction. His plan directed the state to reestablish a government loyal to the Union. To do so required Louisiana to have its people take an oath to "henceforth faithfully support, protect, and defend the Constitution of the United States and the Union of the States thereunder" (United States 1863b, 737).

To start Lincoln's process, a seceded state needed a sworn loyal cadre of at least 10 percent of the number of voters in the state in the 1860 presidential election. Louisiana needed 5,051 oath-takers to qualify, and it easily managed that meager minimum. The state then needed to modify its antebellum constitution to recognize an end to slavery. Lincoln encouraged the state to attend also "to the freed people of such state, . . . provide for their education, and [take measures] which may yet be consistent as a temporary arrangement with their present condition as a laboring, landless, and homeless class" (United States 1863b, 737).

Louisiana's 1864 constitutional convention complied straightaway with Lincoln's command for the state to "recognize and declare . . . permanent freedom" for slaves. It titled the first article of the constitution it proposed "Emancipation." It provided that "Slavery and involuntary servitude, except as a punishment for crime, whereof the party shall have been duly convicted, are hereby for ever abolished and prohibited throughout the State." The second article provided that "The legislature shall make no law recognizing the right of property in man." On September 5, 1864, Louisiana's voters approved the state's new constitution (Bennett 1867, 631–643).

So slavery ended in Louisiana—at least in law. How and when slavery would end in fact remained in question. Louisiana's traditions had no substantial place for blacks outside of slavery. Creoles, like Plessy's people, scratched niches for themselves largely in New Orleans. Few suitable places existed for them elsewhere in the Pelican State. A very few with substantial fortunes edged their way into the planter class. Generally their estates lay isolated upriver from New Orleans. They stood closer to whites than they did to blacks in the fields before the war. Yet everywhere clear signs reminded Creoles of their color and, thus, their diminished status. Whatever their wealth, skills, social pretension, profession, or education, they were not whites.

The question of the hour after abolition pressed on all Louisiana's people of whatever color: Where would they stand in their social and political relations without slavery? The question for some simply turned on principle. *L'Union* trumpeted that note. It echoed at least a generation of abolitionism as it cast the Civil War as a clear-cut contest between slavery and freedom. Abolitionists such as Massachusetts native James Russell Lowell, editor of the *Atlantic Monthly* magazine, used that cast from the war's outbreak.

Lowell wrote in 1861 that "the difficulty of the Slavery question is slavery itself,—nothing more, nothing less." The question was one of "political morality," Lowell wrote. It pitted those whose "habits and prepossessions are those of Freedom" against "a great mistake and a great wrong." Lowell insisted further that in any case slavery was doomed: "It is the stars in their courses that fight against their system," he declared of slaveholders. "The spirit of the age" compelled all to abolish slavery, he insisted (Lowell 1861, 120–121).

"Let all friends of Progress unite!" *L'Union* proclaimed on September 27, 1862, in its inaugural editorial. "The hour has come for the struggle of the great humanitarian principles against the vile and sordid interest which gives birth to pride, ambition, hypocrisy, and lying," the newspaper declared. It argued not simply against slavery, but also against what one of its writers described as "social distinctions based upon color." It took aim against white supremacy and its imposed racist subjugation that, the editors declared, "silences the conscience, that voice of the heavens which cries endlessly to man: 'You were born for liberty and happiness! Do not deceive yourself in this and do not deceive your brother!' "

L'Union envisioned what its writer Jean-Charles Houzeau would describe as "a great revolution, one of the greatest in history," as it battled against the "prejudice of skin" (Houzeau 1872, 18–19). It promised to be no short or small war.

Homer Plessy was still engaged in the fight in June 1892 when he boarded his East Louisiana Railroad train in New Orleans. The case that bore Plessy's name was not his alone then. It presented the long trial of his people from almost Louisiana's colonial beginnings.

References

Bennett, Albert P. 1867. *Debates in the Convention for the Revision and Amendment of the Constitution of the State of Louisiana Assembled at Liberty Hall, New Orleans, April 6, 1864.* New Orleans: W. R. Fish.

Blassingame, John W. 1973. *Black New Orleans, 1860–1880.* Chicago: University of Chicago Press.

Corsan, W. C. 1863. *Two Months in the Confederate States Including a Visit to New Orleans under the Domination of General Butler.* London: R. Bentley.

Davis, Thomas J. 1983. "Louisiana." In *The Black Press in the South, 1865–1879*, ed. Henry Lewis Suggs, 151–176. Westport, CT: Greenwood Press.

Desdunes, Rodolphe Lucien. 1911. *Nos Hommes et Notre Historie: Our People and Our History: A Tribute to the Creole People of Color*, trans. and ed. Sister Dorothea Olga McCants. Baton Rouge: Louisiana State University Press, 1973.

Hall, Gwendolyn Midlo. 1992. *Africans in Colonial Louisiana: The Development of Afro-Creole Culture in the Eighteenth Century.* Baton Rouge: Louisiana State University Press.

Houzeau, Jean-Charles. 1872. *My Passage at the New Orleans Tribune: A Memoir of the Civil War Era*, ed. David C. Rankin. Baton Rouge: Louisiana State University Press, 1984.

Louisiana. 1806. "An Act Prescribing the Rules and Conduct to Be Observed with Respect to Negroes and Other Slaves of This Territory," 1806 La. Terr. Acts 150 (June 7, 1806).

Louisiana. 1855. "Act Relative to Colored Persons, Whether Bond or Free," 1855 La. Acts 387 (March 15, 1855).

Louisiana. 1856. *State v. Harrison*, 11 La. Ann. 722 (1856).

Louisiana. 1861. *Ordinance of Secession, Official Journal of the Proceedings of the Convention of the State of Louisiana.* New Orleans: J. O. Nixon, 1861.

Louisiana. 1890. "An Act to Promote the Comfort of Passengers on Railway Trains," 1890 La. Acts 152 (July 10, 1890).

Lowell, James Russell. 1861. "The Question of the Hour." *Atlantic Monthly* 7: 120–121.

Schweninger, Loren. 1990. *Black Property Owners in the South, 1790–1915.* Urbana: University of Illinois Press.

Solomon, Clara. 1862. Clara Solomon Diaries, 1861–1862, May 8, 1862. In *Southern Women and Their Families in the 19th Century: Papers and Diaries*. Series E, Reel 15. Bethesda, MD: University Publications of America, 1998.

Sprague, Homer B. 1867. *History of the 13th Infantry Regiment of Connecticut Volunteers, during the Great Rebellion*. Hartford: Case, Lockwood & Co.

Sutherland, Jonathan. 2004. *African Americans at War: An Encyclopedia*. Santa Barbara, CA: ABC-CLIO.

United States. 1862. "An Act to Suppress Insurrection, to Punish Treason and Rebellion, to Seize and Confiscate the Property of Rebels, and for Other Purposes," 12 Stat. 589 (July 17, 1862).

United States. 1863a. Proclamation No. 17 [the Emancipation Proclamation] (Designating Certain States and Parts of States as in Rebellion, and Declaring the Slaves Therein Free), 12 Stat. 1268 (January 1, 1863).

United States. 1863b. A Proclamation [of Amnesty and Reconstruction] by the President of the United States of America, 13 Stat. 737 (December 8, 1863).

University of Virginia. 2004. *Geospatial and Statistical Data Center, Historical Census Browser*. Charlottesville: University of Virginia.

TWO

The Start: A Colony and Creoles of Color

PLESSY AND HIS PEOPLE were fighting the colorline. The battle stretched far back before the Civil War's start in 1861. It reached to the early European and African migrations that created colonial Louisiana. Americans intensified hostilities, especially after 1803 when France sold its claims to the territory to the United States. The contest for dominance featured violence at every turn. Indeed, war marked Louisiana's emerging character. The battling started with the first colonizers as they fought to displace the aborigines they called Indians. The colonizers fought each other, too. Spain, France, Great Britain, and the United States— all, in turn, vied to command the area. All wrestled to win privileges and property, all aimed for control—control of self and control of others. The fight promoted group identity. It fostered an us-versus-them mentality to cultivate and shelter a select community of shared entitlements. Breaks among and between groups grew along lines of nationality, ethnicity, and culture. Little so colored hostilities as the developing amalgam called race. That was what Homer Adolph Plessy was fighting in the 1890s as his people had fought it since the 1700s.

Spain opened the contest, with Alonso Álvarez de Pineda leading the way. In 1519, he sailed around the small sandy islands called cays or keys atop the coral reefs south of the peninsula Juan Ponce de León in 1513 had named *La Florida*. Pineda headed westward, tracing the rim of the 950-mile-wide North Atlantic basin the Spanish called the Gulf of Mexico. His expedition mapped much of the shoreline to Veracruz, destined to be the chief Atlantic port of what would become Mexico. Along the way, Pineda noted various clusters of substantial native settlements. He particularly described those around what came to be called Mobile Bay and the river later called the Alabama that flowed into it.

Panfilo de Narváez followed Pineda's finds. In 1528, Narváez identified the area New Orleans would come to dominate. His expedition spotted the mouth where what appeared to be a large river spilled into the ocean. The river was, in fact, huge. The main channel of North America's largest river system, it ran 2,300 miles from its headwaters in the northeast lakes region at the continent's center south to its mouth in the Gulf of Mexico. Hundreds of Indian groups had for centuries made the river's banks and valleys home. In their own languages, many called it the "Big River" or the "Great River." In English it became the "Mississippi," mimicking the Great Lakes region Ojibwe people's word *misi-ziibi*.

The French became the first Europeans to settle the area at the Mississippi's mouth. Their colonial reach in the early 1600s penetrated the northern lakes region of the river's headwaters. From various Indians such as the Mohawk and Ojibwe, they learned of the Great River flowing south to the ocean. René-Robert Cavelier, Sieur de La Salle, jumped at riding the river's full flow. He started by tracking his countrymen Louis Jolliet and Jesuit Père Jacques Marquette's 1672 exploration of the upper Mississippi Valley. In a 1682 expedition down the river, La Salle named the basin region *La Louisiane* in honor of the then French king, Louis XIV (r. 1643–1715), claiming for France all he traversed.

France's minister of marine, Louis Phélypeaux, Comte de Pontchartrain, seized news of La Salle's finds. Pontchartrain's duties included control of the navy and overseas colonies. Amid the European rivalry for territory in the Americas, he moved eagerly to enlarge France's share. To follow up La Salle's finds, Pontchartrain dispatched Pierre Le Moyne, Sieur d'Iberville, from France to North America in October 1698.

To start his expedition, Iberville made his way to Saint-Domingue. The French had a foothold there on western Hispaniola, the Caribbean's second largest island (28,544 mi^2). Spain dominated most of the island with its colony of Santo Domingo. Spain's main colony lay to the east in Cuba, the region's largest island (40,852 mi^2). To avoid the Spanish, Iberville headed northwest from Saint-Domingue, moving to the mainland Gulf Coast. He skirted the Spanish colony in Florida and anchored in Mobile Bay in early 1699. Shortly he made his way over to the mouth of the Mississippi. He and his younger brother Jean-Baptiste Le Moyne de Bienville camped in March 1699 where 20 years later the main French settlement rose in the Gulf region. Bienville would name the site for Philippe, Duc d'Orléans, then France's Regent (1715–1723), calling the place *La Nouvelle-Orléans*.

Iberville encountered various Indians. Most in the area were Muskogee Creek, Choctaw, or Chickasaw. Some proved friendly and some hostile. Among them were peoples whose names or words came to identify places— Atchafalaya, Bayogoula, Biloxi, Bogalusa, Caddo, Houma, Maringouin,

Mobile, Natchez, Natchitoches, Okelusa, Pascagoula, Pensacola, Quinpissa, and Tangipahoa, for example. The Bayogoula, Mongoulachas, and Houmas particularly helped Iberville navigate the lower Mississippi's flow about 300 miles upriver from its mouth. On their trek, the Frenchmen passed a place of tall red cornstalks they called *Baton Rouge*. They canoed through marshlands that came to be called *bayou*. The big salt lake they named "Pontchartrain" lay among many features they recorded.

Iberville recognized the strategic value of the Mississippi Delta, and he set about to secure it for France. He picked Biloxi Bay as the best spot in the area for an immediate post. It provided easy ocean access and a shorter supply line than points such as *La Nouvelle-Orléans*, located farther west. Iberville laid out a fort on the bay's eastern shore and set up a chain of command to hold the place while he sailed to France. When he returned early in 1701 with reinforcements and supplies, he brought French settlers from Canada and also sugarcane plantings from Saint-Domingue. He then sallied forth to set up forts as marauding English and the Spanish from Florida spurred the French to strengthen their position.

Bienville carried on the work after his brother died in 1706. The first order of business required populating the place with settlers, but numbers remained slim. In 1708, the official count of residents recorded only 339 persons in the colony. Soldiers, seamen, and others attached to the crown formed the single largest group, numbering 122. Hardy French Canadian pioneers called *coureurs des bois* numbered 60. A mix of other Europeans and enslaved Indians made up the remaining 157 residents officials counted as French Louisiana's people.

The venture suffered from poor funding. The crown simply lacked cash, so it turned to private financing. Adopting a model from the English and Dutch, the French crown chartered commercial monopolies such as the *Compagnie du Mississippi* and the *Compagnie d'Occident*—the Company of the West, later called the Company of the Indies (*La Compagnie Française des Indes*)—to develop Louisiana. Prospects of reaping riches drew financing, and private investors recruited French, German, and Swiss emigrants to boost colonization. Enslaved Indians and European prisoners added to the numbers, yet settlers remained too few. As elsewhere in the Americas, the demand for bodies reached to Africa.

To bolster its claim to Louisiana, the French followed their European rivals in the Americas by importing enslaved Africans, as they had done earlier in Saint-Domingue. Before Europe's War of the Austrian Succession (1744–1748) spilled into the Atlantic and interrupted the slave-based traffic, the French imported about 6,000 Africans into Louisiana. The blacks expanded the French enterprise. Indeed, their initial numbers boosted the colony to about 5,000 residents by the 1720s and provided Bienville much of the wherewithal to do what he had envisioned in 1699: He laid out and began to build a major settlement on the banks of the Mississippi, about 100 miles from its mouth. So sprang up the burgeoning city of *La Nouvelle-Orléans*.

Reflecting the growing black population, Louisiana officials in 1724 adopted a *Code noir*. French King Louis XIV promulgated the original code in 1685. The first royal edict's title described it as providing rules for "the discipline and commerce of blacks and slaves." More broadly, it treated "the government and administration of justice and good order in the French islands of America" (Louisiana 1724, 89).

The first French footholds in the Caribbean and along the Gulf of Mexico occasioned the proclamation. The original code contained 60 articles. First and foremost, it sanctioned slavery. It settled the practice as legal, defining what it meant to be a slave or a slaveholder and decreeing who could be a slave and who could be a slaveholder. Also it laid out responsibilities and restrictions for slaveholders and for slaves. But the *Code noir* was more than a slave code. Its title translated as "black code," and it regulated peoples from Africa in and out of slavery. It was, thus, was more a code of race relations.

Like other French colonies, Louisiana adapted the *Code noir* to suit itself. Localities inserted their own peculiarities, but the basis everywhere remained the same. Louisiana's *Code noir* appeared in March 1724 as a royal edict treating the "status and discipline of black slaves in Louisiana." On paper and in practice, the code subordinated Africans. It put them, like Indians, beneath Europeans in hierarchies of colonizers and colonized. It identified the non-Europeans as subordinate peoples.

European ideas of identity at the time fixed non-Europeans generally—and even Europeans themselves—on a ladder of rank. Developing notions of nationality, ethnicity, culture, and civilization put people collectively and individually into categories. Religion, language, ancestry, allegiance, and more mixed to rank people in official and popular standing. For example, the original *Code noir* recognized only Roman Catholics as having full rights; it excluded Jews entirely from any rights. Growing ever more powerful in the 1700s, notions of grouping people in categories called "races" developed to dwarf other distinctions.

The concept of race existed to describe differences among peoples long before the so-called European Age of Discovery or Age of Exploration that started in the 1400s. But earlier it carried a narrower, almost tribal tone.

Race initially signaled broad bloodline affinities; then it spread to cultural and regional connections. Even in the 1700s, for example, some Europeans wrote of the "Christian race." Groupings titled "race" thus shifted; the dividing lines ebbed and flowed. From the 1500s onward, the lines more and more widened. Europeans previously considered distant races merged themselves and others from the continent—sometimes only marginally or reluctantly—into a common race called "whites." At the same time, as a counterpoint to themselves, Europeans came more and more to define various Africans commonly called "blacks." The Iberians gave voice to the concept. *Negro*, the Spanish word for *black*, became a common term for the race until the latter 1900s.

Color came primarily to signal race, but other physical features also served as signals. Appearance at a glance tended to communicate station. So lower status clung to blacks even when they escaped slavery. And as the number of slaves in Louisiana increased, the number of blacks outside slavery also increased. Official counts in New Orleans and its environs marked the relatively rapid increase in the number of blacks. In 1722, the count listed 51 Indian slaves and 514 black slaves. By the 1730s, Africans made up more than half of French Louisiana's people (Ditchy 1930, 208). By the 1780s, Louisiana enslaved more than 15,000 of African descent, who then outnumbered the colony's 9,800 whites.

Some slipped slavery by running away. Taking advantage of the bayou and open frontier, some runaways created their own communities. They joined a line of African peoples in the Americas titled "maroons," as they rebelled against being enslaved and isolated themselves from the slavery surroundings them. Few other places in North America lent themselves so well to maroonage. It occurred more often in the Caribbean and in South America, where maroons formed societies of substantial size and power.

Some Africans in Louisiana slipped slavery yet stayed within the dominant society. Exemplary service won release for some. Enslaved women especially gained favor. Because they were so few, a premium attached to women, whatever their heritage. European colonizers were almost exclusively men. Recruiters did manage to send some family groups from Europe, but later rather than sooner. Even then, European women remained relatively few. The count in 1722 listed 140 women and 448 men in New Orleans, aside from 565 slaves (Ditchy 1930, 208). African women also were relatively few as the demand for heavy labor that drew slave imports early brought in more males than females.

European men in early Louisiana came to take African and also Indian women as mates who became mothers of their children. Some such women became wives and so left slavery. Most served as concubines and remained slaves or left slavery as a later gift or bequest from their slaveholder paramours. European men who lived in Louisiana in the 1700s often disclosed their relations with their African or Indian mates in legal testaments they made to distribute their property after they died.

Wills certified in New Orleans between 1804 and 1812 revealed at least part of the early frequency with which European men joined with African women to form families. About one in three (33.3 percent) of the European men in Louisiana born before 1740 with wills probated in the period recognized unions with women of color. About one in four (25.8 percent) born between 1740 and 1759 recognized such unions, as did about one in five (19.0 percent) of the European men in Louisiana born between 1760 and 1779 (Lachance 1994, 211–242).

The earlier European men entered colonial Louisiana, the more likely they were to enter legally acknowledged unions with African or Indian women. The declining rates of such unions over time reflected migration trends throughout North America. Only as settlement developed did more European women appear in colonial and frontier populations. Their increased availability decreased the frequency of European men's taking non-European women as primary mates. That happened among the Spanish. It happened among the English. It happened also among the French in Louisiana.

Rates of unions between European men and non-European women in Louisiana declined in time simply because of the larger population base. They formed a smaller proportion not because they declined in number but because the number of other unions increased. The population structure also shifted with the enlarging population base—a shift that brought increased pressure to enforce old but ignored rules banning unions between whites and blacks.

The French, like other European colonizers, recognized a rule of endogamy to preserve their identity and with it allegiance and group cohesion. As with the original *Code noir*, Louisiana's 1724 code insisted on black and white endogamy. "We forbid our white subjects, of both sexes, to marry with blacks, under the penalty of being fined and subjected to other arbitrary punishment," the code declared in its Article 6 (Louisiana 1724, 89). It forbade all clergy or chaplains to marry any black to any white. It banned black-white concubinage as well.

Sex was less the concern than children. The code levied harsh penalties if "there be any issue from this kind of intercourse." It imposed on the offenders fines of 300 *livres tournois*. The French monetary unit, like the

English pound sterling, rested on an original metal base weight of a pound of the precious metal silver. If one parent was a slave, the law imposed the 300 *livre* fine on the slave's holder. If the master was himself the father, the law not only fined him but stripped him of his title and possession of the slave mother and her child. The law punished the slave mother and child by declaring that they "shall be forever incapable of being set free."

The code's provisions displayed the clear purpose of segregating blacks and whites. The code aimed to keep each group separate and easy to identify. It feared mingling would confuse who was white and who was not, who was dominant and who was subordinate. Yet reflecting some understanding of human nature and the limits of law, the code fixed on the issue of mixed children more than on sex.

The code appeared to wink at sex. It grasped the reality that promulgating a prohibition on black-white intercourse was easier than enforcing such a prohibition, particularly when many white men primarily had access only to black women. Intercourse that produced no permanent relations created few problems for the code. Sex itself changed little from the code's perspective. But *métis*, as the French called those whom they conceived as mixed race, upset the *Code noir*'s worldview. *Métis* eclipsed the view that saw people as only white or not white. Mixed children undeniably connected what the code declared unalterably separate. That was a major reason the code aimed to prevent mixed children.

Mixing the lines of ancestry raised concern about slave status, but that was not the primary problem in considering mixed children. The code could easily fix lineage; it had an old rule to settle status. Like other European enslavers, the French followed a rule of early Roman law to determine where offspring stood. The rule developed from handling cattle and other livestock. The Latin phrase *partus sequitur ventrem* described the legal doctrine: It decreed that offspring followed the status of the mother. Whoever owned the mother owned her offspring. The sire's status played no part in the offspring's status. The mother's status controlled. And so it was in the *Code noir*: A child of a slave mother was born a slave.

The dominant concern about mixed lineage stretched beyond slavery; it reached identity. The issue was the ultimate problem for all codes aimed to separate people by ancestry. They treated people on the pretended basis that some external fact or condition could and did actually segregate people in their essential qualities and humanity. Such codes pronounced some people naturally unsuited to share all society's benefits. Indeed, such codes decreed some people simply incompatible to mix with others. They laid down rules of endogamy to dictate not simply who could and could not marry whom, but also who should and should not mate or breed with whom.

Some segregation systems recognized multiple groups. Others decreed a simple dichotomy, like that in the *Code noir* and the law developing in Great Britain's American colonies. Excluding Indians as outside settled society, early European authorities divided their colonial inhabitants in the Americas as either whites or blacks. They tended to imagine blacks and whites as completely different beings. If blacks and whites were not exactly opposites, then they were as far apart as the writers of the *Code noir* could conceive.

The code cast blacks and whites as naturally incompatible. Its provisions, however, belied its proposition. Segregation was no more natural than slavery. People—not nature—imposed both. The code existed in part to coerce people to conform to social dictates. Its direction ran contrary to nature, which in no way blocked blacks and whites from mingling or mating. Any inhibition arose from society, not nature. The code's ban conceded as much, and for that reason it tried to prevent *métis*, the definitive proof of the code's futility to thwart nature.

Mixed children exposed fundamental fictions of racial segregation and justifications of slavery. They revealed race as a creature of perception, not as a fixture of nature. They displayed race as an imposed identity, as something agreed to, perhaps even insisted upon, so as to conform to some dictate. Their treatment showed race as a tool of social control used to implement dominance and subordination, functioning in turn to elevate and subjugate. Mixed children proved race to be an arbitrary distinction, not a sure scientific or systematic grouping. Mixed children embodied the fact that identity based on race rested on a range of shifting views and environments.

Mixed children stood as tangible proof that to the degree race existed at all, it was fluid rather than fixed. Who, after all, were mixed children in a world split between blacks and whites? Their very existence begged the question of what it meant to be *black* or *white*. What set blacks and whites apart other than decree? What marked the difference—physical features or other visual characteristics? Did the difference lie merely or mostly in appearance?

Clearly, most Africans appeared different from most Europeans. Their dress, language, speech, manners and other behavior marked them as different. They came from different places to start. Living together over time promised, however, to change how both blacks and whites appeared and acted. Indeed, drawing whites together with Indians and blacks was a big part of what made the Americas a New World. It was also a big part of what made the Americas a frightening place for many European social thinkers, such as those who crafted the *Code noir*. Even French thinkers among leaders of the so-called Enlightenment movement in the 1700s that elevated reason and humanistic values, refused to see blacks as equally human or slavery as repulsive. To such minds, mixed children embodied frightening change because they personified not only uncertain identity but lost identity.

The French who implemented Louisiana's *Code noir* in 1724 could see firsthand what writers of the original code in 1685 might merely have glimpsed, yet their purposes remained the same. The *Code noir* of 1724, like that of 1685, aimed to keep unchanged an order based on identity. Its segregationist decrees projected images of people divided by unbridgeable gaps. It cast blacks and whites as having different essential characters or at least different unique sets of characteristics. It aimed to forever perpetuate and preserve white dominance and black subjection.

For the code to work as intended, blacks and whites had not only to stay separate, but also to stay readily recognized as black or white. A visible dichotomy needed to be maintained. Yet the code's own provisions recognized the reality of mixed children's becoming radically changed in appearance and behavior—so changed as to be immediately unidentifiable as black or white. Moreover, mixed children threatened to transform what it meant to be black *or* white. They promised to be both and neither.

Law might use lineage to distinguish identity. Tracing bloodlines from some point in time might label people, but that provided no sure, practical identifier. Everyday matters demanded more instant means of identity than a genealogy chart. Yet markers of pedigree came to stamp mixed children, at least in popular imagination or on paper. More than calling them simply *métis* as the French did, labels stuck to distinguish generations of mixed children.

The Portuguese and Spanish fixed the early European terms. The Iberians first penetrated Africa in the 1400s. They came to call persons of mixed race *mulato*—a term developed from the Spanish and Portuguese word *mulo*, meaning "mule." It reached back to the Latin word *mulus*, meaning the offspring of a female horse and a male donkey. That cross symbolized mixed breeding. The English picked up the term as they became more involved in the Americas. They came to spell the word as *mulatto*. It signaled a person as well as a tawny color—a light brown or tan, rather than the dark or pale called black or white.

From mixed race generally, the term *mulatto* came to specify the offspring of one white parent and one black parent. It represented a first generation of mixed black-white children: half-black and half-white. Labels developed also for later generations, emphasizing how many immediate ancestors were black or white. Such labels reached back from parents to grandparents and great-grandparents. The term *quadroon*, for example, identified the child of a mulatto and a white. The term came ultimately from the Latin *quartus* and more immediately from the Spanish *cuarto*, meaning one-fourth. *Quadroon* labeled a person as having one black and three white immediate forebears and so identified the person as one-quarter black. *Octoroon* developed to identify the child of a quadroon and a white. It tagged black ancestry as a further generation removed. An octoroon had one black and seven white immediate forebears and so identified the person as one-eighth black. By then, the person rarely showed any features typically considered black. Often, in fact, such a mixed-race person appeared white.

Homer Plessy announced himself an octoroon. The term most closely reflected his ancestry in Louisiana's accounting of racial lineage. Both his father and his mother were children of fathers born in France and mothers whose fathers had been born in France. Moreover, the mothers' mothers were themselves at least mulatto. Plessy swore to the U.S. Supreme Court that he was "seven eighths Caucasian and one eighth African blood." He further averred that "the mixture of colored blood was not discernible in him." He looked as "white" as, or more so than, many Italians and other Mediterranean Europeans in Louisiana in the 1890s (United States 1896, 541).

Octoroon, quadroon, mulatto, and other racial lineage labels tagged legal constructions more than anything else. They identified conceptions, pointing to how people such as the writers of the *Code noir* and other colonial laws saw themselves and others. American law would long persist in tracking lineage as a measure of race. Local law would decide how to figure identity from ancestry. U.S. states would fix measures to determine what mix of lineage identified a person as black or white. Mississippi developed the noted "one-drop rule." Moving for so-called racial purity, lawmakers pretended to reach the full extent of lineage. They declared anyone with any black ancestor could never be deemed legally white in Mississippi. Such laws perpetuated the black/white or nonwhite/white dichotomy.

The early color-coded labels fit the needs of colonizers to classify people. The French followed their own system. Each of the European colonial powers pursued its own peculiarities. In general, they arranged colonial inhabitants in one of two patterns, adopting either two-tiered or three-tiered color-coded hierarchies.

The British in mainland North America adopted a two-tiered system, in which they and their descendents recognized only two castes. Their pattern divided people as either white or not white, and they attached immutable social positions, privileges, and status to each caste. The relatively small black population in British mainland North America allowed for it to be more easily marginalized.

In settings where blacks formed the majority, such as the Caribbean, British colonials behaved differently. There they adopted a three-tiered system, more like the French had in their islands and in Louisiana. The three-tiered system allowed nonwhites a bit of flexibility and mobility, for it recognized positions, privileges, and status between black and white.

White supremacist segregation dominated both patterns. It everywhere exalted whites and debased blacks. Slavery sustained all colonial systems in the Americas. It divided whites from nonwhites, for only nonwhites slaved. It everywhere used the base of race, usually described as color. Slaves might slip their shackles, but nowhere could blacks escape their color. Yet shades of color came to mean different things in different places and times. The two-tiered system typically turned a legally blind eye to shades of color. It recognized only white and not white. The three-tiered system recognized colors between black and white and allowed other than whites to enjoy positions and privileges beyond those available to blacks.

The three-tiered system offered opportunities in the chasm between whites and blacks. It invited mixed-race persons to be intermediaries. It let some stand as neither black nor white, as neither slave nor fully free. Only people considered fully white could be considered fully free. Those in Louisiana who came to be called "free people of color" could live and work in a social space between enslavers and enslaved. They escaped rigid restrictions on slaves and enjoyed chances to advance their own position and property.

Law often accorded license to such intermediaries. They grew to share with the groups at both poles. They often grumbled with blacks against impenetrable white supremacy, for being seen as other than white limited what they could do and how far they could rise. They grumbled also with whites about slave primitiveness and black vulgarity. They were not slaves, and they hastened to not be confused with slaves or unlettered blacks. The intermediaries in the three-tiered system hovered in an in-between world.

The colorline persisted in three-tiered societies, to be sure. Indeed, it remained a bright line. Yet three-tiered societies opened selected partitions rather than simply deepening the black-white divide. Such societies let those not white and not enslaved scratch out space for themselves. The arrangement allowed contacts and dealings seldom available to nonwhites in two-tiered societies. Not simply custom and practice but law itself

typically accorded license to nonwhite intermediaries in three-tiered societies. It permitted them to become what the French called *petit-bourgeois*.

While remaining below whites, nonwhites in three-tiered societies selectively gained legal personality and standing. They successfully developed a
common economic and social stake as a *petite bourgeoisie*. They could
own shops and operate crafts and other small-scale, labor-intensive
enterprises. Unlike planters and whites generally, they typically worked
hand-in-hand with those whom they employed. Frequently they ran family
ventures. Often pooling resources in mutual cooperation, they gave one
another material aid, and developed a recognized community.

Common mixed heritage drew Creoles of color together. Indeed, they
developed shared collective and individual identities. Preserving their
French culture and language distinguished them, as did their appearance.
Their identity grew as a rallying point. Their opportunities turned, in large
part, on their distinctive identity. They would in time mobilize more and
more to support, protect, and defend their collective sense of self and their
place. They developed as pragmatic and proud people jealous of their distance from slaves and blacks generally, yet envious of white privilege.

Louisiana grew to epitomize the three-tiered system in North America.
Its acknowledged mixed-race population led the nation in numbers and
notoriety. It persisted in practicing open racial mixing when others had
stopped. Early English colonists in the Chesapeake and Carolinas, for
example, were not so unlike the early French in Louisiana in mating with
non-European women. By the early 1700s, however, rates of interracial offspring fell sharply in the British colonies. Yet rates remained relatively high
in Louisiana, as in the Caribbean, into the 1800s. Mixed-race communities
developed not simply in size but in stature. In Louisiana, those whom the
French first called *métis*, came to be called Creoles or free people of color.
They gained remarkable education, status, and wealth. The initials *f.m.c.*
(free men of color) or *h.c.l.* (*hommes de couleur libre*) became badges of
distinction.

French colonials seeded Louisiana's free colored community. Injecting
color, culture, and language, they defied the *Code noir* to mix with Africans
and Indians. The personal pull of sex proved stronger than the official push
for segregation. The French in early Louisiana lay hardly alone. The paucity
of European women led to similar behavior throughout the Gulf region.
Frenchmen in the Caribbean also indulged themselves. In Saint-Domingue,
where by 1754 there were about 14,000 whites and 170,000 blacks, disap-
proving authorities repeatedly complained about white-black mating. One
commissioner on the island colony huffed in 1760 about "the too intimate

intercourse of the whites and blacks, the criminal intercourse that most of the masters have with their women slaves. If the master is not married, and that is mostly the case (marriage not being popular, and libertinage more tolerated)," the report continued, "the inconstancy natural to the men of this climate makes them change or multiply their concubines" (Davis 1928, 23).

The Spanish proved perhaps more promiscuous than the French. They also took Indian and African women as early mates. Three in four persons counted in Spanish Santo Domingo in 1725 appeared of mixed blood. Those traditions came together in Louisiana in the 1760s.

France lost most of its presence in the Americas in the 1760s. Its empire suffered much from the nearly global Great War for Empire. In North America, British colonists called the struggle from 1754 to 1763 "the French and Indian War." In Europe it ran from 1756 to 1763 and carried the name "the Seven Years War." By whatever name, the French lost.

Anticipating the sad end, French King Louis XV (r. 1722–1774) did a deal with his Bourbon dynasty cousin, Spanish King Carlos III (r. 1759–1788), to keep their common foe Great Britain from getting all of French North America. In the November 1762 Treaty of Fontainebleau, France secretly ceded to Spain "the country known as Louisiana, as well as New Orleans and the island in which the city is situated."

France and Spain then negotiated peace with Britain. The resulting Treaty of Paris of February 1763 said nothing of the 1762 French-Spanish deal. France ceded Canada to Great Britain, along with all claims to the undefined territory east of the Mississippi. France saved for itself only New Orleans and the North Atlantic group of fishing islands of St. Pierre and Miquelon, south of Newfoundland.

The French thus handed over to Great Britain what had been the bulk of *Nouvelle-France*. Before officially leaving, French leaders negotiated concessions for residents. They got the British to agree in Article IV of the 1763 Treaty of Paris to allow "the liberty of the Catholic religion to the inhabitants of Canada." The British agreed also to allow free emigration from Canada for 18 months. French Canadian inhabitants got the right to "retire with all safety and freedom wherever they shall think proper" (Great Britain 1763).

Thousands took the opening. They would not abide living under British rule. An exodus began particularly from the Canadian areas the English renamed Nova Scotia, New Brunswick, and Prince Edward Island—an area the French had called *Acadie*. The British had been seeking to push out the

French there since the early 1700s. They had deported hundreds during the French and Indian War, and they would deport another 1,500 or so after the French helped the fledgling Americans in the War for U.S. Independence (1775–1783).

With the thousands who departed before 1766, the exiles became part of what Acadians dubbed *Le Grand Dérangement* (the Great Upheaval). Some exiles returned to France. Others went south to Saint-Domingue, favoring French rule but not life in France. Many immigrated to New Orleans, and even more to an area about 150 miles east of the city. They settled between the Vermilion River and Bayou Teche, not yet knowing France had ceded the region to Spain.

The fresh French settlers from Acadia became "Cajuns" in Louisiana. Over time, they mixed with many others while preserving their special ethnic heritage. Like Creoles, they proudly retained their French language, heritage, and culture. Their attachment to things French allied them with earlier settlers in French Louisiana when Spain moved to assert its rule in the ceded territory. The upstarts expelled Antonio de Ulloa, the first governor Spain sent in March 1766: In the so-called Rebellion of 1768, Cajuns, Creoles, Germans, and other residents of former French Louisiana sent Ulloa packing.

Spain soon settled the most pressing local grievances. Ulloa's clumsy handling, more than anything else, had rubbed French settlers the wrong way. His ouster and a more adept, no-nonsense governor in the Irish-born, Catholic Spanish Field Marshal Alejandro O'Reilly promised less future friction in what the Spanish named *Luisiana* and administered from Cuba as a district in the *Virreinato de Nueva España*.

The viceroyalty of New Spain thus replaced New France as old Louisiana's official home. " 'Bloody' O'Reilly," as some locals dubbed the governor, soon calmed conditions with an iron fist in a velvet glove. Yet Spanish officials remained wary as they moved to learn what would settle residents. They worried that the bulk of French colonists simply wanted Louisiana to return to French rule. Sensing tenuous allegiance, the Spanish sought to make local allies. In the process, they reached out to Creoles of color.

Spanish officials understood the in-between position of free blacks and Creoles. They had ample experience using them as bulwarks and as intermediaries in slave societies. From the Yucatán to Chile, Spain had used blacks early as conquistadors. Juan Garrido, for example, fought in Hernán Cortés's company in 1519 against the Aztecs and for 30 years shouldered arms for Spain in Mexico and Cuba. Officials throughout *Nueva Espana* learned to use free colored militia. In many ways, they saw color as a blend rather than a simple separation. They allowed nonwhites status and privilege, according them distinct identities from slaves. Granted, *Negros* and *pardos*, as the Spanish referred to blacks and the browns of mixed race, never became Spaniards—that line remained sharp. Yet Creoles of color early found positions for themselves under Spanish rule. They could walk and talk with masters and slaves, with blacks and whites and Indians. And they could stand with or against any other group.

So the Spanish in Louisiana moved to get on their side those they called *libres*, free persons of color. Creoles of color, as the French called them, shared ties to France with other French settlers. Yet they, too, had grievances. The colorline left them bereft of positions they craved. Indeed, the bulk of Creoles remained enslaved along with blacks under French rule. Mixed blood had brought manumission to only a few. When France formally left, Louisiana had only about 150 free persons of color and more than 12,000 slaves. The transition to Spanish rule opened avenues for Creoles to advance, and it opened chances to increase their number free from slavery.

Slaveholders in French Louisiana made scant use of the *Code noir*'s process for manumitting slaves. The action required an officially registered writing. It could be a last will and testament, if the master wanted to wait until his death to part with the slave. It could be a deed, like one transferring property. Either writing released the slave from the control and rule slavery imposed: It made the former slave her or his own person. Manumission removed the legal label and status *slave*. Technically it put nothing in its place. It was a legal withdrawal, rather than a grant. It took away rather than gave; it put the ex-slave on his or her own.

The *Code noir* required all manumission writings to be filed with the Superior Council, which acted as Louisiana's colonial registry. It held all legal records, including deeds and debts such as mortgages, and it kept the colony's vital statistics. The king appointed the Superior Council's members. They constituted the French colony's chief court for all matters civil and criminal. The Council recorded few gifts or legacies of manumission. Immediate and potential profits in the slave society from exporting timber, staves, furs, rice, and sugar prompted holders to tighten, rather than release, their holdings of slaves.

Shifting from French to Spanish law liberalized manumission policies and multiplied the number of free people of color in Louisiana. The transition itself brought manumission to some. Departing French settlers set a few slaves free on leaving. More departed with their slaves in tow. Several prominent planters and more than a few New Orleans merchants headed to

Saint-Domingue with their slaves. The prospect of Spain's closed commercial policies repelled them. Some also appeared put off as they understood Spanish law let slaves have a significant say in their own manumission.

Notably, Spain's rule allowed slaves to hold property of their own and to buy their freedom. A slave entered in Spanish Luisiana's judicial records simply as "Miguel" early illustrated the practice of self-purchase. When his mistress refused to set a price for his release from slavery, Miguel petitioned local authorities. The law throughout Spain's empire gave him and all other slaves a right to have a self-purchase price. In the absence of a price master and slave negotiated, Spanish law directed local judicial authorities to appoint an impartial arbiter to determine the slave's fair market value. Miguel got his price set at 500 pesos (the Spanish silver coin common in the Americas). The court directed Miguel's holder to execute a contract for manumitting him on his paying her the set 500 pesos. Miguel was not alone: Spanish Luisiana's judicial records showed repeated petitions to exercise self-purchase provisions between 1769 and 1800 (Porteouos 1939, 269–271).

The population of free persons of color in Louisiana expanded markedly under Spanish rule. Their number increased particularly in commercial enclaves where slaves could turn time off from their masters into their own coin of freedom, and New Orleans became a premier place for such transactions. Other seaboard cities also drew free people of color. Mobile and Pensacola—New Orleans's sister cities along the Gulf of Mexico—also had small communities of free persons of color. Along the Atlantic, every major port featured a cluster of mixed-race persons along with free blacks. Savannah, Charleston, Wilmington, Richmond, Petersburg, Baltimore, Philadelphia, New York, and Boston all developed significant communities of nonwhites seeking to be free and stay free of slavery.

New Orleans and her sister seaport cities served as safe harbors. They were the bane of conservatives who insisted on rigid social controls. The crush and rush of people simply allowed fewer restraints. The energy, the coming and going, the buying and selling, the flow of people in and out made cities more comfortable places for many who elsewhere found themselves marginal. Many secured urban niches unavailable elsewhere. And the bigger the city, the more space was available. So it was in New Orleans that the seeds of Homer Plessy's fight sprouted its long roots.

References

Davis, H. P. 1928. *Black Democracy: The Story of Haiti*. New York: Dial Press.

Ditchy, Jay K., trans. 1930. "Early Census Tables of Louisiana." *Louisiana Historical Quarterly* 13 (April): 205–229.

Great Britain. 1763. *The Definitive Treaty of Peace and Friendship, between His Britannick Majesty, the Most Christian King, and the King of Spain Concluded at Paris, the 10th Day of February, 1763: to Which, the King of Portugal Acceded on the Same Day*. London: E. Owen and T. Harrison.

Lachance, Paul F. 1994. "The Formation of a Three-Caste Society: Evidence from Wills in Antebellum New Orleans." *Social Science History* 18 (2): 211–242.

Louisiana. 1724. "Black Code of Louisiana." In *Historical Collections of Louisiana*, ed. Benjamin F. French, 89–95. New York: D. Appleton & Co.

Porteous, Laura L. 1939. "Index to Spanish Judicial Records." *Louisiana Historical Quarterly* 22: 180–271.

United States. 1896. *Plessy v. Ferguson*, 163 U.S. 537.

THREE

The Takeover: French, Spanish, American

PLESSY'S PEOPLE fought against a tightening colorline after the United States took over Louisiana in 1803. Americans insisted on sharper racial divisions than the French or Spanish as they imposed their expanding system of American Negro slavery. Their brand of white supremacy pushed a stark black/white divide. Their racial practices and principles recognized no intermediary positions. Creoles of color fell, then, on the dark side of an officious American divide. They were not so easily separated, however, from the special spaces they constructed for themselves particularly in and around New Orleans.

Creoles' place in Louisiana suffered sharp ups and downs as winds of a shifting world order buffeted the territory. In the span of little more than a generation, claims to the land bounced from French to Spanish to French to American hands. None of the powers paid more than scant attention to Indians who lived on the land, possessing it as they had for centuries. Instead, Europeans and many of their American progeny tended to credit only themselves and those who appeared like them. They deemed themselves alone worthy of ownership and command. That attitude would long persist.

Between 1762 and 1803, much changed in Louisiana along with the claimed right to rule. Conflicting directions and developments flooded the lower territory around New Orleans with tides of fresh challenges. Each wave threatened settled foundations, often washing away old understandings and leaving only contested socialscapes. The surge rushed against diverse peoples with long roots in the soil; Homer Plessy's forebears were among those peoples.

Plessy's roots reached back through his paternal grandmother Catherina Mathieu Deveaux, and her mother, Agnes, and through his mother Rosa

Debergue and her mother, Josephine Blanco. They and others of his Creole people struggled in the welter to secure their place.

Only at a distance did Louisiana's Creoles get notice of European or American dictates determining the legal framework of their lives. To start, the secret November 1762 Treaty of Fontainebleau transferred from France to Spain the land where Louisiana's Creoles lived. The next year, in Article 7 of its February 1763 Treaty of Paris with France and Spain, Great Britain won guaranteed "navigation of the river Mississippi . . . in its whole breadth and length, from its source to the sea" (Great Britain 1763). On securing recognition of their independence, Britain's former American colonists clung to guaranteed access to the river, but opening the Mississippi to them proved to be about more than simple passage.

Article 8 of the Anglo-American Treaty of Peace signed in Paris on September 3, 1783, declared that "the navigation of the river Mississippi, from its source to the ocean, shall forever remain free and open to the subjects of Great Britain and the citizens of the United States." Article 2 had granted the United States all British claims to the lands east of the Mississippi, from the Great Lakes down to the "thirty-first degree of north latitude" (United States 1783). That line lay a bit below what decades later became the state of Missouri's southern border. Spain then held claim below the line. Most importantly, Spain controlled the mouth of the Mississippi; it held New Orleans and access to and from the Gulf of Mexico and thus from the lower North American interior to the Atlantic world.

Without Spain's assent, U.S. rights to navigate the Mississippi fell short of reaching their real aim—access to the ocean for the U.S. West. Only in the October 1795 Treaty of Friendship, Limits, and Navigation between Spain and the United States, signed at San Lorenzo el Real (sometimes called simply the Treaty of San Lorenzo) did Spain recognize any right of U.S. citizens to navigate the Mississippi through Spanish *Luisiana*. Also Americans won access to New Orleans. They gained the privilege of tax-free deposit, which enabled them to store in the port goods for transfer. Americans cheered the long-sought benefit as a big boost for their western trade, but the concession failed to satisfy Americans for long. They craved more. They wanted New Orleans itself.

Spain held claim to the territory only briefly after its 1795 treaty with the United States. It returned the claim to France in the October 1800 Treaty of San Ildefonso. The French Republic had by then replaced the Bourbon monarchy. The French Revolution, signaled by the fall of the Bastille in July 1789, had toppled the *Ancien Régime*. Also it triggered the series of massive conflicts called the Wars of the French Revolution (1792–1802).

The fighting engulfed Europe, and spilled over to the Americas as well. France and the United States entered the so-called Quasi-War from 1798 to 1800. On the U.S. side, the undeclared war mostly produced bruised feelings and skirmishes at sea. Prospects for more serious fighting flared, however, as France reclaimed Louisiana.

The French Revolution produced serious battles in the Caribbean, where common winds carried it with significant consequences for France and the United States. Intense fighting enveloped what was then France's chief colony, Saint-Domingue. Sitting on the western third of the Caribbean island of Hispaniola, Saint-Domingue had risen to riches in the latter 1700s from tropical plantation products. Cotton, tobacco, indigo, cacao, and coffee all proved profitable, but sugarcane led all moneymakers. The lure of wealth pulled tens of thousands of Frenchmen to Saint-Domingue. The colony easily outpaced Canada in growth. Only about 65,000 French settlers and few others than Indians inhabited Canada in 1763 when France ceded to Britain claim to the millions of mostly frigid square miles. By comparison, Saint-Domingue's tropical 10,714 square miles boasted about 40,000 Frenchmen when the Bastille fell in 1789. It had 10 times that number of enslaved blacks.

Saint-Domingue slaves led their fellows in the French Caribbean in thrilling to the sound of *"liberté, égalité, fraternité."* The French Republic took the phrase as a revolutionary motto. An early version declared *"liberté, égalité, fraternité ou La Mort."* Slaves in the Caribbean showed themselves ready to face *La Mort* (death) to claim their share of "liberty, equality, fraternity."

French forces struggled initially even to suppress black rebels on the tiny island of Martinique (436 mi^2 [1,128 km^2]), where slaves rose up almost immediately on hearing the echoes of the 1789 revolution. Moving west 800 miles from the eastern Caribbean to Saint-Domingue, suppressing fervor for liberty among its more than 450,000 slaves proved harder. What became known as the Haitian Revolution roiled the erstwhile French colony from 1791 to 1804. It ended in the declaration of the *République d'Haïti*—the second independent nation in the Americas.

Thousands fled Saint-Domingue to escape the fighting. Among them was Germain Plessy—Homer Plessy's grandfather. Some escaped to other Caribbean islands; some, like Germain, headed to the North American continent, trickling early into U.S. Atlantic seaports. Charleston, Baltimore, Philadelphia, and New York got a share of the refugees. So did New Orleans, although it was not so inviting before 1800 when it reverted from Spanish to French hands.

Only an estimated 100 Saint-Domingue refugees arrived in New Orleans between 1791 and 1797. Another 200 came between 1797 and 1802. They proved to be only the first dribbles, yet they excited concerns about the character and future of what in 1800 had again become French Louisiana. The infusion of fresh French blood enlivened the Creole community. New *gens de couleur* and those whom the French called *affranchis*, denoting former slaves, expanded the community of French-speaking free people of color. The strengthening French presence disturbed many Americans.

President Thomas Jefferson stood chief among Americans who frowned at France's reclaiming Louisiana. He eyed the territory as primed for a U.S. takeover long before the French repossession. He envisioned the uncharted lands as extending his dream of a U.S. "empire of liberty." On taking office in March 1801, Jefferson almost immediately began scheming to acquire the territory, or at least New Orleans. The city sat as the entry and exit to and from lower North America's heartland.

Jefferson directed U.S. minister to France Robert R. Livingston to probe French intentions for Louisiana. A skilled diplomat, the prominent New Yorker had served from 1781 to 1783 as the first U.S. secretary of foreign affairs. Yet Jefferson in his ardor refused to leave the business solely to Livingston. The president wanted a closer hand in any deal, so he dispatched his Virginia friend and neighbor James Monroe to work with Livingston. As well as knowing Jefferson's wishes, Monroe knew the French scene. He had served earlier as U.S. minister to France in 1794.

Jefferson authorized Livingston and Monroe to spend $10 million to buy New Orleans. The city's strategic location made it essential to U.S. development. Under foreign control, it formed more than a bottleneck. The French irritatingly demonstrated the point in 1801. On retaking New Orleans, they had closed the port to U.S. citizens. The United States could not abide having its western commercial outlet blocked, and its concerns spread to more than the city.

U.S. fears focused on possible French designs to establish an empire in western North America. The French appeared to be moving with bravado to reestablish their control over their Caribbean colonies. France's brash new leader, first consul Napoleon Bonaparte, sent his brother-in-law General Charles Leclerc to suppress rebels in the French Caribbean, primarily in Saint-Domingue. A force of 40,000 troops sailed with Leclerc in December 1801 from Brest in northwestern France. The captain-general arrived at Samaná Bay in January 1802, and in February retook the ruined provincial capital of Cap François. Jefferson and others paled at the prospect of France's reestablishing its empire in the Americas. That worry spurred U.S. efforts to get title to France's North American claims.

What secured U.S. western dreams resulted less from U.S. efforts and more from black success in Saint-Domingue. There, the rebels repelled French forces. General Leclerc successfully used subterfuge early in 1802 to capture rebel leader Toussaint L'Overture. He deported the one-time slave to exile in France, where Toussaint died in April 1803. But his capture failed to end the revolution. Increasingly desperate, Leclerc ordered a ruthless counterinsurgency. He unleashed 1,500 dogs trained to hound and rip apart their prey. "Terror will precede me and woe to those who will not obey me," Leclerc announced. "I make terrible examples, and since terror is the sole resource left me," the French commander declared, "I employ it" (James 1938, 284–285). But that, too, failed.

Rebels in Saint-Domingue refused to submit to restoration of the slave regime. Their steadfast resistance, combined with the ravages of yellow fever, killed more than 50,000 French troops. General Leclerc himself died in Saint-Domingue in November 1802, and the surviving French forces withdrew in November 1803. The wreck of Leclerc's expedition shattered Napoleon's dream of a revived French empire in the Americas and moved him in disgust to offer the United States all France's claims on North America.

With its debacle in Saint-Domingue, France became eager to sell and the United States stood eager to buy. Each side thought itself favored in the sale. U.S. minister to France Robert Livingston pronounced the deal "equally advantageous to both the contracting parties" (Hosmer 1902, 135). French First Counsel Bonaparte got what he wanted—60 million francs ($15 million) to fund war against Britain. He was not happy with the circumstances that brought France to the bargain, but he saw the deal as necessary. "I require a great deal of money for this war, and I would not like to commence it with new taxes," he confided to his chief negotiator, treasury minister François de Barbé-Marbois. "I know the value of what I abandon. I renounce it with the greatest regret. To attempt obstinately to retain it would be folly," the French leader explained about France's North American claims (Barbé-Marbois 1830, 275).

Negotiators closed the sale in 15 days. The U.S. agents agreed to more than they had been authorized to spend. Their budget was $10 million, but that had been for only New Orleans and its immediate surroundings. They got New Orleans along with claims to approximately 828,800 mi^2 (2.15 million km^2) of French lands. Securing the French claims nearly doubled U.S.

territory. Livingston exulted after the treaty signing. "Today, the United States take their place among the powers of the first rank," he declared in April 1803. "[T]his is the noblest work of our lives," he beamed (Hosmer 1902, 142).

Overstating the historic import of the Louisiana Purchase would be difficult. In his monumental *History of the United States of America during the Administrations of Thomas Jefferson* (1889–1891), Henry Adams declared the "annexation of Louisiana was an event so portentous as to defy measurement. It gave a new face to politics, and it ranked in historical importance next to the Declaration of Independence and the adoption of the Constitution—events of which it was the logical outcome" (Adams 1889, 2:334–335). Acquiring a swath of the continent's broad middle opened the nation to an expansive future for so-called Manifest Destiny to spread the United States across North America from the Atlantic to the Pacific. It led in time to the U.S. acquisition of Texas, the Mexican Cession, the Oregon Territory, Alaska, and more.

More than enlarging America, the Louisiana Purchase amplified contention over what America was and was to be and over what it meant to be American and over who would be deemed American. That ultimately was what Plessy's case was about. The Purchase started to position contending forces in the running war that produced the battle in the historic case of *Plessy v. Ferguson*. The fight proceeded along a broad front. Becoming or being American, both in substance and on the surface, would engage the United States in enduring conflicts far beyond the place that shortly became the State of Louisiana. Yet its socialscape set the battle there apart, particularly in the special place that was New Orleans.

Opponents of Jefferson denounced the acquisition as the beginning of the end for the new nation. South Carolina's Federalist congressman John Rutledge, Jr., conceded that "New Orleans . . . was absolutely necessary for us to get." Yet he complained that "in *substance* [New Orleans] is all we have got for our fifteen millions." He deplored "the purchase of a trackless world." He worried that the larger territory would prove "A country which when worth the holding will I have no doubt rival and oppose the Atlantic states." Further, he rued, "This seems to be a miserably calamitous business—indeed I think it must result in the disunion of these States" (Bacot 1917, 56–57).

The contentious Missouri Compromise of 1820, Bleeding Kansas in the 1850s, the Civil War in the 1860s, and more in time may have proved Rutledge right. At his writing in October 1803, clear contention percolated over what the "trackless" purchase meant for America and Americans.

In no place was the test of absorbing and incorporating the vast territory and different cultures and peoples more immediate than in and around New Orleans.

The United States came to administer New Orleans and its surroundings almost naively. The venture was a first for the new nation. Aside from achieving its own independence, it had never before taken over any European colony. The nation had acquired territory earlier. In its 1783 Peace of Paris with Britain, the freshly minted United States got claims to lands east of the Mississippi. Much of that area was wild, however. The nation had no experience in governing any settled place previously administered with European-based laws outside the Anglo-American tradition. Indeed, the United States had less than 15 years' practice in governing itself under its Constitution of 1787.

The United States in 1803 lacked even a firm understanding of whether the Constitution authorized the national government to purchase foreign territory. The Constitution provided in Article IV for Congress to admit new states, but it nowhere said anything directly about Congress's authority to buy territory. And it nowhere authorized the U.S. president to commit the nation to buying lands. What President Jefferson and Americans like him then dreamed of doing in the Louisiana Purchase was clearer than how they would actually do it. No guide or plan or precedent existed for making New Orleans and the larger Louisiana territory *American*.

Even whether the United States could and would succeed in holding its purchase remained in question at least until after the January 1815 Battle of New Orleans at the close of the Anglo-American War of 1812. In the first years of U.S. occupation, Secretary of State James Madison fretted over losing the prize. Threats to break off the territory or at least part of it alarmed him. What became known as the Burr Conspiracy in 1805–1806 illustrated the early fragility of the American presence. That former U.S. vice president Aaron Burr was implicated in a treasonous plot with U.S. Army officers to set up an inland empire shook U.S. political foundations, to say nothing of stirring questions about the tenuous U.S. hold on the territory. Also the reported conspiracy sparked smoldering ill will with Spain and its colonies on the Louisiana territory's borderlands to the east and particularly to the west.

The United States simply entered a new frontier with its Louisiana Purchase. The territory stretched beyond known limits. Indeed, exactly what land the United States bought in 1803 was not entirely clear. Indeed, to at least glimpse what the nation had bought, President Jefferson commissioned his fellow Virginia-born Meriwether Lewis and William Clark to map part of the purchase dimensions. The Lewis and Clark expedition of 1804–1806 captivated American popular imaginations. President Jefferson, himself, imagined finding a route for immediate U.S. trade to China.

The lower purchase territory lay as the immediate focus of attention. About one-third of the territory's official population, which excluded Indian tribes, lived in Orleans Parish when U.S. administrators arrived in 1803. The area had long shimmered in American eyes. It was indeed a prize. At acquisition in 1803, New Orleans immediately ranked as a major U.S. urban center. With 17,242 residents, it trailed only New York (96,373), Philadelphia (53,722), Baltimore (46,555), Boston (33,787), and Charleston (24,711) in population when it first appeared in the U.S. Census in 1810 (Gibson 1998: tab. 4; University of Virginia 2004, 1810).

The United States entered an essentially exotic place in New Orleans. It encountered people who in mix, language, and culture differed notably from people any other place under U.S. control. Granted, the original states were hardly uniform. Their language, culture, and mix of people varied widely. Yet little in its brief national experience prepared the United States for incorporating the vast area of its 1803 purchase or the densely populated part in and around New Orleans.

Having the place in hand provoked questions of how to handle it. New Orleans was essentially foreign. In sight and sound the residents were exotic. They were not strikingly different the way Indians were; most were deemed "civilized." Nevertheless, they were distinctive. Visitor after visitor remarked on how its people distinguished the place. They were polyglot, as were the populations of many U.S. cities. Yet they formed the most concentrated multilingual locale in the United States. French, Spanish, German, Irish brogue, Caribbean patois, Benue-Congo, Kwa, and other African languages were heard there along with Amerindian tongues. English was foreign, and a minor tongue at that.

Language became an immediate battleground, and it would long remain so. In itself and as a sign or symbol of allegiance, language marked volatile front lines in culture wars that promised to be long-lasting. Speech came to signal to some who was or was not a true American. It was not the only indication. Race immediately designated nonwhites as not Americans, whatever their tongue. Among whites, however, language served to assure some of loyalty. And loyalty was, indeed, much in question as the United States came to administer its newly acquired Louisiana territory.

Questions of rights attached to language and culture. Also they were emotional issues of identity. Creoles like Plessy's people particularly held fast to their French legacy. They insisted that law guaranteed them the right to be who they were. The 1803 Franco-American purchase treaty had, in fact, promised the ceded territory's inhabitants a range of rights. Article III provided for incorporating them into the United States and stated that "they shall be maintained and protected in the free enjoyment of their liberty, property and the Religion which they profess." France's chief purchase treaty negotiator, treasury minister François de Barbé-Marbois, reported that Napoleon himself insisted on such protections. "Let the Louisianians know that we separate ourselves from them with regret; that we stipulate for everything they can desire," Napoleon reportedly told his envoy (Barbé-Marbois 1830, 293).

Article III provided for the ceded territory's inhabitants to be "admitted as soon as possible according to the principles of the federal Constitution to the enjoyment of all these rights, advantages and immunities of citizens of the United States." But the U.S. Constitution specified no principle other than naturalization for receiving foreign-born persons as citizens. For that matter, the Constitution's Article I, section 8, simply authorized Congress "To establish a uniform rule of naturalization." Nothing prescribed any fixed policy or process for treating people such as Louisiana's pre-treaty residents.

Again, the United States had no precedent for handling the purchase territory's people. Fitting the lands and populations into the United States as fully functioning fixtures tested the self directed process of nation-building. In many guises, identity stood at the core of the process. With less than a generation since its 1776 Declaration of Independence, the United States had hardly fixed its national identity by 1803. That construction would be long ongoing. Part of it rested on developing governmental structures. The most important part rested on developing attachments and harmony among the people.

Achieving harmony proved difficult in what Congress designated in March 1804 as the "territory of Orleans" (United States 1804, 283). Recognizing the area's distinction, Congress separated it from the rest of the Louisiana Purchase Territory, dividing the French cession at 33 degrees north latitude—a line that later became the Louisiana-Arkansas border. Anglo-Americans migrating there with their own fixed ideas of who their fellow Americans should be or how they should look and act or live entered an open-ended struggle.

To start, the territory of Orleans's population was mostly nonwhite. Only South Carolina had a similar majority. More than 6 in 10 of the inhabitants in Orleans Parish had an African forebear when the United States took over the territory. Yet differences ran deeper. Creoles of color added dimensions different in size and significance from any other place in the United States. These were Plessy's people. The U.S. Census in 1810 labeled them "freemen and women and children of color." It counted 5,727 such persons in New Orleans (University of Virginia 2004, 1810).

To be clear, other U.S. cities then had sizable free populations of color. In states that had outlawed slavery or were in the process of doing so, several places outstripped or came close to New Orleans in numbers. Philadelphia led U.S. cities in 1810 with a population of 10,514 in the category the federal census labeled "other free persons." New York City followed with 8,137. Connecticut's New London (1,579) and the Massachusetts capital of Boston (1,484) trailed. None of the South's slave states had a city that topped New Orleans's 5,727 free persons of color. Only the Maryland city of Baltimore came close with its 5,671 free colored persons. Charleston, South Carolina, trailed with 1,783, and Richmond, Virginia, lay further back with 1,189 (University of Virginia 2004, 1810).

Numbers told only part of the story. Plessy's people shaped more by their presence and prominence than simply by their size. They stood nonpareil. In no other American place did the community of free people of color approach the accomplished and varied dimensions of that in and around New Orleans. They formed the base of what became the wealthiest community of free people of color in the United States. Visitors to antebellum Louisiana repeatedly remarked on the property and standing of Creoles of color. They included plantation and farm owners. They included slave-owners, too. They included professionals, such as physicians. They included a host of artisans in various crafts. Most were literate and many were well-educated graduates of European schools.

In 1803 the community was not what it would become, but it had well formed its foundations from generations of mixed African and European offspring. The American takeover prompted formal recognition of such unions. Uncertainties in the changing legal regime moved hundreds of European-born men to register their coupling with, and offspring from, African and Afro-American women. Recorded wills in Orleans Parish beginning in 1803 displayed acknowledgments with property and other support for the women and children of these consensual unions. Women such as Charlotte Trudeau thus came to manage significant property, and her six children with Louis Alegre grew to inherit significant property. Families of color such as that Alegre formed with Trudeau, whom he described in his will as a *négresse libre* (free Negro woman), grew into a vibrant community (Lachance 1994, 214).

A last wave of Saint-Domingue refugees expanded the Creole community's reach and resilience. In 1809, roughly 10,000 refugees from the former French colony arrived in New Orleans. They had first fled to Cuba, but finding them too troublesome amid the continuing Napoleonic Wars, Spanish colonial officials in 1809 expelled them. That launched a flotilla of boat people mostly from the southeastern ports of Baracoa and Santiago de Cuba, which sat directly across the Windward Straits from what had become Haiti. Baracoa lay only 150 miles northwest of Cap-Haitien, Haiti. Santiago de Cuba lay 250 miles from the Haitian capital of Port-au-Prince. New Orleans lay about 1,100 miles northwest of the two Cuban ports. Reportedly only one boatload of refugees landed in New Orleans from Havana, 670 miles away (Lachance 1988, 109–111).

The arrivals seemed a human tsunami. Some people saw the inflow as an invasion. Many Anglo-American migrants feared being swept aside in a flood of what they viewed as alien beliefs and behaviors. The Virginia-born migrant lawyer James Brown, who in 1813 would become one of Louisiana's first two U.S. senators, denounced the refugees as "the forces of Bonaparte." They bode ill in his view. He counted them as un-American and feared they would delay, if not derail, the project of Americanizing New Orleans and its environs.

"Our American population since the Cession has perhaps increased about 2,000 whilst we are indebted for the last 12 months alone for the introduction of from 10 to 15000 French," Brown complained in February 1810 to his fellow Virginia-born friend and ambitious political ally Henry Clay, then lawyering in Kentucky and soon to be a force for 40 years in U.S. politics. "The refugees . . . have collected in this City & Territory where they find their own manners, laws, and I may add government," Brown grumbled (Padgett 1941, 931–932).

The Saint-Domingue refugees did, in fact, alter dynamics in and around New Orleans. So many came so quickly that they could only have altered prevailing living patterns. Their numbers multiplied the Orleans Parish population by about one-third in less than a year. Orleans in 1806 counted 17,001 residents. From October 1809 to the end of the year, New Orleans Mayor James Mather reported 9,059 arriving refugees (Lachance 1988, 109–112).

And it was not simply the refugees' gross numbers that altered New Orleans. Complexion, gender, and status added weight to their impact. Most of the 9,059 refugees arriving in late 1809 were nonwhites. The 2,731 whites accounted for less than one-third (30.1 percent) of the arrivals.

The 3,226 slaves (35.6 percent) and 3,102 free persons of color (34.2 percent) predominated.

The nonwhites and whites differed markedly in gender distribution. Men predominated (66.1 percent) among the 2,076 whites aged 15 years or older. In fact, men made up almost exactly half (50.2 percent) of the 2,731 white refugees. In contrast, women predominated (42.8 percent) among the 6,328 nonwhite refugees.

The proportion of children, counted as persons younger than 15 years, was also higher (35.3 percent) among nonwhites than among whites (22.7 percent). The percentage of children was highest among free persons of color (41.8 percent). Among the 1,805 adult free persons of color, the number of women (1,377; 76.3 percent) was more than triple the number of men (428; 23.7 percent). Women and children accounted for the bulk (86.2 percent) of the 3,102 free persons of color. Some were clearly attached to white men as family.

Fewer than 3 in 10 (29.0 percent) of the 3,226 slaves who arrived with the refugees were children. Most of the arriving slaves (41.2 percent) were women. But the arrival of foreign slaves of any sex or age was a problem. In fact, all such arrivals were more than a problem: They were illegal. Congress had prohibited every place under U.S. jurisdiction from receiving slaves from abroad on and after January 1, 1808. That was the earliest date the Constitution authorized such a prohibition to reach any of the original 13 states without their permission. Congress had moved earlier to prohibit importation of slaves into U.S. territories.

On creating the Territory of Orleans in March 1804, Congress prohibited "any person or persons to import or bring into the said territory, from any port or place without the limits of the United States . . . any slave or slaves." The law provided for a fine of $300 for every slave imported in violation of the prohibition. Such a levy amounted to $967,800 for the 3,226 the New Orleans mayor counted as slaves arriving with the Saint-Domingue refugees from October 1809 to January 1810. The law provided also that on a finding of a violation of the statute, "every slave so imported or brought, shall thereupon become entitled to, and receive his or her freedom" (United States 1804, 286).

Territorial Governor William Charles Cole Claiborne initially refused to allow any slaves to land with the refugees. He ordered arriving slaves detained aboard their transports, and he impounded the ships. That furthered havoc. Claiborne insisted that the law was the law and was to be upheld, whatever the circumstances. Yet he would not long hold to that position in the face of the practical costs of confining and providing for the slaves. He had to consider landing the slaves at least for health and safety. Then, too, there was the matter of money spent and money lost in confining the slaves.

Claiborne complained of having limited choices in handling the arriving slaves. He whined about lacking funds either to take care of them or turn them away. "To have them sent out of the Territory, would have been attended with an expense which I had not the means of meeting nor was it easy to select a proper place," he wrote a confidant in July 1809. "To have confined them in Prison, would have been an inhuman act, it would more-over have been attended with an expense which I was neither authorized or prepared to incur," the governor explained (Lachance 1988, 119).

Congress relieved Claiborne of his worries, at least over the arriving slaves. It heeded entreaties and petitions from refugee sympathizers who pled for humanity or a higher law to override technical legalities. "Undoubtedly the laws of the country forbid the introduction of slaves, but the divine law, the laws of humanity make it our duty not to repell those wretches from our shores," implored one petition published in the May 24, 1809, issue of the New Orleans newspaper *Le Courrier de la Louisiane*.

Such pleas ignored the inhumanity of slavery itself. They failed to argue simply to free the slaves. Then and there, slaves had few advocates other than themselves. They found no ready supporters in Congress, which at the end of June 1809 voted to suspend U.S. law so as to permit "bringing into any port or place within the jurisdiction of the United States, any slave or slaves, owned by any person or persons, who shall have been forcibly expelled from the island of Cuba, by order of the government thereof . . . provided also that such slave or slaves shall have been brought into the United States in the same vessel and at the same time as their owner or owners" (United States 1809, 549).

The blacks held as slaves in the 1809 refugee wave proved a lesser problem—at least for the moment. Once their status was settled, they seem-ingly blended into the background. They helped, however, to immediately darken New Orleans as they pushed the number of slaves from 8,378 in 1806 to 10,824 in 1810. Even so, the proportion of slaves fell from 49.3 percent in 1806 to 44.1 percent in 1810. The proportion of whites also fell, from 37.1 percent of Orleans Parish's 17,001 residents in 1806 to only 32.6 percent of the 24,552 in the 1810 census.

The big change in and around New Orleans came in free persons of color. They jumped from 13.6 percent of the parish population in 1806 to 23.3 percent in 1810, as the refugee influx conspicuously augmented the Creole community. The enlarged presence of French-speaking free persons of color reinforced two already ugly battles. The smaller conflict pitted the forces of white supremacy against Creoles insistent on personal and communal rights. The larger was the clash between Anglophone and Francophone forces.

Territorial Governor Claiborne reported to U.S. Secretary of State Robert Smith in July 1809 on how the influx had "much excited" conflicts in and around New Orleans. "The native Americans, and the English part of our society . . . (with some few exceptions) appear to be prejudiced against these strangers, and express great dissatisfaction that an Asylum in this territory was afforded them," Claiborne noted. He further reported in August on how "clamorous" opposition had become, as he explained that "many good Americans are dissatisfied with so great an influx of foreigners" (Lachance 1988, 115).

Claiborne's comment about "good Americans" told something of his leanings. He clearly viewed the scene as a cultural tableau. His political instincts or distrusts cast the sides either as friends or foes. Perhaps the ongoing Napoleonic Wars with their spillover into the Caribbean heightened the governor's concerns. He was hardly alone in worrying about how Europe's titanic struggles surrounding Napoleon's France might affect the local balance of power in America. Claiborne feared the 1809 refugee influx had brought the English/French battle to his territory.

Claiborne's remarks provoked even more profound questions: What or who made "good Americans"? The questions would be long debated. A big part of the discussion in Louisiana in 1809 and later focused on foreign ties. That issue turned on what exactly was *foreign*. In turn, the question came back to what exactly was *American*. At one extreme, some asked if the foreign-born could ever truly be American. Others asked not *if* but *when*. They raised questions about language, religion, and values: What mix might there be in persons deemed "good Americans," to use Claiborne's phrase?

The governor's comments and community response in 1809 exposed hesitations and misgivings about who was who and about who was for or against what and whom. "The foreign Frenchmen residing among us take great interest in favour of their countrymen, and the sympathies of the Creoles of the Country (the descendants of the French) seem also to be much excited," Claiborne noted in July 1809. He and others seemed concerned that perhaps Napoleon was not truly finished in America. They seemed, at least, to fear some form of French repossession or domination—culturally, politically, or both (Lachance 1988, 115).

The refugees provoked more than local concerns about their "Frenchness." And in an Atlantic world at war, their treatment required official tact. For despite the 1803 Louisiana Purchase Treaty, Franco-American relations remained tense. They had been strained since the outbreak of the French Revolution in 1789. They had persisted in a nervous condition of neither peace nor war. Anti-French feelings provoked the four Alien and Sedition Acts Congress passed in June and July 1798 as internal security measures against persons "dangerous to the peace and safety of the United States" (United States 1798, 571).

Hostilities flared in the so-called XYZ Affair of 1798 and the Quasi-War at sea from 1798 to 1800. The Treaty of Mortefontaine, also known as the Franco-American Convention of 1800, calmed tensions enough to avert open war. But no real conciliation followed the 1800 convention. Wrangling persisted over French trade policies and U.S. rights as a nation neutral in Europe's Napoleonic Wars. Depredations by French privateers hardly improved relations.

The handling of Louisiana remained delicate, then, diplomatically and domestically. France was more than sensitive to how America treated persons of French heritage. Governor Claiborne's dispatches to Secretary of State Smith reflected an understanding of the sensitivities.

Louisiana's French community undeniably embraced the 1809 refugees, reveling in them not simply as kindred but almost as reinforcements. The welcome was clear in New Orleans's two leading French-language newspapers. The older was the *Moniteur de la Louisiane*. Reputed to be the first newspaper published in Louisiana, the *Moniteur* opened in 1794. The younger was *Le Courrier de la Louisiane*, which first published in 1807. Both cast the refugees as "victims of the horrors of war," as the *Courrier* described them in its May 24, 1809, issue. Both also published assurances that the refugees were hard working and law abiding. The fresh immigrants had, the *Courrier* insisted, always shown "submission to the laws of the country where they had found an asylum." Both the *Courrier* and the *Moniteur* projected the refugees as assets to advance Louisiana.

Not all refugees counted equally. Even the French-speaking community embraced some more than others. White refugees were most welcome. The *Courrier* reflected that perspective in its May 24, 1809, issue as it identified the refugees in its sights as "unfortunate planters." Most of the arrivals, even among the whites, nowhere approached such status. In writing of the white refugees, Mayor Mather called Governor Claiborne's attention to "many poor women both old and young, and some old or disabled men who can not provide for themselves" (Claiborne 1917, 4:405). That group hardly confirmed the bulk of white refugees as members of the cultivator class. Yet with its paternalist, white male perspective, the *Courrier*'s

spotlight fell on the fewer than one in seven refugees who might have qualified for Louisiana's most elite status—white planters.

Homer Plessy's paternal grandfather, François Germain Plessy, stood
among those nowhere near being "unfortunate planters." He arrived well
before the 1809 wave. Nevertheless, he had emigrated among those refugees noted as *petits blancs*—the little whites. He came with no major property. He held no slaves. His main asset was himself. He was a journeyman
carpenter. He arrived in New Orleans with his brother Dominique.

Born about 1777 in France's southwest city of Bordeaux, Germain—as
he preferred to call himself—had set sail with Dominique for a better life
in the Americas. They had headed first to a tropical Caribbean isle,
Saint-Domingue, but it quickly proved no paradise. The fighting there
pushed them to flee. And so they came to be among the French refugees
in Louisiana.

Germain came to prosper well enough in New Orleans. The expanding
city called for continuous construction, so Germain's carpentry skills were
in high demand. He found ample business to operate Plessy & Co., doing
wood-work of various kinds. He earned enough to support a family and
married the Creole Catherina Mathieu Deveaux. She was born in 1782, the
daughter of the French-born Mathieu Deveaux and a free woman of color
named Agnes. Starting in 1804, Catherina bore Germain four sons and four
daughters. The last of the sons and second-to-last child was Joseph
Adolphe Plessy, born in 1822. He would father Homer Adolph Plessy.

Germain's children and grandchildren were Creoles of color like his wife
Catherina and her mother, Agnes, before her. They were Homer Plessy's
people. And they and those like them found themselves increasingly beleag-
uered in the so-called Americanization of Louisiana.

References

Adams, Henry. 1889. *History of the United States of America during the adminis-
    trations of Thomas Jefferson*, ed. Earl N. Harbert. New York: Literary Classics,
    1986.

Bacot, D. Huger, Jr. 1917. "The Louisiana Purchase, 1803[: John Rutledge to
    Harrison Gray Otis of Boston, Oct. 1, 1803]." *South Carolina Historical and
    Genealogical Magazine* 18 (1): 56–57.

Barbé-Marbois, François. 1830. *The History of Louisiana Particularly of the
    Cession of That Colony to the United States of America*, trans. William Beach
    Lawrence. Philadelphia: Carey & Lea.

Claiborne, William Charles Cole. 1917. *Official Letter Books ... 1801–1816*.
    Jackson, MS: State Department of Archives and History.

Gibson, Campbell. 1998. *Population of the 100 Largest Cities and Other Urban Places in the United States: 1790 to 1990*. Washington, DC: U.S. Census Bureau.

Great Britain. 1763. *The Definitive Treaty of Peace and Friendship, between His Britannick Majesty, the Most Christian King, and the King of Spain Concluded at Paris, the 10th Day of February, 1763: to Which, the King of Portugal Acceded on the Same Day*. London: Printed by E. Owen and T. Harrison.

Hosmer, James Kendall. 1902. *The History of the Louisiana Purchase*. New York: D. Appleton and Company.

James, C. L. R. 1938. *The Black Jacobins: Toussaint Louverture and the San Domingo Revolution*. New York: Dial Press.

Lachance, Paul F. 1988. "The 1809 Immigration of Saint-Domingue Refugees to New Orleans: Reception, Integration and Impact." *Louisiana History* 29 (2): 109–141.

Lachance, Paul F. 1994. "The Formation of a Three-Caste Society: Evidence from Wills in Antebellum New Orleans." *Social Science History* 18 (2): 211–242.

Padgett, James A., ed. 1941. "Letters of James Brown to Henry Clay, 1804–1835." *Louisiana Historical Quarterly* 24: 921–1177.

United States. 1783. *Treaty of Paris of 1783*. Washington, DC: U.S. National Archives and Records Administration, 1972.

United States. 1798. "An Act Concerning Aliens." 1 Stat. 570 (June 25, 1798).

United States. 1804. "An Act Erecting Louisiana into Two Territories, and Providing for the Temporary Government Thereof." 2 Stat. 283 (March 26, 1804).

United States. 1809. "An Act for the Remission of Certain Penalties and Forfeitures, and for Other Purposes." 2 Stat. 549 (June 28, 1809).

University of Virginia. 2004. Geospatial and Statistical Data Center, Historical Census Browser. Charlottesville: University of Virginia.

FOUR

The Colorline: Becoming American

FROM THE OUTSET of U.S. administration of Louisiana in December 1803, free Creoles of color sought recognition as full members of the public community. They fought to be accepted as full citizens. It would be a long campaign. It was the crusade in which Homer Plessy enlisted. His case, which the U.S. Supreme Court would decide in 1896, was part of the struggle. It was part of the Creole drive for law to recognize them as they wished. The colorline repeatedly blocked their quest.

As Homer Plessy demonstrated more than 90 years after the 1803 Louisiana Purchase, color was not a solitary barrier. As with Plessy, complexion and other physical features hardly distinguished Creoles of color from whites. The colorline was a proxy for a capricious complex within an Anglo-American creed of white supremacy manufactured in terms of race and culture to define not only citizenship but identity itself.

The intolerant dogma rested on more than visible features. It backed a political and social regime seeking to dictate the character and value of personal identity. To privilege its own self-image, it propagated a self-absorbed ideology that imagined individuals as types, projecting them as less and more than themselves. It envisaged everyone as representing a circumscribed group and as being imbued with exclusive group characteristics. The view, in many ways, extended a tribal mentality that locked people into predefined positions. It cast personal and group identity as objects to fit Anglo-American white supremacy's own self-centered fabrications. The doctrine demanded to regulate who people were on its terms and required law to recognize persons only in skewed ideological views.

Anglo-American white supremacy worked more to exclude than simply to differentiate. Appearance marked only its first line of attack. It charged far beyond. It pretended to scrutinize the unseen. It presumed to inspect and categorize ancestry and descent. It weighed not only behavior but beliefs, customs, and culture. It further assumed the function of pronouncing judgment on people. In line with its own preconceptions, it declared who people were or were not and whether or where they fit in society. It was transparently political in asserting its norms and standards. It deployed privilege and propaganda in its campaign to enshrine its own self-image and to stigmatize alternative values and views.

Louisiana's Creoles of color challenged the white Anglo-American creed. Their very presence refuted the rationality of official or popular divisions of people into mutually exclusive, homogenous categories cast as absolutes. They embodied the simple fallacy of the black-white dichotomy. Their lineage proved the distortion of branding people as nothing but white or nonwhite, European or Other. Their French heritage further shaped the contest as their refinement showed Creoles as hardly uncultured.

Creoles' conflict fixed on more than their being pushed on the wrong side of the Anglo-American racial divide. Their struggle centered on their identities and individualities. They fought to be themselves and to get official recognition of who they were. They confronted successive governments that refused to acknowledge their character and community as different yet legitimate and fully acceptable. They resisted having any government ignore or rebuff them or the ancestry and heritage that made them who they were. With an acute sense of self-identity as a community and as individuals, they detested being rejected for who they were not.

Creoles of color denounced whiteness as the sole badge of public acceptability or standing. They felt a slap in the face when Congress made being white the sole mark of membership in Louisiana's developing body politic—the sole criterion specified in the act of March 1804 organizing the Territory of Orleans. The only political rights Congress provided in the act went to "free white male persons" (United States 1804, 286).

Tying rights to gender and race was typical U.S. policy. Subordinating women surprised few at the time, and excluding enslaved or even emancipated blacks raised no eyebrows. But Creole free men of color presented a different issue. At least in their own self-view, they embodied composite black-white images. Many were more than mulattoes. Their mixed ancestry reached generations beyond having one white parent. Many had multiple white forebears. The dimensions of their mixed ancestry exposed the fraud of the invented Anglo-American racial dichotomy that ordinarily operated in the United States. Given Louisiana's culture of interracial intimacy, framing Creoles' mixed ancestry contradicted developing U.S. social norms.

Creole free people of color refused to be quietly subordinated in a government intent on brutalizing or marginalizing them simply as nonwhite.

They spurned the straitjacket of the Anglo-American racial dichotomy. They rejected *white* as a singular identity. They did not claim to be white. Their very appearance, however, raised the question of what it meant to be *white*. Like Homer Plessy, many certainly looked white. Many had relatives accepted as white, and they exalted that heritage. Surrendering it seemed to abandon their communal and personal identities. Most refused to do that. They insisted on standing distinct.

Creoles of color had to be careful what they wished for. Standing distinct had advantages and disadvantages. Louisiana's first territorial legislature in June 1806 codified the Anglo-American racial dichotomy. It provided Creoles of color no separate distinction. It lumped them into a category described as "free negroes, mulattoes or mustees." Typical of U.S. practice, the law grouped together all persons with any non-European heritage, whether their ancestors were all Africans or whether some were Europeans, as with mulattoes, or some were American Indians, as with mustees. Anyone with any ancestor not recognized as a European fell outside the privileged circle U.S. law generally prescribed as "white."

Louisiana's 1806 "Act prescribing rules and conduct to be observed with respect to Negroes and other Slaves of this Territory" put Creoles of color nowhere near where they wished to be. It defined them in a narrowing black-or-white position they adamantly opposed. The hardening racial regime since the U.S. takeover implacably thrust Creoles of color closer to blacks. Indeed, it recognized them only as sorts of Negroes and not as any sorts of whites. And the act's title told the tale of the official view of Negroes: It equated *Negro* and *slave*.

The 1806 act recognized differences in status between free people of color and the enslaved. So Creoles of color stood apart to a degree, but not as they wanted. They remained legally distinct from slaves, yet they also remained subordinate as nonwhites. They escaped some of the law's rigid restrictions on slaves whom the law commanded to submission in "absolute obedience." Free people of color enjoyed a freedom of movement and right to travel denied to slaves, whom the law confined to their worksites unless accompanying their holder or carrying a valid pass authorizing their going to and from specified places. The law further classified slaves as property, not persons; it categorized them as real estate subject to mortgage, seizure, sale, and property tax. Slaves could own nothing. They could sell nothing. They could not legally ride a horse, buy liquor, or carry a weapon. They could not marry. The law recognized none of their unions or their children. It refused to see slaves as legitimate couples or as parents. Slaves were simply not persons in the eyes of the law.

As elsewhere in the United States, what became Louisiana's initial Black Code dehumanized and depersonalized slaves. Louisiana's 1808 *Digest of the Civil Laws* summarized the abject condition's definition. "A slave is one who is in the power of a master and who belongs to him in such a manner that," the law decreed, "the master may sell him, dispose of his person, his industry and his labor, and who can do nothing, possess nothing, nor acquire anything, but what belongs to his master" (Louisiana 1808, 10).

Louisiana's new regime simply adopted the usual U.S. rule that, in the eyes of the law, slaves were nonpersons. They had no civil rights. Free people of color had at least some civil rights and a measure of legal personality. Louisiana's 1806 Black Code granted them a right to trial by jury, similar to whites, for instance. Also it let them legally carry weapons if they got a permit to do so from a justice of the peace. Free people of color had rights to property. They could own, buy, and sell goods, services, and land. They could inherit, albeit within limits attached to restrictions on marriage and the legitimacy of children.

Louisiana law persisted in recognizing no interracial unions or their offspring as legitimate. It denied to free women of color and their children with white men valid family status and the legal identity of husband-and-wife and father-and-child. The colorline dammed the legal flow of regular blood relations. In inheritance, it blocked free women of color and their children from claiming full shares of estates from their white mate or parent without a valid and verified will directing distribution of his property.

The onset of U.S. law in 1804 pushed hundreds of European-born men to file testaments with the Orleans Parish recorder of wills between 1804 and 1806. They legally documented their children from, and their consensual unions with, free women of color and provided them rights to share fully from their estates. In doing so, they sought to enable those who were, in fact, their wives and children to defeat the incapacities U.S. law imposed on people of color. Thousands of white men in and around New Orleans similarly filed testaments with the Orleans Parish recorder of wills down through the decades to the Civil War to protect their relations in what the French termed *le ménage de fait* and the English called common law marriage.

Article 8 in Louisiana's 1808 digest of the civil code continued to prohibit marriage between free persons of color and whites. Also it prohibited marriage between free persons and slaves. That restriction rested not on the colorline but on slaves' legal incapacity to act as persons. Louisiana law did not, however, prohibit interracial cohabitation. It perhaps yielded in practice to a *fait accompli*, accepting the historical evidence that a significant segment of Louisiana's population lived on both sides of the arbitrary white/nonwhite colorline.

Fact at times trumped law, for what the law denied as interracial marriages persisted. The registers at New Orleans's St. Louis Cathedral attested to the fact. The parish, established in 1720, maintained two marriage registers: one for whites and one for free persons of color. Interracial unions appeared in both, but with a twist. The mixed pair entered the register as unmixed. For the purposes of the marriage, one of the couple adopted a color for the ceremony, standing either as white, to be recorded in that register, or as a person of color, to be recorded in that register. Homer Plessy's grandparents so stood.

François Germain Plessy married Catherina Mathieu Deveaux in the rebuilt cathedral—completed in 1793–1794 after the calamitous fire of 1789 destroyed the original edifice built over six decades. For Creoles of any standing, as for prominent whites, wedding in the structure was a social must. It validated the union as a matter of public record. The Plessy ceremony preceded U.S. administration in December 1803, not that American law proved any more effective than French law in barring such unions.

Born in France's southwest port city of Bordeaux about 1777, Germain—as Plessy preferred to call himself—was indisputably white. Catherina was not. She was a mixed beauty, one of a multitude for which New Orleans was long much noted. Her father, like her husband, was born in France. She, like her mother, was a free woman of color. The law of the day banned Catherina's marriage, as it had her mother's before her. Yet both marriages were fact. And more than the apparent *ménage de fait* of her parents when she was born in 1782, Catherina had her marriage to Germain solemnized in the St. Louis Cathedral register.

Starting in 1804, Catherina and Germain had four sons and four daughters. Born in 1822, the last of the sons and second-to-last child was Joseph Adolphe Plessy. He would be Homer Plessy's father. The generations of Plessys suffered with others an American push-back against officially or publicly accepting the likes of them.

With U.S. administration, a campaign of exclusion unfolded against free people of color in of Louisiana. Even as territorial law distinguished them from slaves, it reduced what free persons of color legally could do. Legal action pushed them off lands and out of certain occupations. It limited their owning and operating taverns. It restricted their work as midwives. It curbed their public market access. It prohibited their holding white indentures. With such measures segregation increasingly seeped through

Louisiana society as an American custom. The Episcopal Christ Church—
the first Protestant church in the Louisiana territory—exemplified the
trend: It admitted only whites when it opened in 1805.

Creoles battled against the growing exclusion of segregation, but they
fought from tenuous positions. The unfolding political and social terrain
offered them little refuge. No place they preferred opened to shelter them.
Louisiana's developing character under U.S. administration left Creoles to
pick one of the two sides in the Anglo-American racial dichotomy: They
could ally with ruling whites or enslaved blacks.

What choice was that? Who would choose to be black in circumstances
where that choice meant being a slave? Choosing to be white, for any
who could do so, brought wholesale privileges. Yet Creoles' basic self-
perception rejected the choices in principle for their community. Either
choice in their view threatened to destroy their separate identity. Nor did
either appear before the Civil War to accord them the recognition and
status they desired.

Creoles viewed the black/white dichotomy as a false dilemma that failed
to reflect reality. Events early required them to choose a side, however.
They had no fence on which to sit. Everyday decisions pressed continual
choices on them. They had immediate consequences to consider as they
pursued their ultimate communal goal of full public recognition and accep-
tance. They wanted as much freedom as they could muster as long as they
could have it. They could not stand isolated. From almost any perspective,
to preserve what freedom they had demanded that Creoles distance themselves from slaves. Some saw a need even to side with slaveholders.
A few became slaveholders. Others served as plantation overseers or slave
drivers or rode as slave catchers.

The biggest early public test of where Creoles of color stood as a community in regard to slaves in U.S. Louisiana came in the first weeks of
1811. What some have called the largest slave uprising in U.S. history broke
out 35 miles northwest of New Orleans. The area then carried the name the
German Coast or German Coast County. Early French colonials had called
it *Côte des Allemands*. The name originated from the 1720s pioneers from
the Rhineland, Alsace-Lorraine, and other German-speaking regions who
built thriving settlements in what became part of St. Charles and St. John
the Baptist parishes in the French colony.

The outbreak started on Wednesday, January 9, at Manuel Andry's plantation. Slaves attacked Andry (also spelled Andre) and his son. The assailants gathered other slaves as they moved southeast on the River Road
running to the territorial capital. Runaways living as maroons in the bayou

joined the band. Their number swelled from a few dozen to more than 100. Exaggerated estimates reached 500.

Sugar plantations dominated the area, so it was dense with slaves. The local ratio of slaves to whites topped 4:1 in many spots. The St. Charles population in 1820 counted 2,987 slaves and 727 whites; St. John counted 2,209 slaves and 1,532 whites. Yet the rebel core in 1811 likely counted no more than 200. They were not that many when they invaded Jacques Fortier's plantation, about 15 miles east of Andry's estate. Virginia's scowling *Richmond Enquirer* newspaper reported that at Fortier's plantation, the rebels "commenced killing poultry, cooking, eating, drinking and rioting" (Thompson 1992, 8).

Quick reports of the uprising sent whites scurrying. The alarm also rallied local militia and volunteers to suppress the slaves. At an initial encounter on January 10 with their numbers favoring them, the rebels "full of arrogance," according to an on-site report, stood their ground against about 80 local militia and volunteers. A few rebels had horses seized in their progress, but they lacked weapons for any formal battle. Their arms were mostly tools for working cane: machetes and other cane knives, hoes, and axes. The band was certainly no match for U.S. Army General Wade Hampton's regulars and two companies of militia who rushed from New Orleans with a company of dragoons and another of light artillery down from Baton Rouge.

A rout ensued. By midnight on Friday, January 11, the retaliatory carnage totaled 66 blacks dead, 17 missing, and 16 jailed for trial. On January 13, St. Charles Parish Judge Pierre Bauchet St.-Martin convened a summary court of five local property owners, as Louisiana law directed. The three-day proceedings acquitted three slaves and bound over six for further investigation. It condemned 21, who were immediately shot and then decapitated. The court ordered the heads posted on poles "as a terrible example to all who would disturb the public tranquility in the future" (St.-Martin 1811, 20).

The uprising conjured up terrible specters. It projected for many whites glimpses of wholesale death and destruction. Such images arose more from anxious imaginations than from actual results of what was called the German Coast Uprising. Only slaves had suffered slaughter; the rebels killed only two whites. In a speech to the territorial legislature on January 29, 1811, Governor Claiborne described the dead whites as "two highly esteemed Citizens . . . cruelly massacred" (Claiborne 1811, 5:123). Yet many whites feared much worse. Like others in American slave societies, Louisiana's whites lived uneasily in the midst of slaves they dismissed on the one hand but saw as dangerous on the other.

Questions of loyalty headed the list as locals assessed the episode. The Anglo-American black/white divide at the extreme marked such uprisings as race war. Recent history enlarged that view in lower Louisiana. "A Gentleman at New-Orleans," as one writer was styled in a letter dated January 11, 1811, connected the local events to broader currents. "We began on Wednesday last to have a miniature representation of the horrors of St. Domingo," he opined in his much reprinted missive that appeared in the February 19 *New York Evening Post*. His reference reflected the scare the Haitian Revolution threw into U.S. slaveholders.

Anxieties early fixed on slaves brought in with the Saint-Domingue refugee influx in 1809–1810. Suspicion had surrounded such slaves since their arrival in U.S. ports in the early 1790s with the first refugees from violence in the French colony. Watching mayhem unfold there between 1791 and 1804 spread deep apprehensions throughout the United States. Many feared the Caribbean bloodbath would entice imitation on the North American mainland and moved to isolate the Haitian Revolution. Congress in time enacted an embargo against Haiti in February 1806, and little direct U.S. trade would occur until the 1820s. The United States refused to officially recognize the Haitian Republic until 1862. U.S. slaveholders wanted to quarantine what they viewed as a viral infection. They dreaded slaves' being exposed to thinking violence could lead to freedom. The irony of such a position in light of the United States' roots in its own War for Independence appeared lost on slave owners.

The German Coast Uprising refreshed concerns about slave insurrection nationally. At least 90 percent of the newspapers publishing in the United States at the time carried reports of the episode. It flashed as something of a national event. Commenting widely on its meaning, at least 122 papers outside Louisiana took editorial stances with regional differences. Everywhere some mention of the prospects of large-scale U.S. slave uprisings appeared. Also the episode everywhere appeared as a cautionary tale. The press in heavy slaveholding areas cast the episode as a warning for slaves to behave and for slaveholders and whites generally to be on guard. In areas given to antislavery, the press tended to rue the severity of the suppression and cast the episode as a warning against the inevitably bloody consequences of slaveholding (Thompson 1992, 5–29).

Legislatures and municipal councils in slaveholding areas from St. Louis to Tennessee, Kentucky, and Virginia took notice. Many toughened their slave control provisions, and several states reorganized their militia to deal more efficiently with slave unrest in the wake of the Louisiana uprising, if not because of it. Their cue came in part from Louisiana's own responses.

News of the outbreak moved territorial Governor Claiborne to order 200 militiamen to patrol New Orleans and to impose a 6:00 P.M. curfew on black males. The city council rushed to curb paths for slave mischief. After all, New Orleans was then not only the center of U.S. Louisiana but the site of its most numerous and dense slaveholding. Orleans had more slaves than any other parish. It had 14,946 slaves in 1820, twice as many as second-place West Feliciana parish (7,164). So New Orleans acutely felt the threat of slave violence.

Within 10 days of the uprising, New Orleans had fresh ordinances tightening its slave controls. The measures closed the city to all slaves not residing or working there. The city council sanctioned stopping and searching any suspicious slave—meaning any nonwhite person in the city. It authorized summary punishment of slaves found out of place, making them liable to be fined, jailed, and whipped. It banned slaves from congregating outside of work. They could not legally gather on their own in public or private except with the mayor's permit for funerals and daytime Sunday dances. Uneasiness over slaves being armed went so far as banning slaves, unless blind, from carrying canes. Violators suffered 25 lashes and loss of the walking stick. The territorial legislature followed suit in tightening slave controls.

The moves to prevent future slave violence carried disturbing reflections on who had instigated and participated in the uprising. Frightened whites seldom knew what to think in the face of threatened or actual slave violence. Such a terror-filled countenance challenged their thinking about themselves and their slaves and also about slavery and the wider world. They found themselves caught in contradictions.

U.S. slaveholder ideology posed American Negro slavery as basically benevolent and slaves as characteristically servile. If that were true, what did slaveholders or their society have to fear from slaves? Moreover, whites by and large disparaged blacks' intelligence. So how could slaves plan and execute any insurrection posing any real danger to whites generally? Either slaves were truly docile or they were truly dangerous.

Whites' reactions to the 1811 German Coast Uprising, like those to earlier and later such episodes, fell back on many a familiar formula to explain events. To calm themselves at least in part, many whites shifted the troublesome center of unrest from an axis within their slaves and society to outsiders. General Hampton, for example, immediately pointed the finger at foreigners. He fixed particularly on Spanish instigators, as he had the Spanish on his mind. The general happened to be in New Orleans at the time of the uprising only because he and his troops were in transit to fortify the U.S. frontier against Spain. Hampton insisted in a January 12 report to Governor Claiborne that "the plan is unquestionably of Spanish Origin" (Dormon 1977, 401).

Many American worries in the South at the time fixed on the Iberian empire. It then bordered the United States in the southeast with its colonies in East and West Florida. Also it bordered in the southwest with its colony of greater Mexico, then at the start of its war for independence that raged from 1810 to 1821. Some worried about a tit-for-tat syndrome, aware of U.S. instigation to break off from Spanish control Mobile and other parts of what became Alabama, Florida, and Mississippi in the so-called West Florida Rebellion of 1810.

Others blamed French intriguers, and there Creoles of color fell under increased suspicion. Anglo-Americans distrusted the Creoles' mixed heritage. They doubted their loyalty. The Creoles' French language and ways cast them as un-American in some eyes. Their so-called tainted blood that identified them as less than white also identified them as likely allies of enslaved blacks and as generally less than trustworthy in many whites' eyes.

Outside agitators perennially served as convenient foils to cover internal failings. Self-serving provincial views frequently fixed the cause of local troubles on interlopers, usually foreigners or outcasts. The usual self-delusion declared that absent the presence of worrisome outsiders all would have been, and would be, well locally. The view suggested all was well before the outsiders appeared.

So in and around New Orleans in the aftermath of the 1811 uprising, people hunted for persons lacking long and deep local roots. Saint-Domingue refugees immediately surfaced in popular views. Even slaveholders among the exiles or those sympathetic to them fell under suspicion. False reports heaped scorn on plantation owner Barthélémy Macarty, for example, for failing to aid sufficiently in suppressing the uprising. His real fault was being of French descent.

One set of accusations charged recently arrived French colonial slaveholders with not knowing how to treat slaves properly in the American manner. "They are unfriendly and inhuman," claimed a widely reprinted letter, describing exiled Saint-Domingue slaveholders, whom many considered of a class that had long before displayed ineptitude in losing their homeland to slave rebels. "The ill treatment of the slaves is said to be the cause of their late rising," said the letter in the March 30, 1811, *New York Weekly Museum* newspaper. "Americans, who have negroes, are under no fear; they are well treated, and their masters boast they could sleep in the huts with them and be perfectly safe," asserted the writer (Thompson 1992, 20–21).

The coup for accusers of Creoles of color and exiles at large came in fixing the uprising's leader as the mulatto commonly called Charles Deslondes. Some accounts described him as a free person of color; others correctly identified him as a slave brought to Louisiana among the Saint-Domingue exiles. The widow Jean-Baptiste Deslondes held title to him, accounting for the surname attached to him. Charles appeared to be a man with some ability to command. Widow Deslondes had hired him out as an overseer on the Andry plantation, where the uprising began.

The most embellished accounts had Charles organizing his rebel forces into military companies. Some asserted that he appointed officers, selected flagmen to carry colors and signals, and designated drummers to lead his parading formation as it marched to the cry "On to Orleans!"

Several accounts went so far as to title the episode the "Deslondes Slave Revolt." The slave Charles became something of a legend. Facts about his actual part in the 1811 uprising remained thin, however. The central and certain facts were his being from Saint-Domingue and being of mixed blood. That stirred already strong feelings against Creoles of color.

On first news of the uprising, free men of color in New Orleans rushed to prove their allegiance. They recognized the suspicion surrounding them, and they seized the widespread scare as an opportunity to rally in support of the government. They immediately petitioned Governor Claiborne to let them muster as militia to help suppress the rebellious slaves. Like other nonwhites throughout U.S. history, many Creoles viewed armed service as a means to prove themselves worthy of respect and trust. They saw the opportunity as one to show themselves acting the same as white men in taking up arms and risking life and limb to defend the society. They hoped such service would gain them recognition and rights denied them.

Military necessity early and often accorded men of color the opportunity to serve in U.S. armed forces. Governor Claiborne commended the free men's militia service in 1811, and he championed letting them continue to stand as militia even when many other whites, especially slaveholders, pressed to disband and outlaw such militia. Acting on Claiborne's insistence, the legislature in September 1812 authorized the muster of 256 property-holding free men of color in four militia companies. More than the governor alone, threats from the U.S. War of 1812 against Great Britain moved Louisiana's lawmakers to acquiesce to recognizing and raising free men of color in arms. When hard pressed in the climactic Battle of New Orleans in January 1815 that elevated him as a national hero, U.S. Army

General Andrew Jackson mustered two battalions of free men of color. They acquitted themselves with distinction, but their worthiness in battle left their civil status unimproved.

Serving the government under arms in Louisiana put free men of color on the side of ruling whites and against enslaved blacks. It reflected their choice—not that they had many real options. Power resided on the side of Anglo-American whites. Whether they liked it or not, free people of color stood to gain little and lose whatever they had by siding with slaves. The tenuous security they had lay with the ruling whites, at least for the time being.

Material and social success pointed toward whites and away from blacks, so that many free people of color distanced themselves from slaves at every turn. Anglo-American white supremacy infected them, too, with color prejudice. In one way or another, many accepted complexion as a measure of personal worth and social standing. The nearer to white a person appeared, the more acceptable the person appeared—even among people of color. Social strivers among nonwhites often simply accepted whites' standards and imitated them, even while not necessarily wanting to be white themselves or different from who they were. They were not necessarily posers; prejudice had insidiously poisoned them.

No matter how light-skinned their complexion, free people of color in antebellum Louisiana had to face the fact of their exclusion as nonwhites. The state's developing legal and popular structures systematically relegated them to diminishing status. As so-called republican institutions expanded adult white male privilege in Louisiana and elsewhere in the United States, the rule of race further distanced free people of color from the privileges, immunities, and rights of citizens. Evolving civic and political values emerged for whites only. Indeed, keeping public goods and processes free from the corruption associated with nonwhites increasingly appeared in itself as a popular value for whites. Freedom had the cast of color.

While segregating free people of color from whites, Louisiana law continued to distinguish them from enslaved blacks. The distance sometimes yawned; sometimes it narrowed. Keeping a clear space became crucial to Creoles. So long as slavery reigned, whatever legal standing free people of color had depended on their standing apart from slaves. Such a stance, however, reinforced white supremacy. It supported the colorline and merely begged for it to bend enough to protect Creoles' positions. The attitude was self-serving, but it arose from self-protection. Even more, it was an act of self-preservation.

Scrambling to stay clear of enslaved blacks sent free people of color to court again and again. It was not that they were essentially quarrelsome; they simply were necessarily vigilant. They walked a thin line as any bump might push them into the abyss with slaves. So they defended their position against encroachment, exercising their cherished right to take legal action. Slaves had no such right, as Louisiana courts repeatedly noted.

The state's first civil code entitled a slave to bring no action except to claim and prove he or she was not a slave. As elsewhere in the United States, the law in Louisiana presumed blacks were slaves. They carried the burden of proving they had somehow gained liberty. Free people of color in Louisiana escaped that burden as a result of the 1810 case of *Adelle v. Beauregard*. Hearing the case, Louisiana's Superior Court sitting in New Orleans distinguished persons of color in regard to slavery attached to what the court described as "the presumption arising from colour" (Louisiana 1810, 184).

The Louisiana court acknowledged the general U.S. rule, citing the 1802 North Carolina case of *Gobu v. Gobu*. The court there expounded the principle "with respect to the presumption of every black person being a slave." It explained that "because the negroes originally brought to this country were slaves . . . their descendants must continue slaves until manumitted by proper authority. If therefore a person of that description claims his freedom," the North Carolina Court instructed, "he must establish his right to it by such evidence as will destroy the force of the presumption arising from his color" (North Carolina 1802, 188-189).

The presumption of slavery generally attached to blacks did not suit people of color, the Louisiana court explained. "Persons of colour may have descended from Indians on both sides, from a white parent, or mulatto parents in possession of their freedom," the court reasoned. If slavery depended on descent, then when descent appeared to be other than purely black the slavery connection changed, the court noted. Slavery was automatic only for blacks, it said, but no such self-evident condemnation attached to persons of mixed heritage. "Considering how much probability there is in favor of the liberty of those persons," the court ruled in 1810, "they ought not to be deprived of it upon mere presumption, more especially as the right of holding them in slavery, if it exists, is in most instances capable of being satisfactorily proved" (Louisiana 1810, 184).

Adelle's case in 1810 established the fact as the rule in Louisiana. Beauregard had brought Adelle as a girl from the West Indies. He sent her to a New York boarding school for finishing. When she matured sufficiently for his purposes, he had her returned to New Orleans to serve him as a slave. But Adelle had perhaps learned too much for Beauregard's position: She refused to serve him as he wanted. Fleeing his house, she sued to deny his holding her as his slave. Adelle's appearance, which plainly captivated Beauregard, proved his undoing. She appeared white enough to require him to prove his title to her as a slave. He failed, and the court ruled her a free woman.

A rule of appearance thus cut in favor of persons of color in Louisiana. The whiter they appeared, the wider their distance from slaves. The darker they were, the closer they appeared to slavery. Blacks carried the burden of proving they had somehow gained liberty. Persons who appeared clearly of mixed heritage escaped that burden. Claiming them as slaves required proof of title. Their color furnished them the presumption of freedom. So ruled the court in 1810.

Not every person of color prevailed as Adelle did. The legal presumption in favor of people of color operated amid a welter of rules and practices. Some cut in their favor; others cut against them. They moved to and fro as pawns in cultural wars between Anglo-Americans and remnants of colonial Spanish and French rule and generations of immigrants. Anglo-Americans pushed for the rule of U.S. law without modification. It promised unrestrained slavery and a simple black-white dichotomy. People of color cringed at its prospect. The continental European civil codes offered them at least slivers of liberty.

Slavery and more generally what was called race relations served as prime terrain in the battling over legal culture. In simplest form, the issue became what was to be Louisiana law. The reality was that the law was not being created from scratch at the start of the 1800s. The U.S. takeover could not simply erase Louisiana's colonial heritage. The original U.S. states had themselves built on their colonial law as it existed when they became independent in 1776. So the fledgling state of Louisiana built on its colonial law at the U.S. purchase in 1803. Its reception of law brought together different legal systems. It did not wipe out the old law; it reformed it.

Louisiana Supreme Court Justice Pierre Derbigny early explained the state's reception process. "It must not be lost sight of, that our civil code is a digest of the civil laws, which were in force in this country, when it was adopted," he wrote in the 1817 case of *Cottin v. Cottin*. "Those laws must be considered as untouched, wherever the alterations and amendments, introduced in the digest, do not reach them, and that such parts of those laws only are repealed, as are either contrary to, or incompatible with the provisions of the code," Justice Derbigny instructed (Louisiana 1817, 94). Resisting simple adoption of Anglo-American practices, the French-born Derbigny insisted on continuity with the continental code civil, and his position had backing as he became in 1828 the state's sixth governor.

Court battle after court battle into the 1860s Civil War showed how people of color found their claims to liberties and freedom itself swayed with the leanings of Louisiana law. The way in which the state's courts treated a condition termed *statuliber* exposed something of the vulnerable in-between status of people of color in antebellum Louisiana. *Statuliber* descended from the ancient Roman law of slavery. The Spanish had adopted it and put it in place in Louisiana during their colonial rule, and in U.S. Louisiana it acted as something of a bulwark against the stark 1806 Black Code.

Statuliber created a status that might be described as conditional or temporary slavery. Cases such as *Poudras v. Beard* (1816) and *Metayer v. Metayer* (1819) gave the doctrine early effect. Derbigny, then Louisiana secretary of state, helped write the principle into Article 37 of the 1825 civil code. It defined "*statu liberi*" as the condition of "slaves for a time." It described them as "those who have acquired the right to being free at a time to come, or on a condition which is not fulfilled, or in a certain event which has not happened; but who, in the meantime, remain in a state of slavery" (Louisiana 1825, 66).

Statuliber served as a crucial doctrine in cases treating the force of last wills and testaments and other writings promising manumission. It allowed also for an oddity in U.S. slave law—emancipation by prescription. It sanctioned slaves' freeing themselves essentially by self-possession over time. The formula laid down in *Metayer* in 1819 recognized as emancipated a slave who escaped his owner's control for 20 years or who had lived as free in his owner's presence for 10 years.

Statuliber frequently appeared at issue in cases treating people of color's status. Often the parties were blood relations, some of whom were recognized as whites who claimed some of their legally unrecognized kin as slaves. Such suits arose at times also among related persons of color, as illustrated in the much noted 1836 case of *Berard v. Berard*. There a niece sued her aunt for freedom for herself and her five children. The court referred to the plaintiff niece simply as "Berard." She identified herself as a free woman of color. Her status was, of course, exactly what was at issue.

Berard claimed to have been born free in Saint-Domingue and come to Louisiana as a refugee with her father's sisters, distinguished for convenience as Jeane and Louise. Berard described living with both aunts "as one of the family." After Jeane died in 1814, Berard continued to live with Louise until she, according to Berard, "conceived the idea of making her and her five children slaves" (Louisiana 1836, 157–158).

Louise objected, arguing that she never claimed Berard as her slave. She insisted, however, that Berard was in fact a slave. Jeane had title to Berard, which descended on Jeane's death to her natural children and legal heirs, Celina and Antoine Garidel, Louise testified.

The crucial question at trial became who had to prove what. Berard relied on the 1810 rule from *Adelle v. Beauregard* requiring a presumption "in favor of the liberty of [colored] persons" and calling for anyone claiming a person of color as a slave to have "satisfactorily proved" in court "the right of holding them in slavery, if it exists." But 1836 was not 1810. The early presumption in favor of people of color being free had faded in Louisiana. The trial court refused to invoke any presumption in Berard's favor. It treated her as a slave unless she could prove otherwise.

Louisiana's Supreme Court affirmed that position. "A slave cannot stand in judgment for any other purpose than to assert his freedom," the court ruled. Berard could only state her claim. She lacked standing in court to argue, challenge, or dispute further. For as the state Supreme Court noted in concluding *Berard v. Berard*, a slave "is not even allowed to contest the title of the person holding or claiming him as a slave" (Louisiana 1836, 158). But how was Berard, or anyone else, to prove their case if the court denied them standing to offer evidence?

Louisiana law thus adjudged Berard a slave. By blood she may have been a cousin to those invested with title to her, but not in law. And as she was adjudged a slave, so were her five children. It made no difference who their father was; their mother's status descended upon them. In Louisiana, as elsewhere, the law followed the Latin legal doctrine *partus sequitur ventrum*—the offspring follow the womb. As with the law controlling cattle and other livestock, a slave mother's owner owned all her offspring. *Statuliber* saved the children of mothers enslaved under that condition: When she became free, so also did they. They were meanwhile slaves nevertheless.

Slavery's cutting edge continually menaced Louisiana's Creoles of color. They could fall into bondage at any moment. It could happen by law, as with Berard. Or it could happen outside the law. As elsewhere throughout the antebellum United States, kidnapping for slavery was rampant, and complexion offered no immunity.

Antebellum Americans frequently heard stories of what they called "white slaves." U.S. writer Richard Hildreth illustrated the point with his 1836 novel *The Slave: or Memoirs of Archy Moore*. To heighten attention to his work, Hildreth made the title of his enlarged 1852 edition *The White Slave; or, Memoirs of a Fugitive*. Hildreth's title character revealed the crux of the tale early. "From my mother I inherited some imperceptible portion of African blood, and with it, the base and cursed condition of a slave," he reported (Hildreth 1836, 7).

Archy Moore insistently exposed the absurdity of his condition and legally imposed identity. "Though born a slave," he declared, "I inherited all my [white] father's proud spirit, sensitive feelings and ardent temperament; and as regards natural endowments, whether of mind or body, I am bold to assert, that he had more reason to be proud of me than either of his legitimate and acknowledged sons" (Hildreth 1836, 7–8). Moore's commentary on his life questioned both what marked a person as a slave or as white.

Moore's character attacked both the racial foundation of slavery and the conception of race itself. Brutal domination alone constructed slavery and race, he suggested. "I had found, by a bitter experience, that a slave, whether white or black, is still a slave; and that the master, heedless of his victim's complexion, handles the whip, with perfect impartiality," Moore explained (Hildreth 1836, 41).

In Louisiana, the story was commonplace, yet it occasioned extraordinary episodes. The so-called lost German girl was one such incident. It flared in New Orleans in the spring of 1843. German immigrants identified a young woman as one of their kin kidnapped 20 years earlier. She had unusual birthmarks and striking resemblances to Dorothea Müller, then dead, whom the immigrants said was the girl's mother. They claimed the young woman was the long-lost Salomé Müller. She was then living with the name Sally Miller or Mary Miller.

New Orleans café owner Louis Belmonti held the woman as a slave he purchased from a reputed Southern gentleman named John Fitz Miller. But Miller could produce no original title or evidence of having acquired the girl legitimately. Twenty years distant from coming into Miller's hands when she was only six years old, the woman had no recollection of how she came to be with him or of her life before then.

Who and what the woman was became the heart of a *cause célèbre*. She stood as a mystery. What would determine her identity? Would it turn on who people said she was, in light of the fact that she did not know who she was, who her parents were, or where she came from? Her status, whether slave or free, depended on her identity. That was the hard issue in the politics of her case. But what were to be the indicators of identity?

No Louisiana court, or any court in any other slave state, could determine the woman's legal position merely on her looks, given that she was not visibly black. Releasing every slave who appeared white would not work as a practical matter. Slaveholders would not accept the economic loss. More broadly, Anglo-American white supremacy would not abide accepting mere appearance as proof of public standing as white. It maintained a politics of purity in which *white* designated infinitely more than a category of appearance. *White* carried cultural and social substance and meaning.

Not just anybody could be accepted as free and white in antebellum America. Especially in Louisiana, stiffening boundaries of personal identity increasingly stressed sharp divisions among peoples. Odd lines developed with the U.S. takeover. Anglo-American immigrants to the new territory that became a state in 1812 pushed to distinguish themselves not only as whites but also as different from others who might consider themselves whites. They featured a nativism with a bias against foreigners, identified as immigrants from outside the United States. Place of birth loomed large in Louisiana's political and social scales. It served as an element in the state's culture wars. The conflicts included elements also of race and religion.

So the question in 1843 of who the young Miller/Müller woman was carried much the same core as the question in 1896 of who Homer Plessy was. Would appearance tell the tale or would lineage determine the outcome? Little, if anything, in color would distinguish Miller/Müller from Homer Plessy. The issue for both would become lineage. Plessy knew well who his people were. Miller/Müller claimed no memory of who her people were, yet their testimony saved her. A host of German immigrants came forward as her people to convince Louisiana's courts that Miller was Müller and that she was German, white, and so not a slave.

Plessy's lineage lay open Louisiana's disputable lines of official identity. His French grandfather Germain and grand-uncle Dominique demonstrated the twisted character of personal identity Anglo-American white supremacy imposed. Germain married the Creole free woman of color Catherina Mathieu. Her father, like her mother's father, was born in France. Yet Catherina and Germain's descendents became forever marked as other than white. Dominique married a South Carolina-born woman, Nancy Roe. She was reputed as white. So were their three sons—Adolphus, Germain, and Dominique, Jr.—who came to sign their family name as Duplissey.

Louisiana's law and dominant society drew a bright line between the Plessys and the Duplisseys, as they dew a bright line also between non-whites and whites. But what was the difference? None appeared in physical features. Yet the different designations *white* and *free person of color* made all the difference in the world in Louisiana before and after the Civil War.

One label opened recognition as full members of the public community. It provided full citizenship with all the rights and privileges attached thereto. The other description assigned diminished legal and social status, it denied equal rights, and it ignored the full ancestry that marked the personal identity of persons such as Homer Adolph Plessy.

References

Claiborne, J. F. H. 1811. *Letterbook, 1790–1820*. Jackson, MS: Mississippi Department of Archives and History.

Dormon, James H. 1977. "The Persistent Specter: Slave Rebellion in Territorial Louisiana." *Louisiana History* 18 (4): 389–404.

Hildreth, Richard. 1836. *The Slave: Or Memoirs of Archy Moore*. Boston: John H. Eastburn.

Louisiana. 1808. *A Digest of the Civil Laws Now in Force in the Territory of Orleans with Alterations and Amendments Adopted to Its Present System of Government*, comp. Louis Moreau Lislet. New Orleans: Bradford & Anderson.

Louisiana. 1810. *Adelle v. Beauregard*, 1 Mart. (o.s.) 183 (La. 1810).

Louisiana. 1817. *Cottin v. Cottin*, 5 Mart. (o.s.) 93 (La. 1817).

Louisiana. 1825. *Civil Code of the State of Louisiana*. [New Orleans]: Published by a citizen of Louisiana.

Louisiana. 1836. *Berard v. Berard*, 9 La. 156 (E.D. La. 1836).

North Carolina. 1802. *Gobu v. Gobu*, 1 N.C. 188 (N.C. 1802).

St.-Martin, Pierre Bauchet. 1811. St. Charles Parish, Original Acts, Book 41, 1811, #2, 17–20.

Thompson, Thomas Marshall. 1992. "National Newspaper and Legislative Reactions to Louisiana's Deslondes Slave Revolt of 1811." *Louisiana History* 33 (1): 5–29.

United States. 1804. "An Act Erecting Louisiana into Two Territories, and Providing for the Temporary Government Thereof." 2 Stat. 283 (March 26, 1804).

FIVE

The City: *Vive la différence*

THE FRENCH-BORN IMMIGRANT Germain Plessy saw his Louisiana family increasingly squeezed before he died in 1863. The pressure was more political and social than economic. Plessy & Co. did well enough so that his wife and children proved better off than many other Creoles of color. The business prospered sufficiently to occupy him and his four sons born between 1804 and 1822. As a carpenter, Germain found ample work in the expanding antebellum New Orleans.

Growing along the lower Mississippi River's sweeping curve that supplied the nickname "Crescent City," New Orleans soared from 27,176 residents in 1820 to 168,665 in 1860. From the fifth largest U.S. city in 1820, it jumped to third in 1840. It then trailed only New York City and Baltimore, Maryland, in population. New Orleans stood as the lower South's leading city. It dwarfed Charleston. The South Carolina port had been a rival in 1820, when it was America's next largest slave city. Its 24,780 residents had ranked it sixth overall in the nation. By 1860 it had fallen to 22nd. Its 40,522 residents numbered less than one-fourth of New Orleans's population. Among U.S. slave cities in 1860, only Baltimore's total population of 212,418 topped New Orleans's. Only New York topped it as a U.S. commercial port (Gibson 1998, tab. 5–10; University of Virginia 2004, 1820–1860).

No other U.S. city matched New Orleans's mix of New and Old World charm. European visitors often complimented it. Antebellum New Orleans beckoned as an oasis of civilization in the eyes of many foreign and domestic travelers. To many, the city lay also as a siren. Its Catholicism sounded the tones of an alien religion, which rang prominently among Creoles of color and the French and Spanish populations lingering from their colonial rule. The city stood more than blemished by such people. Even worse in many eyes than the city's collection of racially indistinct people was the fact that native-born Anglo-American whites sat as a minority. Early

American New Orleans was, after all, a dark city. Its harshest critics deemed it un-American; its boosters hailed its cosmopolitan image. Not everyone shared the same picture of what New Orleans was or should be.

Bitter battles raged along a range of fronts in and around New Orleans. The city's center itself became much contested terrain as the metropolis grew as a cluster of competing enclaves. Fighting long persisted over where the center should be—above or below Canal Street. Would the center be the old town, the *vieux carré*, or elsewhere? Political and popular struggles to grasp control of the city targeted every advance and development. Skirmishes erupted from time to time almost street-by-street as cultural and ethnic groups, reveling in their distinct identities, fought for turf.

Acknowledging the divides in 1836, the state legislature partitioned New Orleans into three separate, self-governing units imaginatively called the First, Second, and Third Municipalities. The French-heritage population occupied the First Municipality, which spread from the old colonial city center. Creoles of color, like the Plessy family, lived there and on its expanding margins called *faubourg*.

Canal Street separated the First Municipality from what contemporaries called the "uptown" Second Municipality, considered the "American" section. Esplanade separated the First Municipality from the immigrant "lower" Third Municipality, where Germans and Irish predominated. Germans lived principally at the foot of Jackson Avenue. The sons and daughters of Erin congregated around Constance and Euterpe streets, and the area became known as the Irish Channel.

All three "municipalities" fronted the Mississippi. The river gave life to all. The three shared it, a mayor, and a common council, but little else. They competed for prominence. They collaborated on little and cooperated on less. Each preferred to develop its own facilities and amenities. Their boundaries resembled national borders. Thoroughfares changed names, for instance, crossing Canal Street between the so-called American and French quarters. St. Charles Avenue became Royal. Camp became Chartres. Magazine became Decatur. The populations lived apart, worked in separate businesses, frolicked in separate parks, and worshipped in separate churches. When they died, their remains lay in separate cemeteries.

Almost no spirit of shared community engaged the city's residents. More than anything else, outside pressures alone from time to time pushed people in New Orleans onto common ground. Even after 1852, when the legislature abolished the separate municipalities and restored unitary city government, popular separation persisted.

New Orleans lay split not only among its cultural and ethnic factions; it lay divided from much of the rest of overwhelmingly rural Louisiana, where many persistently plotted against the city's dominance. Their first notable success came in the 1820s, when the legislature moved the capital 60 miles upriver to Donaldsonville, touted as a more central location for the state. Advocates applauded the exodus from too-crowded, too-noisy New Orleans—but it proved brief. In 1831, the capital returned to the city. In 1849, the legislature again moved, this time going farther upriver to Baton Rouge. Union occupation during the Civil War returned the capital to New Orleans, and it remained there until 1882, when it went back upcountry to stay in Baton Rouge.

New Orleans's character prompted persistent debate, and in the antebellum era the continuing contest over culture and identity figured prominently in disputes. The confrontations harkened back to old questions of what it meant to be *American.* Preserving—indeed cultivating—New Orleans's European flavor clashed from many perspectives with the push to make the city *American.* Some focused on the feel of the place, arguing over its ambiance, architecture, and layout. Most arguments fixed ultimately inhabitants. Who lived in the city made all the difference in how people felt about it. Also the population mix determined who ruled. Newcomers pushed for more than footholds or handholds, angling for commercial and political control. They moved to grasp the reins of power and make the city their own.

Struggles over civic and personal identity lay at the heart of the contest to control New Orleans. This contest figured in internal and external relations. Not confined to the city itself, it reverberated throughout Louisiana and beyond. It crossed U.S. borders. Few major elements in the nineteenth-century Atlantic world escaped it. Assimilation, culture, ethnicity, immigration, inheritance, language, miscegenation (then usually called amalgamation), race, religion, and more roiled the antebellum Crescent City. And churning in the midst stood Creoles of color—including Germain Plessy's wife and children and their like, Homer Plessy's forbears.

New Orleans was developing as a telling site for the future of the U.S. South. It pointed toward directions for the nation's growing cities. It drew immigrants like no other city in the lower South. Unlike northern cities, it had a relatively large nonwhite population. In regard to race and identity, then, New Orleans represented a prophetic mix for modern America. It prefigured converging clashes of race, religion, immigration, ethnicity, and class and culture amid competitive commercialism. It projected anxieties over controlling the cast and content of American-ness.

New Orleans had not entered the 1800s as an American city, and many at mid-century doubted its progress toward being *American*. Its population reassured few. It appeared more a city of foreigners and people of color than of native Anglo-American whites. It sat predominantly nonwhite into the 1830s. Thereafter the inflow of Europeans turned the Crescent City into the nation's second-largest immigrant reception center. More than 50,000 arrivals came to it annually before the Civil War. With a nod to New York and other East Coast ports, some by 1850 were calling New Orleans "America's back door."

Irish and German immigrants led the pack. Most who entered through New Orleans moved on. The bulk steamed up the Mississippi. Germans, for example, found St. Louis, 700 miles upriver, especially hospitable. Newcomers also made the 1,000-mile journey to Chicago. Even while the bulk moved on, many immigrants stayed in New Orleans. Few strayed elsewhere in Louisiana. Of the state's 24,266 Irish-born residents in 1850, only 16.8 percent lived outside the city. German-born residents congregated in New Orleans less than the Irish. Old German settlements from Louisiana's colonial era welcomed kindred new blood, yet 11,220 (64.1 percent) of Louisiana's 17,507 German-born residents in 1850 lived in New Orleans (Spletstoser 1996, 288–289).

Louisiana's population of 68,233 born outside the United States made it very different from its sister slave states in 1850. None approached its 13.2 percent foreign-born. Neighboring Texas came closest, with 8.3 percent of its residents being born outside the United States. Florida (3.1 percent) was the only other Deep South state with more than 2.0 percent foreign-born residents in 1850 (University of Virginia 2004, 1850).

New Orleans looked even more different from its southern sisters. Its population was 42.9 percent foreign-born in 1850. That contrasted also with most of the rest of Louisiana. Aside from Orleans's neighbors Jefferson (36.7 percent) and St. Tammany (10.1 percent), no other parish counted more than 9.0 percent foreign-born residents. Only three other parishes— St. Bernard (8.7 percent), Plaquemines (7.6 percent), and East Baton Rouge (8.4 percent)—had more than 5.0 percent foreign-born residents (University of Virginia 2004, 1850). Thus the Crescent City stood alone like no other place in the Pelican State, in the slave South, or in the nation.

Boosters trumpeted New Orleans's antebellum population mix. "When we state that in no city in the New or Old World is there a greater variety of nations than in this, or a greater diversity of different and distinct races and people to be met with than here, we are but asserting an established truism," declared the *Daily Picayune*. "New Orleans is a world in miniature, subdivided into smaller commonwealths, in every one of which distinctive traits of national character are to be seen, and the peculiar language of its people to be heard spoken," boasted an editorial in the September 23, 1843, edition.

New Orleans's leading newspaper flaunted what the city could not hide. Yet many considered the city's diversity no virtue. More than a few, in fact, deemed it a vice. Such insiders and outsiders determined in their own ways to save the city from its colored, foreign, multiplying, and polyglot hordes. They wanted to cleanse New Orleans, to make it whiter, more *American*. Their quest ran against the tide—except in regard to people of color. There it converged with a rising white tide. It rose with the influx particularly of pre-famine Irish immigrants. The flow in the 1830s eddied to reverse the earlier buoying that had sustained Creoles of color and blacks generally.

Early opportunities in the mushrooming city had advanced nonwhites' numbers there. Creoles of color particularly thrived with New Orleans's growth in the early 1800s. Their community sprouted with it. Along with other free persons of color, Creoles rose in numbers in the 1820s to account for almost one in four of the residents in and around the city. From 17.4 percent of the Orleans Parish population in 1820, their community expanded to represent 23.9 percent in 1830. Their numbers grew almost two-thirds (65.6 percent) over the decade. From 7,188 residents in 1820, they grew to 11,906 in 1830. Orleans itself grew only 20.5 percent over the same decade; the parish's total residents went from 41,351 in 1820 to 49,826 in 1830. Whites increased much more modestly at 10.6 percent, going from 19,244 in 1820 to 21,281 in 1830 (University of Virginia 2004, 1820–1830).

The decade of the 1820s marked the relative high point for nonwhites in antebellum New Orleans. Their numbers then dominated the population. In 1820, free persons of color and slaves together formed 53.5 percent of the Orleans Parish population. In 1830, they were 57.3 percent. Thereafter decline set in, relatively and in some years absolutely. The proportion of nonwhites fell steadily after 1830. It stood at 41.8 percent in 1840; it was almost half that at 23.5 percent in 1850. And in 1860 nonwhites accounted for only 14.6 percent of the Orleans population. Declining slave numbers explained much of the drop. After reaching a high of 23,448 in 1840, slaves in Orleans Parish numbered about the same in 1860 (14,484) as they had in 1820 (14,946). At the same time, however, their share fell from 36.1 percent to 8.3 percent of the parish population. Free persons of color fell to 6.3 percent of the Orleans population in 1860, down from their high of 23.9 percent in 1830 (University of Virginia 2004, 1820–1860).

The decline in the number of free persons of color in Orleans fit with the trend throughout the lower South. Their proportion dwindled regionally

amid hostility that became palpable in the 1840s. Their number in the
region declined 16.3 percent during that decade, continuing a trend that
began earlier. The downturn sank free persons of color from 3.5 percent
of the lower South's population in 1820 to 3.1 percent in 1840 and 1.5 percent in 1860. In 1840, about 1 in 10 (10.7 percent) of all free persons of color
lived in the lower South. In 1860, fewer than 1 in 8 (7.6 percent) lived there,
according to the U.S. Census (University of Virginia 2004, 1820–1860).

Most of those free persons had what the census deemed mixed racial
ancestry. The 1850 count put the proportion of free persons of color with
mixed racial ancestry at 68.6 percent in the lower South. Such persons usually found cities more hospitable than the countryside. The New Orleans
population reflected that fact. In 1860, 58.7 percent of Louisiana's free persons of color lived in the Crescent City. Similarly, throughout the lower
South, 53.2 percent of all free persons of color in 1860 lived in cities.

The fast-growing number of whites reduced the relative proportions of
free persons of color and of all other nonwhites. More than a growing white
population, the decline represented a concerted drive against nonwhites.
Free persons of color suffered most there, particularly during the 1840s.
Hostilities cut their number nearly in half (–48.2 percent) in Orleans Parish.
From 19,226 in 1840, they dwindled to 9,961 in 1850 (University of Virginia
2004, 1840–1850). A white supremacist tide eroded and at times threatened
to wipe away free people of color in antebellum New Orleans. Their presence
and their place came under siege as immigrants swelled the city's white ranks.

Fresh European arrivals and U.S. migrants, too, swarmed antebellum
New Orleans. Many Germans and Irish who crowded in were counted as
whites, although often of a different hue than Anglo-American Protestants
with whom they frequently clashed. They clashed also with free people of
color and with slaves.

Competing for jobs and social space, fresh European immigrants and
other white migrants embraced any advantage. Touting their whiteness
proved one such advantage. German craftsmen used it to displace many
Creole artisans. Irish and later Italians used their whiteness to push blacks
from the docks and other work. The newcomers became no more socially
acceptable, yet their whiteness established their standing above the black
bottom with its colored upper layer.

Grappling to gain the upper hand, white newcomers made New Orleans
a battleground. They rallied there in notable concentrations. Nearly
3 of every 4 (75.1 percent) foreign-born whites in Louisiana in 1850 lived
in Orleans Parish. Their numbers grew by 1860 to more than 8 in 10
(81.9 percent) (University of Virginia 2004, 1850–1860).

At times the white immigrants' position proved ironic. They often won jobs because employers pegged them as cheap and disposable. Irishmen, for example, dug the New Basin Canal in the 1830s. They got the job by default. Few slaveholders were willing to risk their investment by exposing their slaves to the yellow fever, malaria, and cholera infesting the swamplands to be cleared for the shipping channel between Lake Pontchartrain and the Mississippi River. At least 8,000 Irish workers—some estimates ranged as high as 20,000—died to earn $1 per day building the 3.2-mile-long passage, which opened in 1838. Slaves proved too expensive for such work.

Irishmen and other whites pushed nonwhites out of much work in the city. They could not dislodge household slaves, but they could, and did, in places dislodge free persons of color from domestic service. They sought also to displace nonwhites, whether free or slave, from municipal works. They fought, for example, to do street cleaning and levee maintenance. The earthwork embankments stood alone to save the city from flooding. Many sections sat precariously below sea level; no section stood on truly high ground. As a consequence, levee maintenance proved necessary and steady work. It was also filthy drudgery. The hard work that remained reserved for blacks lay in the fields.

Enslaved blacks retained exclusive hold on Louisiana's sugar and cotton plantations. The state led the nation in extensive slaveholdings. No state in 1860 had more holdings of 100 or more slaves (University of Virginia 2004, 1860). And on the state's plantations slaves had no competitors. Replacing them was simply too costly for planters even to contemplate. But the hold went beyond money: The race-based social order dictated blacks' place and position, as well as the place and position of whites.

White supremacy cleaved a stark black/white divide in rural Louisiana. It isolated black slaves in a world where most rarely interacted with whites other than their overseers. Many slaves rarely caught even a glimpse of their plantation owners, who were often either absentee or distant. Except on special occasions, Louisiana's plantation slaves seldom interacted with anyone beyond their own holding. At most, interaction reached only to neighboring plantations. Racial separation was virtually complete.

Rural Louisiana's black/white split presented a deceptively tidy social image. It extended beyond slavery and appealed even to whites who envisioned themselves as better off if the place were rid of slaves. Most such whites preferred to do away with nonwhites altogether. But blacks were going nowhere as long as slavery persisted. And in the planter-dominated world of Louisiana and the Deep South more broadly, slavery appeared a fixture before 1860. Sharp racial separation that isolated nonwhites served, then, as the only alternative to getting rid of them. It satisfied white supremacists, whatever their stance on slavery.

A sharp racial divide marked American life. It stretched beyond slavery. The South manifested it most visibly, but the colorline was obvious throughout the United States. Whites publicly and socially shunned non-whites. The overwhelming majority of whites preferred simply not to be around nonwhites. A privileged few whites had nonwhites to serve them personally. The larger white population let nonwhites do what they preferred not to do themselves. The poorest whites resented even that presence as they eked out a living, competing against nonwhites for jobs and social space. At the bottom, they clung fiercely to white supremacy. They closed their eyes to class exploitation. They turned blind eyes to cultural and ethnic snubs so they, too, could line up in the ranks of whites and stand separate and superior to nonwhites.

Prejudice against blacks was blatant. They were hardly the only non-whites set apart, however. The Indian removal President Andrew Jackson pushed in the 1830s brazenly reopened an even more extensive exclusion. It further isolated Indians from what the likes of Jackson deemed American society. Jackson's removal policy uprooted southeastern tribes such as the Cherokee, Choctaw, and Creek from their homelands and displaced them west of the Mississippi in what U.S. officials dubbed "Indian country." It paved the way to segregating Indians on reservations.

Louisiana maintained its racial divide mostly through its slave code. The bulk of its nonwhite population were slaves, after all. Only South Carolina (57.2 percent) and Mississippi (55.2 percent) ranked ahead of Louisiana (46.9 percent) in slaves as a proportion of total population in 1860. Thirty-one of the Pelican State's 49 parishes in 1860 had slave majorities. In all but three parishes—Calcasieu (19.7 percent), Winn (19.7 percent), and Orleans (8.3 percent)—slaves formed more than one-fourth of the population (University of Virginia 2004, 1860).

Most worries about nonwhites breaching the racial order in Louisiana focused on slaves. Whites' anxieties arose especially from their contradictory expectations. They imagined slaves as docile, yet simultaneously envisioned slaves as wild. The profile was racial: It was about not being white, more than it was about being enslaved.

The 11 death-penalty crimes Louisiana codified in 1855 for nonwhites, whether enslaved or not, displayed what whites most feared. Assault headed the horrors. It ranged from murder to attempted murder to merely drawing white blood. It included means and methods such as cutting, drowning, poisoning, shooting, stabbing, or strangling. Assault included rape or attempted rape. Such attacks by nonwhite men on white females stoked outrage, perhaps even more than arson and insurrection. Even a hint of such a threat could cost nonwhites their lives.

As the lumping together of crimes suggested, Louisiana's slave code lay within its broader Black Code. The title "Black Code" translated into English the colonial French *Code noir*. It reflected the common European bias in the Atlantic world that equated "black" with "slave." Moreover, it fixed "black" as an overall category for persons within colonial society who were not white. This view excluded Indians, cast as being outside society. Such labeling exposed the law's white supremacist basis. It linked all nonwhites to slaves. They all sat legally subservient to whites.

Although they vigorously resisted the linkage, Creoles and other free persons of color in antebellum Louisiana never escaped the shadow of slavery. No matter their complexion, as long as they were identified as non-whites, they remained connected to slaves. Louisiana's 1855 "Act Relative to Slaves and Free Colored Persons" exhibited the connection. The state Supreme Court drew a bright line in 1856 to distinguish slaves and free colored persons in law, but the two remained linked in fact.

Antebellum Louisiana tolerated slaves better in many ways than it did free persons of color. Planters and those who profited from slavery craved as many slaves as they could lay hands on. Conversely, few, if any, whites wanted to see more free persons of color in the state. Indeed, the legislature moved early to exclude them. Even before becoming a state, the freshly minted U.S. territory of Louisiana prohibited free persons of color from entering its borders. The territorial legislature in April 1807 passed "An act to prevent the emigration of free negroes and mulattoes into the territory of Orleans," which provided for arresting and expelling violators. Nonwhite seamen sailing into Louisiana ports had to depart within 30 days or suffer the act's penalties. Conviction for a first offense carried a sentence of one year at hard labor. Any further conviction brought life at hard labor.

Legislators acted also to remove nonwhites already resident in Louisiana. The 1807 law gave slaves later emancipated in Louisiana 30 days to leave, and it banned their return. It banned all nonwhites from returning to Louisiana if they ever left. The lawmakers clearly deemed the departure good riddance—at least in general. In 1831, they made exceptions for "free negroes, mulattos, or other persons of color, who have not entered this state in violation of the laws." It provided for those who were "owners of property . . . and exercise a useful trade, and who have always conducted themselves in an orderly and respectful manner . . . [to] be permitted to

depart from the state and to return thereto, as their business may require."
The legislators continued to refine the prohibitions, adding notable restrictions in 1816, 1830, 1841, 1843, 1852, and 1855.

Louisiana's 1830 "act to prevent free persons of colour from entering
into this State" delineated categories of descent among banned nonwhites.
It included "negroes," understood as persons of unmixed African ancestry.
It distinguished them from "persons of color," understood as having mixed
ancestry or blood. The statute used several terms to distinguish further
among persons of color. It used "mulatto" as a general term for all persons
of so-called mixed blood. In more specific use, it applied "mulatto" to refer
to the child of a person considered of unmixed African ancestry and a person considered of unmixed European ancestry: A black parent and a white
parent produced a mulatto child. A mulatto parent and a black parent produced a child the law called a *griffe* (also spelled griff). A mulatto parent
and a white parent produced a child called a *quadroon*. A quadroon and a
white produced an *octoroon*.

The lawmakers did not seek to label every possible combination, but
rather identified what they considered the most common mixtures among
persons of color. The labels recognized a tendency among persons of color
to decrease their black blood and increase their white blood, thereby
"whitening" their generations. The trend fit notions of white supremacy that
projected being white as the desired human standard. It assumed a universal aspiration to be white. Given that they considered white the most superior form of humanity, white supremacists considered a trend toward
whiteness as progress. But there it exposed an irony, if not an obvious
inconsistency.

Mixed mating produced ambivalent offspring in the view of white
supremacists. They damned such mating as staining white purity. Yet if
such mating blemished whiteness, it also whitened, or at least lightened,
the population. It produced people who were not quite white. Being not
quite white, of course, they were not white at all in the eyes of white
supremacists, nor were they white in the eyes of the law.

Louisiana followed a rule technically called *hypodescent*. Used throughout the United States, the rule assigned so-called mixed offspring to the
ancestry of the parent with lower social status. Mixed children could thus
technically never be white in Louisiana or in many other places in the
United States—at least not in law. That effect reflected the notorious "one
drop rule." Any African ancestor, however remote, relegated a person to
being forever some version of black. Such a person could never be white

under the rule. Looks were another matter, but distinguishing ancestry by appearance could be devilish.

Families such as that of Germain Plessy confounded "eyeball tests" of identity. They failed to fit white supremacists' simplistic social vision. The Plessys and their like distressed the simple-minded, one-dimensional dichotomy that depicted people as either white or nonwhite. The Plessys personified aggravating indeterminacies. Ambivalence persisted about who they were and thus about how they were to be treated in Louisiana's race-dominated societal scheme. They presented problems in practice more than on paper. In theory, the law easily assigned their identity. On the streets and elsewhere, however, who was to say who they were?

Germain's birth settled who he was legally, at least in part. Birth was, in fact, supposed to settle all identity. Yet U.S. law itself enshrined achieved identity over identity birth ascribed. Naturalization allowed persons—at least free white persons—to become Americans regardless of their birth. Thus birth did not settle all identity, at least not forever. U.S. law allowed people to acquire national identity. And beyond law, America beckoned people to come and change themselves into whoever they wanted and worked to be. That was part of the dream of America. Not everyone had access to making the dream real, however. Images of their African ancestors appeared to forever bar some persons from becoming and being full members of the public community, accepted as full citizens.

Germain stood in contrast to his family. Yet the racist atmosphere cast him in shadow, too. He was white by any reckoning. He was no Anglo-Saxon white Protestant, of course. He was an American citizen, yet his being born in France churned ambivalence in some circles about how *American* he was. His marriage to the nonwhite Catharina Mathieu further clouded his identity. How could he be a true white American and be married to a woman of color?

And Germain and Catharina's four sons and four daughters, who were they? Like their father, they were French in culture and speech. In the nomenclature of Louisiana law, the Plessy children were at least octoroons. Their mother was herself probably an octoroon. The Plessy children were nowhere black in appearance. They were more white than anything, by looks. They lived in something of a separate world, occupying an in-between space. They were neither white nor black. Many, if not most, of New Orleans's free people of color by 1850 were much the same as the Plessy children. The federal census listed 8 in 10 free persons of color in the city as "mulatto." Only 2 in 10 were listed as "black."

The Plessys inhabited an ambivalent social space. They had comforts, but they faced continual conflicts and uncertainties. Except for Germain, they were neither black nor white. They mixed with both, yet they fit with neither. In appearance and manners, they blended in more with whites than with blacks. Being associated with blacks meant being associated with slaves, which in turn carried the danger of being enslaved. No free person of color wanted that fate, so free persons of color like the Plessys kept a distance—socially if not physically—from blacks. Many in their caste suffered from color prejudice as much, if not more so, than the most rabid whites. They took their own complexion as a mark of superiority. They embraced whiter as better and darker as worse. Even so, their own mixed ancestry denied them entrée anywhere as whites.

The Plessys might have passed as whites, but they did not. Others like them did. Leaving the locale where they were known, they let their appearance speak for who they were. They let their visual identity be their personal identity. Their French culture and language promised not necessarily to betray them in a polyglot world filled with the foreign-born and other migrants who spoke less than standard English, if any English at all. The Plessys showed little interest in pretending, however, to be who they were not. Like other committed Creoles of color, they were proud of who they were, even as the politics of the day denied them freedom to be who they want to be.

Within the colorline, the Plessys lived between the rock of white supremacy and the hard place of slavery. They escaped the ban against literacy under which slaves labored. Louisiana in January 1830 made it a crime for "all persons who shall teach, or permit or cause to be taught, any slave in this state, to read or write." The Plessys also escaped the privations of the least fortunate of those of their light-skinned fellow Creoles. They had ample sustenance. The four Plessy boys—Honoré, Gustave, Jean Livie, and Joseph Adolphe—helped their father in business. They operated Plessy & Co., carpenters, at 53 Elysian Fields. *Cohen's New Orleans & Lafayette Directory for 1851* listed the shop. The Plessy girls—Clarice, Marie, Catherine, and Louise—apprenticed with their mother for the day each would keep her own household. Like their brothers, they were raised to keep to their own. Marrying within the group was the rule.

Joseph Adolphe illustrated the pattern in marrying Rosa Debergue. Her family traced its roots back to a patriarch who emigrated from northern France's Ville de Bergues. Joseph Adolphe and Rosa would have three children. Their second child and only son arrived on March 17, 1862—the Roman Catholic feast day of St. Patrick. They named him Homère Patris Plessy, and he began life amid a chaotic world of war.

Before war came, the Plessys tasted some, but hardly all, of the privileges of the elite of their caste. They enjoyed literacy, schooling, and free association and movement within their community. Their relative freedom operated within conspicuous restraints and restrictions of race, class, and caste. Strict segregation set groups apart. The Plessys' New Orleans functioned like a maze. It stationed people on their own strips of society. Wealth, reputation, nativity, lineage, color, culture, and myriad other identifiers tagged their piece of the world and the paths they might trod.

Social distance regulated antebellum New Orleans life. The city was hardly alone there. Louisiana and, in fact, all the United States shared much the same social patterns. The rules turned on more than slavery. They operated by common consent—at least from whites. Race was a primary marker. So was sex. But those markers were hardly alone. Religion, sect, national origin, language, ethnicity, and more marked people.

Social distance not always meant physical distance. As determined as groups may have been to have their own space in antebellum New Orleans, many could not avoid contact with others where they lived and worked. Housing patterns displayed that fact of life, as the antebellum city showed little of the gross residential segregation that increasingly marked its post-bellum character. Before the 1860s class, ethnicity, and national origins marked differences among the city's neighborhoods and sections more than race did. Slavery sustained racially integrated housing.

One in three New Orleans households in 1860 held at least one slave as a live-in domestic. That was a primary station for city slaves, but there were various others. The city's labor market featured slaves with an array of skills. Available for hire, their work ranged from artisan to day laborer. Their hiring out allowed people without the wherewithal or wish to own slaves to rent slave labor by the job, day, or longer.

The antebellum New Orleans slave market was the nation's busiest. It thrived not only on sales but also on rentals. Yet most slaves in the city served as domestics. Households of the day demanded such labor. It passed between luxury and necessity for those who could afford it. The more elaborate or elegant the household, the more extensive the labor it required. Cooking, baking, cleaning, laundering, personal care, and toilet called for intensive labor. Also, elite households required coachmen, grooms, stable hands, and others in livery. Because they often needed to be at hand, these workers lived on the site. That often meant slaves lived in the most fashionable households.

Living in the same household did not necessarily mean living in the same house. Antebellum New Orleans's residential patterns carved out racial and social space within households and neighborhoods. The design fit what urban geographers came to call the "backyard pattern." It featured close but separate living spaces, which allowed nonwhites to live almost everywhere in the city. Indeed, in the 1850s, nonwhites lived in about equal numbers in all seven New Orleans wards. Their character differed from ward to ward. Creoles of color clustered between Canal and Esplanade. Germain Plessy's family lived there at 53 Elysian Fields.

The largest concentration of slaves lived west of Canal Street in what between 1836 and 1852 was officially the Second Municipality. Unofficially known as the "American sector," it housed the richest Anglo-Americans. Mansions fronted the major boulevards. Behind them spread slave and servant housing. The best of the slave quarters usually were small four-room, single-level structures. The pattern created a white periphery and a dark core. Jefferson, Napoleon, and St. Charles Avenues bounded a half-square-mile interior that exemplified the pattern.

No extensive white-only or colored-only sections existed then in the city. Noticeable dark clusters grew at its edges in the 1850s. Their development signaled some of the results of the increasing push against nonwhites, as well as the growing population pressure on housing. This force pressed most strongly on outlying areas most removed from the city's advantages. Prime residences spread above the business and commercial districts along the Mississippi.

More than race divided New Orleanians then. Religion, national origin, language, ethnicity, culture, color, and more also split the population. The cuts ran in varying directions and pierced some more than others. Some cuts ran deeper. Some severed people such as the Plessys from civic life. They left Creoles of color such as the Plessys shorn of civil liberties and rights. Whatever they enjoyed came only at sufferance. They had no recognized inalienable rights. Lawmakers could revoke or take away whatever Creoles had. What they held legally distinguished them from slaves, who, of course, held nothing legally. But the depth of the difference ebbed and flowed.

Antebellum Louisiana law distinguished free people of color from slaves. The state supreme court emphasized the distinction in *State v. Harrison*. The December 1856 decision declared that "in the eye of the Louisiana law, there is . . . all the difference between a free man of color and a slave, that there is between a white man and a slave." The court illustrated what the law allowed a free man of color. He "is capable of contracting. He can acquire by inheritance and transmit property by will. He is a competent witness in all civil suits. If he commits an offence against the laws, he is to be tried with the same formalities, and by the same tribunal, as the white man," the court observed (Louisiana 1856, 724).

In the same breath, the *Harrison* court noticed significant distinctions between white men and free men of color. The likes of Germain Plessy's sons, the court noted, stood marked "with the exception of political rights, of certain social privileges, and of the obligations of jury and militia service." They had no voice in the political process. They had little recognized public voice at all. They could not hold public office, nor could they vote. They remained legally silent on all subjects that marked full manhood in the society. They lacked recognized standing as citizens.

Niceties aside, free people of color were really little different from slaves. So insisted Louisiana Supreme Court Justice Henry M. Spofford in his dissent from the *Harrison* court. The New Hampshire-born graduate of Amherst College in western Massachusetts argued that free people of color and slaves "both compose a single, homogeneous class of beings, distinguished from all others by nature, custom and law." Distinguishing them from each other was a matter of semantics, not substance, Spofford maintained. The sole substantial difference, he noted, separated colored persons from white persons. The 1845 migrant to Louisiana accepted a stark non-white/white dichotomy. Persons of color were, in his view, "*persons of color, whether bond or free,*" he emphasized. "The division of this class of persons into bond and free" was a matter of convenience, he explained. It was nothing more than "an attempt to simplify and expedite the . . . law," he concluded (Louisiana 1856, 725–726).

Spofford's position anticipated U.S. Chief Justice Roger B. Taney's March 1857 pronouncements in the Dred Scott case. Persons of color, whether in slavery or out, were "never confounded with citizens of the State," Spofford noted. "No white person can be a slave; no colored person can be a citizen," Spofford declared. Taney agreed.

In *Scott v. Sandford*, the U.S. chief justice denied the one-time slave Dred Scott had ever been or could ever be "a citizen . . . within the meaning of the Constitution of the United States." Taney further agreed that those whom he described as "persons who are the descendents of Africans" had only conditional rights and privileges, at best. Such persons, he declared, "whether emancipated or not . . . had no rights or privileges but such as those who held power and the Government might choose to grant them." More simply, he insisted, "whether they had become free or not," such persons "had no rights which the white man was bound to respect" (United States 1857, 407).

Such pronouncements from the highest legal authority dampened Creoles' hopes for recognition as full members of the public community, let alone as citizens. Their continuing exclusion failed, however, to douse their ardor. Indeed, their passion to be accepted fully as Americans intensified in the nation's Civil War.

References

Gibson, Campbell. 1998. *Population of the 100 Largest Cities and Other Urban Places in the United States: 1790 to 1990*. Washington, DC: U.S. Bureau of the Census.

Louisiana. 1856. *State v. Harrison*. 11 La. Ann 722 (1856).

Spletstoser, Fredrick Mar. 1996. "The Impact of Immigrants on New Orleans." In *A Refuge for All Ages: Immigration in Louisiana History*, ed. Gless R. Conrad and Carl A. Brasseaux, 287–322. Lafayette, LA: Center for Louisiana Studies.

United States. 1857. *Scott v. Sandford*. 60 U.S. 393 (1857).

University of Virginia. 2004. *Geospatial and Statistical Data Center, Historical Census Browser*. Charlottesville: University of Virginia.

SIX

The War: Slavery and Segregation

CREOLES OF COLOR seized the Civil War as the promise of a new day. It dawned hazily, however. The first signs of war drew some Creoles to hasten to prove their local loyalty, as they had in earlier Louisiana's crises. Some rallied to save their own stakes. Louisiana, after all, had more colored slaveholders (nearly 1,000) than any other state. Some mustered among the 1,100 free men of color in New Orleans who volunteered for the Confederacy. The hopefuls paraded down Canal Street in April 1861; they paraded again in January 1862. Their banner proclaimed them "defenders of the native land," and they adopted the regimental title "Native Guards."

Their offer to serve the South gained Creoles no official recognition. Whites continued to shun them as nonwhites and, so, unworthy to shoulder arms for the cause. Louisiana's legislature persisted in exclusively conscripting "free white males capable of bearing arms," as the rebel state's February 1862 call commanded. Only in retreat from the Crescent City did southern forces find a use for Native Guards. Confederate General Mansfield Lovell ordered Native Guards to police duty in the city in early April 1862. As the South's commander of New Orleans's defenses, he shortly abandoned the city and the Native Guards.

Daybreak emerged for Creoles at large as Union forces occupied New Orleans at the end of April 1862. They hoped the Union's advance would advance their own position. They longed to stand beyond the veil of color and saw the wrenching changes of war as offering opportunities to produce what they sought. The war already seemed to signal a swift and sure end to slavery. Earlier in April, the U.S. Congress had abolished slavery in the District of Columbia, which suggested a federal commitment to abolition.

Many Creoles wanted something more. They espied light on their long distant hope of being recognized as full citizens and escalated their fight to secure their aim. Some trooped to battle for the Union after the

U.S. Congress in July 1862 authorized enlistments of "persons of African descent . . . for the suppression of this rebellion." Three regiments mustered under the Stars and Stripes as the 1st, 2nd, and 3rd Louisiana Native Guard. More than Creoles or other free men of color filled the regimental ranks: Slaves fresh from the fields, some black as night, joined as well. Color and class prejudice moved more than a few Creoles of color to refuse to muster alongside those they deemed beneath them. Many white U.S. Army soldiers were no more accommodating. The battlefield hardly eliminated racism.

Some Creoles suffered ambivalence about soldiering. Many nonwhites recurrently did. The double world of their existence ever stirred anxiety and uncertainty. So in war they sometimes wavered, unsure where their self-interest lay. Some wondered whether others would recognize their contribution. Some saw service as risking too much for too little. Some saw nothing changing if they served. Some saw service as doing their duty to themselves and their larger communities. Some saw service as a sure way to advance their recognition and rights. Some saw armed service as a chance to make their world a better place.

The former slave and renowned abolitionist Frederick Douglass insisted during the war that military service would boost black men's stature. "Once let the black man get upon his person the brass letter, *U.S.*, let him get an eagle on his button, and a musket on his shoulder and bullets in his pocket, [and] there is no power on earth that can deny that he has earned the right to citizenship," Douglass declared at an 1863 Philadelphia mass meeting to inspire enlistments. He urged his fellow men of color to "go into this war to affirm their manhood" (Foner 1952, 3:370). His urgings echoed in New Orleans.

Douglass hoped the Civil War would spur America's moral growth. He viewed it as "a war of ideas . . . a battle of principles . . . a war between the old and the new, slavery and freedom, barbarism and civilization" (Douglass 1878). Influential New Orleans Creoles shared that view. They rallied to the frontlines of the struggle of ideas and the battle for public opinion, deploying the press as a primary weapon.

In September 1862, Creoles launched *L'Union*. Published on Saturdays and Wednesdays and sold for a nickel per copy, the biweekly emerged as the first newspaper in the South colored people owned, edited, and published. It marked in the South the milestone New York's *Freedom's Journal* had marked in the North in March 1827, declaring "We wish to plead our own cause. Too long have others spoken for us."

The New Orleans newspaper in its inaugural issue declared, "We inaugurate today a new era in the destiny of the South." *L'Union* launched itself into what it saw as "the cause of the rights of man and of humanity." It adopted what it took up as a progressive call to end slavery and segregation as part of eradicating the racial practices and principles that entrenched white supremacy.

L'Union trumpeted Creoles' claims to being fully American. Its notes carried the tones of U.S. founding documents. "We take for the base of our platform the Declaration of Independence of the United States," proclaimed the newspaper's inaugural issue. Its motif repeated that "all men are created equal, that they are endowed by their Creator with certain unalienable Rights, that among these are Life, Liberty and the pursuit of Happiness." Its first issue carried the opening installments of a serial printing of the U.S. Constitution.

If American in theme, the newspaper was French in style and language. That duality highlighted Creoles' continuing dilemma of identity. Rigid U.S. dichotomies refused to recognize the diversity Creoles represented. American formalism dismissed hybrid identities, preferring to project oversimplified Anglo-American ideals of their own images as reality. It stereotyped people and set standards to marginalize those it defined as Others. It built an us-versus-them divide, at once simple and yet complex, within a fragmented society. Its Anglo-American supremacy imposed a staid self-perception that ignored Americans' diversity and curtailed American identities. *L'Union* battled such limits, echoing Creoles' long-standing call for full recognition of their manifold identity. As ever, its mixed-race founders rejected the white/nonwhite pigeonhole dichotomy. They embraced their multicultural, multiethnic ancestry within their American identity.

L'Union's language muted its message. Publishing in French reduced its readership and relegated the newspaper in many eyes to being "un-American." Its language positioned the paper to reach mostly Francophones who already agreed with its position. Influencing public opinion broadly required the paper to reach beyond its own community—and it grew to do that. It began printing an English-language edition. The *Union* joined *L'Union* in July 1863 as a sister publication with a more simple and direct message that better positioned Creoles to rise as slavery fell.

Creoles of color had long understood that slavery dragged them down even though they were not themselves slaves. They saw that only when blacks were free of slavery would Creoles have any chance at full civil rights. Yet they had long chafed at being classified or confused with blacks or slaves. They were not slaves. Most had never been slaves nor had their ancestors for generations. Nor were they blacks, not in their own eyes. But even those who distinguished Creoles from blacks sharply distinguished

Creoles from whites. The common view of others set Creoles apart from blacks and from whites, yet left them on the dark side of the black/white dichotomy. Creoles did not want necessarily to be white. Most wanted to be who they were, but they wanted also to have the same privileges as whites. As long as the standard for full legal status excluded all except whites, Creoles had no chance of acceding to the position they so long coveted.

Politics alone promised Creoles the position they desired, but their numbers assured them no leverage in determining public policy. To win in politics required them to ally with others for common cause. Creole leaders understood that. They understood also that picking appropriate allies posed problems. Creoles had few natural allies in America's no man's land of mixed race. At best, they appeared to have mostly allies of convenience. But what might be comfortable to start might change in an instant—lasting arrangements required more.

A few whites with unionist sympathies showed themselves willing to make common cause with Creoles. Such an alliance for political purposes was more or less what Creoles had in mind in working with blacks' being freed from slavery. While Creoles were willing to ally with blacks, they were not so willing to associate with blacks. For their part, many blacks resented Creoles' sense of disdain and distance. So class and color inhibited their alliance. A few pointed to the high road without prejudice, but they had much to overcome.

Politics, more than principles, put Creoles together with blacks in the rapidly changing world of Civil War Louisiana. The two shared common needs to oust the white supremacist slavocracy that oppressed both but did not burden each equally. The disparity bred in slavery alienated many enslaved blacks from many Creoles of color—and from other free people, too. White supremacists exploited differences as part of a divide-and-conquer strategy. Both blacks and Creoles succumbed to scheming that separated them. Each fell blind at times to the monster of prejudice that scorned their common African heritage.

Creoles and whites, whatever their views, saw that whoever controlled blacks would control Louisiana. Antislavery and proslavery forces saw that before the Civil War. The turn of the war against the South set off a scramble to secure control of blacks. Old-guard whites wanted blacks kept in place as plantation labor. Louisiana's antebellum economy depended on slave labor, and the plantation owners who dominated the state refused to lose that labor. Other whites also refused to lose the position white supremacy afforded them. They brooked no change in black subordination.

Even if their positions lost on Civil War battlefield, many southern whites refused to surrender their positions in the race relations they considered part of their way of life.

This was the place Homère Patris Plessy entered at birth in 1862 and his French-born *grand-père* François Germain Plessy departed in death in 1863.

The battle to shape postwar Louisiana was intensifying in July 1864 when new, more aggressive owners took over *L'Union* and the *Union*. A new state constitution was in the offing. It followed President Abraham Lincoln's December 1863 Proclamation of Amnesty and Reconstruction. Lincoln had invited persons in rebel states "to resume their allegiance to the United States, and to reinaugurate loyal state governments within and for their respective states." Union military commander Major General Nathaniel P. Banks supervised compliance in Louisiana. He certified sufficient, qualified loyal voters to elect in March 1864 a governor as well as delegates "to revise and amend the constitution of the State." The convention assembled in New Orleans on the first Wednesday in April 1864. It wrapped up its work in July, sending its proposed document to the general electorate.

The proposed constitution provoked strong reactions among nonwhites. In fact, the debates over its drafting were among developments that launched the takeover of *L'Union* and the *Union*. The new Creole owners reorganized the publication as the New Orleans *Tribune/La Tribune de la Nouvelle-Orléans*. It started as a bilingual, triweekly newspaper with its first issue on July 21, 1864. The revamped publication began with a politic tone in hailing the convention for eliminating slavery. But the delegates could have done no less. President Lincoln's December 1863 conditions for demonstrating renewed loyalty to the Union required the state to "recognize and declare . . . permanent freedom" for slaves. The delegates did that straightaway. They titled the first article of the proposed constitution "Emancipation." The second article provided that "The legislature shall make no law recognizing the right of property in man."

Doing no more than ending slavery amounted to "half-way measures," the *Tribune* railed. Slavery was only part of the detestable system of racial caste, domination, and exploitation. The whole system needed eradicating, the newspaper insisted. The slave code furnished only part of the law of racial exclusion. Outlawing slavery alone left untouched the prejudice against color that persisted as public policy and practice, the fresh Creole voice complained. The more far-reaching task at hand required law to recognize men of color plainly as men. Color made a man no less or more than other men, the paper argued. Finishing the job the Civil War had begun required acting against slavery's basis—totalitarian white supremacy.

The *Tribune* illustrated clear differences about the Civil War's meaning and ultimate effect. It exposed the chasm yawning between whites and non-whites across America. Spokesmen for people of color struggled to bridge the gap. Their reach to link the war to a crisis in American values fell short of what most whites were able or willing to grasp. Frederick Douglass persistently spoke about missing links in U.S. policy. Another escaped slave drew a starker picture in black and white. "The war was begun with the purpose of restoring the nation as it was, and leaving the black man where he was," William Wells Brown explained. "Now the time has come when you must recognize the black man as on the same footing with the white. If not, the mission of this war is not ended, and we must have yet more disasters to scourge us into the right way," he warned at a May 1864 New England Anti-Slavery Convention in Boston (Brown 1864).

Failed public policies on race would indeed torment the United States for generations. The *Tribune* crusaded to get Louisiana to change its course early. Breaking with embedded white supremacist positions was, however, not something the state's leaders in 1864 were ready or willing to do. And they were not alone in their reluctance: Whether Confederates or Unionists, most whites in 1864 tended to view abolition as a means of war, not as an aim of the war. They accepted ending slavery as a result. The proposed Thirteenth Amendment Congress approved in April 1864 appeared to make abolition certain. For many whites, that promised to end the slavery question. And it was as far as they wished to go on what people called "the Negro question." Civil equality among the races appeared out of the question.

One contemporary white southerner described the popular white position succinctly. "It is enough to free them, let them be free as the beasts in the fields," he said (Houzeau 1870, 92). That sentiment rang true also for whites in the North. Slavery had been essentially a dead letter there for nearly a generation before the Civil War, but that brought nonwhites in the North few, if any, civil rights.

White sentiment grew angrier and more emphatic in the South as the Civil War drew to a close. There abolition meant immediate, wrenching change. Outlawing slavery in accounting terms alone meant writing off property valued at $170,733,000 in Louisiana, one delegate claimed during the 1864 constitutional convention (Bennett et al. 1864, 215). The full depth and direction of the changes remained to be seen. The *Tribune* understood that. It understood also the ongoing battle between whites' wishing to moderate change and nonwhites' wishing to maximize change.

The character of Louisiana after slavery became the central object of a continuing civil war. The *Tribune* marked the battle lines during the 1864 convention and into the debates on ratifying the constitution at the polls in September 1864. The radical Creole voice challenged delegates who dug in their heels against people of color.

William Tompkins Stocker represented recalcitrant whites. The prominent attorney declared himself no enemy of slavery itself. He acceded to abolition, he admitted, "not from any sentimental feelings or conscientious feelings I have against slavery." He said he backed the measure only "because I believe our country demands it of us" (Bennett et al. 1864, 181). Without federal pushing, Stocker would have left slavery and slaves as they were.

On the race front, Stocker showed himself unwilling to yield an inch. He announced himself in favor of moving aggressively against all who were not white. "I have no sympathy with the African; my sympathies are with the white man and not the negro," he declared. "My hand is against the African, and I am for pushing him off the soil of this country," he announced (Bennett et al. 1864, 181). An opponent of secession and a Unionist, Stocker was nevertheless no friend of people of color. He hardly stood alone in opposing the progressive platform Creoles pushed in the *Tribune*.

Benjamin H. Orr exemplified convention delegates who took a more moderate stance than Stocker's. "I voted to free the Negroes. I voted for immediate emancipation. I voted for it because I considered slavery to be morally wrong," Orr declared. But he had other principles to balance. He stood for and with the "thousands of poor laboring men throughout the State who toil from morn till night to support their families," he professed. His reference pointed to a clear colorline, as he spoke in sympathy for "white men laboring under the sun day after day." They, not blacks, stood as Louisiana's future in Orr's view (Bennett et al. 1864, 217–218).

Orr and Stocker were among an easy majority of 1864 convention delegates who stood fast against civil equality for nonwhites. Creoles' grand goal—the right to vote—loomed nowhere in the view of such men. "I voted against giving the Negro the right of suffrage; I shall vote against it on all occasions. I do not think he is entitled to it," Orr stated flatly.

The *Tribune* saw little likelihood of changing the minds or sentiments of men such as Orr or Stocker. Unionists though such men might be, they represented whites only, and they would always represent whites only.

Defeating them required changing the electorate, but such a change appeared all but impossible from within. Louisiana's electorate was not going to change itself. The state's whites would not willingly surrender their power and privilege. Only forces from outside Louisiana appeared likely to open the ballot box to nonwhites.

The federal government had power to force change. It exercised that power in moving Louisiana and other states to outlaw slavery, and it had the power to force other changes in law. But President Lincoln preferred not to force change; he preferred to propose rather than to dictate. Lincoln showed that conciliatory side in March 1864 in a private note he wrote to newly elected Louisiana Governor Michael Hahn, confiding a suggestion for Louisiana's new state constitution's provision to "define the elective franchise."

A diffident Lincoln wrote Hahn, "I barely suggest for your private consideration, whether some of the colored people may not be let in." He recommended "the very intelligent, and especially those who have fought gallantly in our ranks." The pragmatic politician in Lincoln saw the need to bolster Union voters in the former rebel state. He foresaw that struggles in and with the South would not end on Civil War battlefields. Colored voters would, he predicted, "probably help, in some trying times to come, to keep the jewel of liberty within the family of freedom." Lincoln declined to push the point, however. Indeed, he shied from making the point openly. He closed his note to Hahn by emphasizing that "this is only a suggestion, not to the public, but to you alone" (Lincoln 1864, 162–163).

The *Tribune* understood, if the president did not, that the bulk of Louisiana whites were not willingly going to push back the colorline. Then, again, Lincoln himself was not much for pushing against the colorline. He articulated that in his losing 1858 Illinois senatorial campaign, when he announced his view of "a physical difference between the two [blacks and whites], which in my judgment will probably forever forbid their living together upon the footing of perfect equality" (Lincoln 1858, 3:16). Lincoln repeated his sentiment in August 1862 to a group described as "free colored men" to whom he spoke at the White House. "You and we are different races. We have between us a greater difference than exists between almost any other two races," the president said. While he repeatedly professed his belief in basic human equality, he confessed to seeing no prospect for black-white equality. "[E]ven when you ceased to be slaves," Lincoln said, "you are yet far removed from being placed on any equality with the white race" (Sandburg 1939, 1:574–575).

Lincoln's position highlighted shades of equality most Americans then saw. Equality never enjoyed more than limited purchase in the United States. In many American minds, equality had no place at all—at least not as a universal term. It sounded like leveling, which traditionally was anathema in America. The idea of everyone being the same in every way always appealed to few, if any, Americans. Even utopian visions limited their homogenous, self-sufficient communities. The land of opportunity was a land of differences and distinctions. It was a place to get ahead, not a place for being like others.

Distinctions of age, sex, and status ran deep in American society and in the American psyche, as did perceived differences of race. And that said nothing about the depth of differences in wealth, resources, and culture. Accommodating such differences as a matter of legal theory or rights posed profound questions and uncertainties. Louisiana struggled with settling on solutions, as did all America.

Even the phrase "equal rights" troubled Americans. It reached too far. In principle and practice, rights in Civil War era America came in various categories. Applying equality across the board was incomprehensible to many legal theorists as well as to most common persons. They rejected equal rights as meaning all persons had the same rights. Children could not have the same rights as adults in their view. Certainly, children could not have the same rights as their parents. If they did, what happened to the family? And how could husbands and wives have the same rights, or men and women for that matter?

Thus equal rights talk invoked issues broader than race; it provoked consideration of the entire social order. Race figured, after all, as an essential ingredient in the leavening of America. It weighed in domination and subordination throughout the nation. Altering its place portended a domino effect, conservatives insisted, and no good could come of it. Who could tell where the inevitable succession of undesirable outcomes would stop? Abolition was not the end; it was, conservatives warned, merely the beginning of the end of America as it was and as they insisted it be.

Conservatives cast abolition as introducing a parade of horrors they cursed as a "nigger crusade." It promised to destroy social order and muddle society, they said. It would allow anyone and everyone access everywhere. It would throw people against their will into close contact with others they would prefer to avoid. It would trample personal freedom of association and force social mixing. Most horribly, conservatives said, abolition would unleash "the spirit of amalgamation." The unbearable result, they claimed, would turn America into "a regenerated nation of half-breeds and mongrels, and the distinction of color [would] be forever consigned to oblivion." An 1863 polemical parody of the traditional Christian Our Father or the Lord's Prayer titled the "Black Republican Prayer" (1864) gave voice to the terrible litany of ugly outcomes of equal rights (Kaplan 1949, 274–343).

The image of black men coupling with white women evoked the ultimate popular horror. An 1864 election tract coined a term for it by joining the Latin words *miscere,* meaning "to mix," and *genus,* meaning "race." It appeared in the full title *Miscegenation: The Theory of the Blending of the Races, Applied to the American White Man and Negro.* The 72-page pamphlet, which appeared anonymously, sold for 25 cents and became an instant sensation. It announced itself as posing questions that "should enter into the approaching presidential contest." The questions were ones the pamphlet declared it "our duty as Americans, as Christians, as humanitarians" to answer. "An Omen" hung over America, the pamphlet advised. The nation faced "The Future—No White, No Black," it concluded (Croly 1864, 69, 75, 78).

Creoles embodied the mixed-race image and reality denounced in *Miscegenation.* The twisted public discourse savaged their ancestry and identity. Few fit the imagined vilified coupling; most descended as Homer Plessy had, from white men coupling with nonwhite women. Such pairings seldom entered the anti-miscegenation discourse that projected white women coupling with black men. Even so, Creoles and other mixed-race issue stood pilloried as unnatural horrors.

Widespread white aversion to mixed-race images excluded Creoles from any hope of being admitted to society as whites. Many Creoles accepted that, but nevertheless insisted on being publicly treated like whites. They demanded no distinction in law based on race or color or ancestry. The only way for that to happen, however, was for all persons to be treated alike—at least in public and by public authority. But how was that to happen? Conservative whites in Louisiana and elsewhere in America insisted it should not happen. They stood firm on the colorline.

Even before the Civil War's cannon seemed cooled, fresh battles heated up on the colorline. Conservative whites insisted that ending slavery in no way ended the colorline. They contended slavery had nothing, in fact, to do with the colorline. Slavery was simply a legal system of property rights in their view. It stood separate from race relations, they insisted. Abrogating all "law recognizing the right of property in man," as Louisiana's 1864 constitution did, ended slavery in their view. The reality of race was something different. To conservative whites, racial difference was immutable. Also, they maintained, natural law decreed white supremacy. Creoles and others attacked that position.

Sorting out the meaning of slavery engaged not only Louisiana but the American nation as the Thirteenth Amendment became part of the Constitution in December 1865. One conclusion emerged as clear on all sides: Outlawing slavery left those released from slavery with no clear civil status. It conferred no certain rights or standing. Louisiana moved, as her sister ex-Confederate states did, to resolve parts of the uncertainty about civil status. Like them, Louisiana produced a retooled Black Code that, critics charged, re-created slavery under a different name.

Louisiana's post-abolition regime adopted the appearance of being race neutral. It stripped terms of race and color from key statutes. Also, it reached back to lessons from antebellum Northern states that held ex-slaves under the guise of contract. Using the legal theory of a voluntary agreement to defeat charges of slavery or involuntary servitude, Illinois and Indiana, for example, had left some ex-slaves tied at times to 99-year indentures. Louisiana did not go that far. It stopped short of the harsh South Carolina and Mississippi codes. But like them and other ex-Confederate states, Louisiana marshaled the force of the state to separate and subordinate nonwhites.

The postbellum South's Black Codes unavoidably revised nonwhites' legal capacities. They necessarily conferred selected civil rights. States such as Louisiana needed, for example, to recognize the right to contract as it formed the legal base of their revamped labor regime. The right to contract extended beyond labor, of course. It brought ex-slaves the capacity to legally marry and to exercise property rights. Louisiana had less far to travel than other states on extending such rights: It basically slotted newly freed people into the position free persons of color occupied before the Civil War.

Many Creoles chafed at sharing the same status as fresh ex-slaves. Their conceit exposed differences among nonwhites. The appearance in April 1865 of another newspaper in New Orleans further bared differences. Those liberated from the fields insisted on having their own say, refusing to defer to others. They embraced their vilified color, and they espoused their own political ambitions. In their publication *The Black Republican*, editor S. W. Rogers introduced himself as "now a freeman [who] was born, and has lived most of his life, a slave." He described his staff as "composed, with few exceptions, of American colored men, most of whom were bondsmen." He drew a clear contrast between his group and Creoles and their *Tribune*. "We mean to maintain our race—not deny it," he retorted (Davis 1983, 157).

Perhaps fatefully, *The Black Republican*'s inaugural issue appeared on April 15, 1865—the day when President Lincoln died. An assassin had shot him in the head the night before in Washington, D.C., while he attended a performance of English playwright Tom Taylor's farce *Our American Cousin* at Ford's Theatre, less than a mile from the White House.

The Black Republican's hearty voice proved undaunted at the death of the president many hailed as "the Great Emancipator." It continued boldly, announcing itself as speaking for "the poor as well as the rich, the freedmen as well as the freemen." It noted the difference between the groups. They might all fit in the general category "colored," but that hardly made them all the same. *The Black Republican* directly confronted the *Tribune*, dubbing itself "the true organ of the American colored people of Louisiana." It published a message of unity centered in common folk, not an elite. "It will be printed in the English tongue, the tongue that brought us freedom," the paper declared to differentiate itself further from the Creole *Tribune*.

The Black Republican assumed no airs. It preferred militancy to elegance. Its primary audience was not the *Tribune*'s. It catered to no *petite bourgeoisie*—no artisans, shopkeepers, or small property holders. It spoke to and for the dispossessed. They had common cause with more privileged Creoles when it came to civil rights. In many ways, however, their positions diverged. They were not one and the same people. In some ways they were like chalk and cheese—yet they were not unlike the variety found among whites. Diversity marked them, too.

The *Tribune* and *The Black Republican* urged joint efforts to secure equal rights. Creoles and blacks could work together for the same end. They could benefit from each other's strengths and shore up each other's weaknesses. Neither was about to forget who they were; their identity stamped each. As Creoles did in the *Tribune*, *The Black Republican* kept its identity centered. "Emancipated brethren, let us come together as one man," it exhorted. "Let us secure the freedom we have received by the intelligence that can maintain it" (Davis 1983, 157).

The *Tribune* and *The Black Republican* both agreed as 1865 closed that freedom was not yet complete for those who were not white. Others also recognized the gap. Demands for full civil rights resounded in the North as well as in the South. Cincinnati's *Colored Citizen* in August 1865, for example, decried the persistent "unwillingness to carry out democratic principles." Speaking from Ohio's largest city and the seventh largest in the nation in 1860, just behind New Orleans in population, the weekly begun in 1863 counseled an easy solution to civil rights issues. "Be simply *democratic*, gentlemen, and all is easy," it advised (Aptheker 1951, 551).

The newly founded National Equal Rights League (NERL) added a concerted voice. The group spun off in 1864 from the National Convention of Colored Men at Syracuse, New York. It held its own inaugural convention in Cleveland, Ohio, in October 1865. There it pointed to the U.S. Constitution as providing clear principles to solve the so-called Negro problem and civil rights issues. The nation's fundamental charter should simply ensure "a Republican form of government" in every state, as guaranteed in Article IV. No law could then distinguish persons "on account of race or color," the NERL explained (NERL 1865, 21).

The Black Codes Louisiana and other ex-rebel states enacted in December 1865 and January 1866 made clear that full civil rights were not coming to the South—at least not by state action. This unavoidable realization moved Congress to act. It produced the nation's first federal civil rights law. Much of the debate during the act's passage focused on an unanswered question: Exactly what were civil rights? No all-encompassing answer emerged. The legislation did, however, recognize and categorize as civil rights a list of economic and political rights. To put those rights under federal protection, Congress attached them to national citizenship.

President Andrew Johnson objected to the congressional action. The North Carolina-born politician had served Tennessee in Congress beginning in 1843; he became a U.S. senator in 1857. Johnson served also as Tennessee governor from 1853 to 1857. He opposed secession, and when federal forces regained control of Tennessee in 1862, President Lincoln appointed Johnson military governor of the state and tapped him in 1864 to become vice president. Lincoln's assassination made Johnson president. While a staunch Unionist, Johnson also staunchly supported states' rights. He vetoed the civil rights bill in March 1866 on states' rights grounds.

The U.S. Constitution left to the states the authority to regulate personal rights, Johnson insisted. That included civil rights. Congress had no such authority in the president's view. Senator Lyman Trumbull of Illinois and Representative James F. Wilson of Iowa and other Republicans in Congress disagreed with the president. They pointed to the Thirteenth Amendment's second section which declared that "Congress shall have power to enforce this article by appropriate legislation." They saw the civil rights issue as an extension of the slavery question. Like other white conservatives, Johnson rejected any such connection. In his view, Congress simply lacked authority to enact civil rights measures.

The issue was not race, President Johnson insisted. "I share with Congress the strongest desire to secure to the freedmen the full enjoyment of their freedom and property and their entire independence and equality in making contracts for their labor," he insisted in February 1866 (McPherson 1871, 74). Yet he had also declared, "Damn the negroes, I am fighting those traitorous aristocrats, their masters." Johnson reportedly responded to Lincoln's Emancipation Proclamation by declaring, "[T]he Administration made a sad mistake in touching the Negro" (Johnson 1983, xlviii). Nevertheless, Johnson maintained the issue at hand was federalism.

The president rested his veto of the civil rights bill on his understanding of the U.S. Constitution's division of authority between the federal and state governments. "Hitherto every subject embraced in the enumeration of the rights contained in this bill has been considered as exclusively belonging to the States. They all relate to the internal police and economy of the respective States," Johnson explained. "They are matters which in each State concern the domestic condition of its people, varying in each according to its own particular circumstances and the safety and well being of its own citizens" (Johnson 1866, 38).

Congress overrode the president's veto. The vote in the Senate was 33 to 12—three votes more than the two-thirds required. In the House of Representatives, the vote was 111 to 38. Thus federal law came to provide that "citizens, of every race and color, without regard to any previous condition of slavery or involuntary servitude, except as a punishment for crime whereof the party shall have been duly convicted, shall have the same right, in every State and Territory in the United States" (United States 1866, 27).

The Civil Rights Act of 1866 stopped short of being an equal rights law. It operated selectively, not completely across the board. It provided for specific rights, beginning with what many thought of as economic rights. The first was the right to make and enforce contracts. It provided for the right "to inherit, purchase, lease, sell, hold, and convey real and personal property." As necessary protection for such rights, the act included the right "to sue, be parties, and give evidence." It came closest to an equal rights measure in providing for personal security. It recognized the right of all citizens "to full and equal benefit of all laws and proceedings for the security of person and property, as is enjoyed by white citizens." It there recognized the white standard embedded in U.S. law. In adjusting the standard to citizens of any color, Congress provided that all citizens "shall be subject to like punishment, pains, and penalties, and to none other" (United States 1866, 27).

Congress voided "any law, statute, ordinance, regulation, or custom, to the contrary" of its pronouncements in the 1866 Civil Rights Act. Some seemed naïvely to believe the act would be all that was necessary to settle civil rights issues stemming from slavery. Many people had initially also

thought abolishing slavery would be all that was necessary. The more practical understood at least some dimensions of the continuing problem of
racial discrimination exhibited in slavery. Supporters of organizations such
as the National Equal Rights League understood that slavery represented
only the most extreme symptoms of white supremacy. Curing the disease
itself demanded fundamental behavioral changes; it required changing attitudes, customs, habits, and more. Many questioned whether that was something law could do—and persistent arguments attached to whether it was
something federal law or any law *should* do.

Johnson's vetoes expressed widely held objections to extending civil
rights to nonwhites. Republicans in Congress had the votes to override
him, but they wanted more than fickle political power to outweigh resistance to federal civil rights. They wanted to fix an enduring foundation for
ending discriminatory state acts. Their focus fell on what later became the
familiar phrase "race, color, or previous condition of servitude." Thus, in
June 1866, Congress proposed a Fourteenth Amendment. Like the Civil
Rights Act, the amendment used terms of general reference, providing for
broad reach. It confirmed federal control of citizenship, and it banned
states from denying or abridging the rights of U.S. citizens. Also it extended
protections to "any person." It provided that "No state shall . . . deprive any
person of life, liberty, or property, without due process of law; nor deny to
any person within its jurisdiction the equal protection of the laws."

Congress aimed the proposed language to quiet any uncertainty about its
authority over civil rights. The fifth section of the proposed amendment
copied the second section of the Thirteenth Amendment. It provided that
"Congress shall have power to enforce, by appropriate legislation, the provisions of this article." The language suggested far-reaching changes in
American federalism.

Rather than silencing opposition, the proposed amendment quickened
resistance. It joined issues that locked the president and the Congress in
mortal struggle. It prompted the Louisiana legislature stubbornly to declare
in February 1867 that it "refuses to accede to the amendment" (Louisiana
1867, 9).

Resistance among ex-Confederate states such as Louisiana moved
Congress to more direct measures. A majority of Republicans saw the need
to change what southern state legislatures and the president were doing.
So, Congress took over Reconstruction. In March 1867, it passed the first
of four Reconstruction acts that put the rebel states under military control.

Only Tennessee escaped the process called congressional Reconstruction. In January 1865, Andrew Johnson as military governor had

initiated the process that restored Tennessee as a recognized legal and loyal state. Taking office as vice president in March 1865 and then within six weeks becoming president, Johnson signed off on the full restoration of his home state. Its 10 ex-Confederate sisters lingered under Congress's dictates.

Johnson became increasingly unable to help his fellow southerners as he fell under siege himself. The House of Representatives impeached him in February 1868. Johnson only narrowly escaped. In May 1868, the Senate voted 35–19 to convict him, falling a mere one vote short of the two-thirds required to remove the president from office.

Congress had taken charge of Reconstruction, and people of color exulted. Congress had opened the way not only out of slavery but to full citizenship. Congress would provide Louisiana's Creoles what they had so long desired. The Fourteenth Amendment confirmed them as U.S. citizens and as citizens of Louisiana. Moreover, congressional Reconstruction brought them voting rights.

Congress understood that to change southern legislatures required changing southern electorates. It did that in two parts. First, it eliminated previous voters who were "disfranchised for participation in rebellion." Second, it added new voters, calling for elections in the state "by the male citizens of said State, twenty-one years old and upward, of whatever race, color, or previous condition" (United States 1867, 429).

A new day had, in fact, dawned in Louisiana.

References

Aptheker, Herbert. 1951. *A Documentary History of the Negro People in the United States*. New York: Citadel Pr.

Bennett, Albert P. et al., comp. 1864. *Debates in the Convention for the Revision and Amendment of the Constitution of the State of Louisiana: Assembled at Liberty Hall, New Orleans, April 6, 1864*. New Orleans: W. R. Fish, printer to the convention.

"Black Republican Prayer." 1864. In *Black Scare: The Racist Response to Emancipation and Reconstruction*, by Forrest G. Wood, 92+. Berkeley: University of California Press, 1968.

Brown, William Wells. June 4, 1864. "Address to New England Anti-Slavery Society, May 27, 1864." *National Anti-Slavery Standard*.

Croly, David G. 1864. *Miscegenation: The Theory of the Blending of the Races, Applied to the American White Man and the Negro*. New York: H. Dexter, Hamilton & Co.

Davis, Thomas J. 1983. "Louisiana." In *The Black Press in the South, 1865–1879*, ed. Henry Lewis Suggs, 151–176. Westport, CT: Greenwood Press.

Douglass, Frederick. 1878. "Speech in Madison Square on Decoration Day, 1878." Frederick Douglass Papers, microfilm reel 15, Manuscript Division, Library of Congress, Washington, DC.

Foner, Philip S., ed. 1952. *The Life and Writings of Frederick Douglass*. New York: International Publishers.

Houzeau, Jean-Charles. 1870. *My Passage at the New Orleans Tribune: A Memoir of the Civil War Era*, ed. David C. Rankin. Baton Rouge: Louisiana State University Press, 1984.

Johnson, Andrew. 1866. "Veto Message of the President." In *Tribune Almanac and Political Register for 1867*. New York: Tribune Association.

Johnson, Andrew. 1983. *The Papers of Andrew Johnson*. Vol. 6, 1862–1864, ed. Leroy P. Graf, Ralph W. Haskins, and Patricia P. Clark. Knoxville, TN: University of Tennessee Press.

Kaplan, Sidney. 1949. "The Miscegenation Issue in the Election of 1864." *Journal of Negro History* 34 (3): 274–343.

Lincoln, Abraham. 1858. *The Collected Works of Abraham Lincoln*, ed. Roy P. Basler. New Brunswick, NJ: Rutgers University Press, 1953.

Lincoln, Abraham. 1864. *The Essential Lincoln: Speeches and Correspondence*, ed. Orville Vernon Burton. New York: Hill and Wang, 2009.

Louisiana. 1867. "Joint Resolution Relative to the Constitutional Amendment Proposed by the Congress of the United States as Article XIV." 1867 La. Acts 9 (February 21, 1867).

McPherson, Edward. 1871. *The Political History of the United States of America during the Period of Reconstruction, April 15, 1865–July 15, 1870*. Washington DC: Philp & Solomons.

National Equal Rights League (NERL). 1865. *Proceedings of the First Annual Meeting of the National Equal Rights League Held in Cleveland, Ohio, October 19, 20, and 21, 1865*. Philadelphia: E. C. Markley and Son.

Sandburg, Carl. 1939. *Abraham Lincoln: The War Years*. New York: Harcourt, Brace & Co.

United States. 1866. "An Act to Protect All Persons in the United States in Their Civil Rights, and Furnish the Means of Their Vindication" (Civil Rights Act of 1866). 14 Stat. 27 (April 9, 1866).

United States. 1867. "An Act to Provide for the More Efficient Government of the Rebel States" (First Reconstruction Act). 14 Stat. 428 (March 2, 1867).

SEVEN

The Reconstruction: Hope for Equal Rights

HOMER PLESSY was too young in 1868 to grasp all the changes emerging in the world around him. He had just turned three years old when the Confederate Army surrendered at Appomattox in April 1865. He was but four when Congress passed the Civil Rights Act in April 1866. He was turning five when congressional Reconstruction started in March 1867. He was turning six years old when Louisiana hailed a new state constitution in April 1868. These milestones would grow in importance in his life; they marked the start of his personal path to the U.S. Supreme Court in 1896.

Older Creoles of color like Homer Plessy's parents had a better grip on unfolding opportunities at the close of the Civil War. They seized the chance to crack the shackles of color against which they and their Creole ancestors had so long chafed. They rushed to lead a transformation in Louisiana to secure what they viewed as their rightful position as full citizens and full members of the public community, recognized for who they were.

Many Creoles saw themselves as natural leaders of the enlarged postwar colored population in which white supremacy lumped them. Being free before the war conferred on them clear advantages over the newly freed. Some Creoles had enjoyed extraordinary white patronage. Indeed, some enjoyed sizable patrimonies from their white fathers. Some amassed their own notable estates. Some had traveled to Europe. Some had attended universities and other schools there. Some had become physicians or entered other professions. Some like Homer Plessy's parents and grandparents had become *petit bourgeoisie*. Homer's father was an artisan, a carpenter like his own father. Such benefits showed themselves during the war, as Creoles emerged as political leaders. Their public campaign in *L'Union* and the New Orleans *Tribune* illustrated their forward position.

Not everyone saw Creoles in New Orleans as Creoles saw themselves, of course. Their superior self-image in Louisiana's hierarchy hardly fit immediate realities. Creoles were a minority. They prided themselves on being a relatively small, stubbornly self-defined group. They stood apart in ancestry, culture, language, and religion. They shared experiences and outlooks with both blacks and whites, yet their experiences and outlooks also separated them from both blacks and whites. They proved more welcoming to whites than to blacks. Yet whites persistently rejected them as nonwhites, and blacks long resented Creoles' customary condescension and insularity.

No shallow divide separated Creoles and other prewar free nonwhites from the postwar freed. Differences among the postwar people collectively called "colored" in polite terms divided them broadly into blacks and tans. Of unmixed African ancestry, blacks for the most part came from Louisiana's fields bearing the brunt of plantation slavery. Tans were mulattoes and others of mixed ancestry. Many were free before the war, but not all. Not all tans were Creoles. Beyond their light complexion, their Catholic French ancestry, culture, and language set Creoles part. Thus those called "colored" were no singular people, any more than whites were all the same. The colorline alone carved the simplistic dichotomy of white or colored.

Differences among colored people were easy to see. U.S. Army Major Benjamin Rush Plumly, who served as a staff officer in New Orleans between 1863 and 1865, noted that fact during the war. Before the war, the Pennsylvania-born merchant allied himself with abolitionist William Lloyd Garrison. From his home and business in Trenton, New Jersey, Plumly before the war abetted fugitive slaves fleeing along the so-called Underground Railroad. In uniform in Louisiana, Plumly organized schools and teachers for the newly freed people. He recoiled at the prejudices in the colored population.

Colored people "divided into castes as sharply defined as those of Hindostan—the free against the bound, the light against the dark," Plumly complained. "There are colored creoles who do not believe in freedom for the black," he exclaimed in an 1863 letter to Garrison. "There are others who would limit colored suffrage to their own class," he added. Sadly, he noted, at least a few Creoles "with all their admirable qualities, have not forgotten that they were, themselves, slaveholders" (Rankin 1979, 133).

The Black Republican pointed up differences between "the poor as well as the rich, the freedmen as well as the freemen." It urged colored unity in spite of differences, as did the Creole-run New Orleans *Tribune*. Both newspapers exhorted all colored people to unite in common cause against white supremacy. The *Tribune*'s issue of January 8, 1865, emphasized "the necessity of being united, and acting as one body." Such a need, the editors hoped, "is now generally understood."

Too few Creoles lived in the countryside to engage them generally in common cause there. Moreover, they showed little interest in economic survival issues that engaged country blacks. Militancy in Louisiana's sugar region in the years immediately after the war, for example, drew little support from Creoles. Grassroots mobilization in places such as Iberville Parish, where blacks outnumbered whites three to one, came to interest Creoles almost exclusively as it touched results at the polls. Labor market concerns crucial to fieldworkers stirred scant sympathy among most Creoles. Yet blacks showed their strength in sugar bowl areas such as Iberville by reshaping their labor arrangement themselves. That was what the end of slavery meant to them: Being freed meant not working as slaves. Citified Creoles usually stood distant from such concerns.

Common cause for Creoles developed more immediately at the state capital. Almost everything there took on a political air and touched the colorline. New Orleans's segregated streetcars became an early example of the ongoing combat there. Whites resisted abandoning the star car system that allowed them to ride any available car while relegating nonwhites to starred cars. This system sometimes resulted in no cars or seats for nonwhites when impatient whites commandeered them. Colored U.S. Army troops refused to abide such segregation. With their arms and numbers, they rode where they pleased. Colored civilians remained relegated, however, to the one-in-three cars designated for them. The *Tribune* persistently campaigned to desegregate streetcars. "We must claim the right of riding for every one of us, and claim it unconditionally," the newspaper declared in its January 13, 1865, issue.

Tensions were taut in postbellum New Orleans. The push and pull of change to the antebellum order strained the colorline. The influx of blacks escaping the fields had immediately begun to erode the old order in the city. Their swelling mass rubbed raw thousands of homecoming Confederate veterans who expected to find the city as they had left it before Union occupation in 1862.

Confederate leaders such as General of the Army Robert E. Lee had surrendered on the battlefield, but returning rebel veterans were unwilling to surrender at home. Many remained rebellious and insisted on antebellum ways and means to fix conservative control of Louisiana. That meant keeping nonwhites where they had been. It meant excluding them from public participation. Slavery may have been gone in law, but the fact remained as segregationist refused to budge. Rebels stood fast on the colorline. They may have yielded on the battlefield, but at home they refused to give any quarter.

The struggle of Reconstruction developed, then, along an old line. It turned on questions of home rule and who would rule at home. With the electorate unchanged, Louisiana's antebellum leaders reemerged in late 1865 and 1866 to reclaim their positions. Elections in November 1865 ousted most white Unionists from state office in Louisiana. Elections in May 1866 removed them from most municipal and parish posts. The same trend swept the South.

To keep power Union occupation had brought them, white Unionists in Louisiana and elsewhere in the South needed colored voters. No other way existed for them to win at the polls. Everyone understood that, but conservative legislatures refused to permit that. Everything turned on who could and would vote. The old Creole touchstone for being accepted as full citizens thus became a flintstone. Sparks flew over suffrage and in July 1866 ignited a conflagration in New Orleans.

Using parliamentary maneuvers, Unionists moved to reconvene the convention that had crafted Louisiana's 1864 constitution. That body had adjourned on a motion allowing it to reconvene on call. Unionists used that provision with an aim to secure nonwhite voting and, thereby, their own political position and power. White conservatives refused to allow it, gathering to protest the convention's reopening on Monday, July 30, 1866, at the Mechanics' Institute.

Union occupation forces had early commandeered the Greek revival-style building on Dryades Street between Canal and Common to serve as the state capitol. It became a disaster site that Monday. Whites and non-whites, convention opponents and supporters clashed outside the building. Gunshots followed fisticuffs. Rioting engulfed the streets. City police did nothing to stem the fighting. Indeed, they added to it, joining in attacking white Unionists and nonwhites. U.S. Army troops came to restore order, but by then 48 men lay dead and more than 200 were wounded. The city remained under martial law until August 2.

The New Orleans riot signaled the upswing of political violence in Reconstruction. Such unrest hit not only the Crescent City but much of Louisiana and the entire South. Three days of rioting in Memphis at the beginning of May portended the coming rise of terrorism. The toll in Tennessee's leading city was staggeringly greater than that 400 miles down the Mississippi in New Orleans. Forty-eight people also died in the Memphis rioting, and 75 were wounded. Arsonists torched 8 black schools, 4 black churches, and at least 91 homes. New Orleans, by comparison, suffered little property damage.

Memphis's size magnified its May 1866 riot. Its population was then nearing 40,000, about one-fifth of New Orleans's population. Although that deepened the city's devastation, scale was not what distinguished the Memphis and New Orleans riots. Rather, purposeful planning set them apart. The Memphis riot represented a general melee. Racial friction spontaneously ignited there. White policemen confronting black U.S. Army veterans sparked an altercation that spilled into rioting. The rampage gained purpose after it started.

In contrast, the New Orleans violence began with purpose. It was political from start to finish. White conservatives decided to block constitutional change by force. They gathered, in their own view, as vigilantes. They aimed not only to disrupt what they saw as an illegitimate convention, but also to intimidate those who supported changing Louisiana's political structure with its unbearable racial consequences.

The July 1866 New Orleans riot accomplished white conservatives' immediate aim: The rump convention collapsed. The political violence provoked a backlash, however, that soon defeated the conservatives' purpose. It intensified reaction to earlier riots and other reported antiblack violence. The New Orleans riot capped a wave of other grim incidents such as the May riot in Memphis and a June riot in Charleston, South Carolina. Such events boosted Republicans nationally in the November 1866 congressional elections. Taking their victory as a plebiscite, Republicans in Congress overrode President Andrew Johnson's wishes in March 1867 to enact radical Reconstruction.

Congress cast its Reconstruction plan as necessary for "peace and good order" in Louisiana and 9 of its 10 sister rebel states. Tennessee alone escaped federal direction to establish "loyal and republican State governments." The congressional program invoked "sufficient military force" for its purposes, which began with a mandate "to protect all persons in their rights of person and property, to suppress insurrection, disorder and violence." It subordinated to federal control all civil government in the 10 southern states (United States 1867, 428).

Congress mandated changes in the fundamental law of the 10 states. It began by altering their electorates. It added voters by enfranchising "male citizens . . . twenty-one years old and upward, of whatever race, color, or previous condition." Also it subtracted voters by excepting from suffrage "such as may be disfranchised for participation in the rebellion." Congress required each of the 10 states to frame a new constitution that included such voting rights. Moreover, it required the 10 states to ratify the proposed Fourteenth Amendment (United States 1867, 428–429).

Congressional Reconstruction supplied a platform for Creoles to reach what they had long prayed for in Louisiana. They at last had the vote in their hands. They were too few, of course, to change white supremacy on their own. With allies among all colored people, however, they could muster the numbers to dominate at the polls. The first registration lists under Congress's adult-male suffrage mandate counted 82,907 of Louisiana's 127,639 voters (64.9 percent) as colored. In fact, colored people formed the majority on Louisiana voting lists from the opening of suffrage to them in August 1867 until 1890, when a virulent campaign to disfranchise non-whites began to crest and wash over the state and the entire South (Du Bois 1935, 466).

Creoles' first chance to vote in Louisiana came in September 1867. They seized it, as did colored voters generally. Homer Plessy's father, Joseph, went to the polls. Voting was virtually compulsory in his circle. Its coming had been too long and difficult for the right to not be exercised. To not vote would be like throwing away a valuable gift unopened. More than simply voting, Creoles and other colored men wanted to see their own in office. And they put them there: The election for a state constitutional convention seated 49 colored delegates and 49 white delegates.

The New Orleans *Tribune* beat the drum for the common theme among colored delegates—at least it was the theme among Creoles. "The extension of equal rights and privileges to all men, irrespective of color or race," expressed the motif for a new constitution's design, the Creole voice insisted in its issue of November 28, 1867, five days after the convention's opening.

The constitution that emerged from the convention brimmed with the language of equal rights. Its opening title echoed cherished phrases from the 1776 Declaration of Independence. It pronounced as part of the state's fundamental law that "All men are created free and equal and have certain inalienable rights." Its second article echoed the federal Civil Rights Act of 1866. It cast protections over "All persons, without regard to race, color, or previous condition of servitude" and provided that "[t]hey shall enjoy the same civil, political, and public rights and privileges, and be subject to the same pains and penalties." Its Article 13 outlawed "distinction or discrimination on account of race or color" in all "places of a public character." That included accommodations, amusements, and other businesses. It included conveyances, too. There was then to be not only "neither slavery nor involuntary servitude in this State," but also no public segregation. The proposed constitution provided also for adult male suffrage.

Under watchful U.S. Army guard in April 1868, nearly 115,000 colored and white Louisiana men voted on the proposed radical change in the state's fundamental law. The vote to adopt the constitution was 66,152 (57.6 percent) in favor, 48,739 against. The 17,413 majority ratified the constitution (Davis 1965, 302).

The tally exposed areas of strength and weakness. It showed Creoles unable to carry the equal rights banner to victory in their own stronghold. The proposed constitution lost in Orleans Parish 14,763 to 14,291. The count showed no black/white breakdown of voters. De Soto was the only other parish to omit such a breakdown. It sat in northwest Louisiana, 300 miles across the state from Orleans Parish. The constitution lost there, too—1,133 to 657. That was odd. The constitution lost in only a few parishes like De Soto where slaves constituted the majority of the population in 1860 (Davis 1965, 303–304).

The results unsurprisingly showed ex-slaves' votes as decisive to sustain any equal rights political structure in Louisiana. Creoles thought themselves important, and they were in many ways. Nevertheless, their votes alone could carry little, if anything, in postwar Louisiana. They might swing something in New Orleans. Outside Orleans Parish, however, Creoles' numbers carried little clout. To advance their political program required Creoles to unite in common cause with ex-slaves.

On some issues, achieving unity seemed easy. Desegregated public transportation appeared to be such an issue. It stood as a simple test of slavery's end. Before abolition, the law so restricted nonwhites' travel in Louisiana that segregated transportation was virtually a nonissue for most people. Creoles in New Orleans muttered about it, but before Union occupation during the Civil War they could muster no challenge to the policy. After the war, the situation changed.

New Orleans's old segregated star car system became a rallying point on both sides of the colorline. The one-in-three mule-team-drawn streetcars bearing large black stars to indicate their availability for nonwhites served as symbols of white privilege. The New Orleans *Tribune* and the *Black Republican* attacked what the cars represented. "All these discriminations that had slavery at the bottom have become nonsense," the *Tribune* railed in its April 21, 1867, issue. "It behooves those who feel bold enough to shake off the old prejudice and to confront their prejudiced associates," the paper urged in opposition to the segregated system.

Scuffles sporadically signaled challenges to segregated streetcars. In the last days of April and first days of May 1867, confrontations escalated. William Nichols's arrest on April 28 kicked off what the unsympathetic New Orleans *Daily Crescent* of May 7, 1867, described as a "pre-concerted design on the part of a number of colored men."

Mass protests exhorted colored riders to refuse black star cars and to ride cars designated for whites only. The largest protest occurred along Rampart Street near Congo Square. A colored crowd estimated at 500 described as men and boys spent Saturday afternoon May 4 confronting segregated cars.

The male protesters had female counterparts. On May 5, two unnamed colored women staged a sit-in on a whites-only car. They refused to budge as white passengers berated them. They sat patiently while others fidgeted and finally left the car, tiring of further delay or unwilling to wait to ride on a car with the protesters. The two women outlasted the white driver as well. He finally acceded to driving the car with only the two women passengers to their destination.

Riots loomed. The *Daily Crescent* newspaper later reported on May 7 of the worries that "a serious, perhaps calamitous disturbance might come upon the city, as a result of the continued agitation of this car question." Visions of the July 30, 1866, Mechanics' Institute bloodbath loomed, except now the image appeared of colored people attacking whites.

One worried railway company manager reported to New Orleans Mayor Edward Heath that "threats have been made by coloured persons that they intend to force themselves on the cars reserved for whites." He reported colored men's warning that "should the driver resist or refuse them passage, they would compel him to leave the car and take forcible possession themselves." The railway executive pleaded with the mayor to take steps to "insure the preservation of the public peace" (Reid 1867, 224–225).

General Philip H. Sheridan, the U.S. Army area commander, refused to dispatch troops to intervene. Instead, he counseled civil authorities to settle the matter. Unyielding colored resistance showed little sign of abating. Railway officials feared for their property and personnel. Other white civic leaders worried over how disrupted service might affect their businesses, customers, and employees. The city's white leaders apparently calculated that the lesser evil they faced was to end the segregated star car system.

On Monday, May 6, 1867, New Orleans Police Chief Thomas E. Adams delivered a neutral-sounding announcement of the desegregation victory. He proclaimed law and order to be on the side of a first-come, first-served system. Instead of arresting colored people for seeking to ride on any car, the police chief promised to arrest whites who resisted a passenger's choice to ride in whichever car he or she chose. "No passenger has the right to eject any other passenger, no matter what his color. If he does so, he is liable to arrest for assault, or breach of the peace," Chief Adams declared according to the New Orleans *Crescent* of May 7.

The streetcar protesters gained a foothold for the desegregation principle in Louisiana. Only further steps would show how firm their position was. Still, the victory secured a starting point. The protesters proved what collective, concerted colored action could do. They had at least in this instance disrupted the old order. They had made the city flinch and alter its public policy. Their direct action made a difference.

City leaders accepted the demand for desegregated streetcars. Eliminating the star car system, however, was not the same as eliminating segregation. That required more than a proclamation. Desegregating streetcars could only marginally impact the broad social system. Such change might be isolated, or it might produce other changes. What those might be became pressing questions. The New Orleans *Daily Picayune* of May 7, 1867, gave voice to white supremacists' immediate concern. The streetcar agitation was "simply the introductory step to more radical innovations, which must materially alter our whole social fabric," the newspaper warned.

Indeed, the streetcar victory spilled into a hasty assault on segregation elsewhere. Colored activists demanded service at previously whites-only eateries, retailers, theaters, and other businesses in New Orleans. They hurried to capitalize on the momentum from Police Chief Adams's May 6 announcement of the star cars' demise. They made little further headway, however, as they got little, if any, service. Almost universally, white proprietors or customers spurned colored persons seeking service. They were rebuffed as intruders. Widespread violence again loomed.

Mayor Heath hurried to avert spreading confrontations. He requested a legal opinion on the law covering public businesses. City Attorney Henry D. Ogden took a convenient position he based shakily on private property rights. Simply being open to the public made no place actually public, Ogden reasoned, so the law of trespass answered the question. Business proprietors had the legal right to refuse service as they pleased, Ogden advised Heath. "Although expecting remuneration from the patronage of the community at large," Ogden explained of retailers, restaurants, and other businesses, "they are nevertheless private property, owned by private individuals or private corporations, and subject to such rules and regulations as the proprietors may deem proper to adopt."

How such businesses differed from streetcars the city attorney failed to explain. Streetcars were private property, too. Private corporations owned and operated them. Did they, too, have the legal right to refuse service as they pleased? If they did, what was the legal basis of the police chief's May 6 proclamation? If they had no such legal right, then how did retailers, restaurants, and other businesses have such rights as the city attorney advised?

Clarifying the law awaited another day. Mayor Heath made the city attorney's opinion public on May 15 and issued a proclamation based on it. He declared simply that the law prohibited "all persons whatever from intruding into any store, shop or other place of business conducted by private individuals, against the consent and wishes of the owners, proprietors, or keepers of the same." The *Tribune*'s May 16 issue carried the city attorney's opinion and the mayor's proclamation with biting commentary.

The *Tribune* relentlessly fought segregation. Equal rights in its view could only mean no public distinction or separation based on race, color, or previous condition. That was what the end of slavery meant to Creoles. They had little patience for gradualism or half-measures. Ex-slaves had waited for centuries for slavery to end. Creoles had waited for centuries for segregation to end. They had prayed for equal rights, not emancipation. Now emancipation had come and Creoles insisted that equal rights come now, too. "When will the right time come?" The Creole voice plaintively asked in its July 31, 1867, issue. The *Tribune* answered its question adamantly, demanding immediate change in principle and practice.

Delay created only further distance, the *Tribune* insisted. It pushed to eradicate the white/nonwhite dichotomy instantly. It maintained that no time was like the present. What would waiting do? When would be a better time, it taunted: "[W]hen we shall have realized the separation of this nation into two peoples?" Left by itself, time would only deepen the divide. It would drop Creoles further into the black/white abyss. It would further entrench the separation that had imposed slavery, the paper's July 31 editorial declared. It virtually shouted its closing message. Wait much longer, the *Tribune* instructed, and "It will, then, be TOO LATE."

The 1868 state constitution answered Creoles' perennial prayers. It incorporated antidiscrimination principles into Louisiana's fundamental law. It prohibited segregation in every public avenue and venue. And it settled the public-private debate. The constitution provided that "all places of business . . . for which a license is required by either State, parish or municipal authority, shall be deemed places of a public character" (Louisiana 1868, art. 13).

The new constitution pushed further to enter the explosive field of schools. It provided what Louisiana had never before had: a statewide system of public schools. Article 135 directed the state legislature to "establish at least one free public school in every parish" and to "provide for its support by taxation or otherwise." The rub came in mandating a unitary system. "All children of this State, between the ages of six (6) and twenty-one (21)," the constitution directed, "shall be admitted to the public schools or other institutions of learning sustained and established by the State, in common, without distinction of race, color or previous condition."

The constitution's wording responded to fierce opposition. To start, many in Louisiana opposed maintaining schools at taxpayers' expense; they simply did not want to pay more taxes. Nor did many want to pay to school children other than their own. The louder opposition came from whites, who overwhelmingly and violently rejected having their children in school with nonwhites.

The *Louisiana Democrat* complained early against plans for such schools. The Alexandria newspaper's February 21, 1866, issue offered among the mildest, if snide, early jibes. It wrote that "negro and white children are to be drawn by a leveling process, into a grand Democratic equality in the Republic of Letters, through the medium of Public schools." The white conservative organ denounced such schools as part of a damnable crusade for social equality.

Whites unable to stomach the image of their children in school side by side with colored children schemed to keep such an event from being realized. Even many white Unionists and Republicans resisted the unitary school idea. The *Tribune* excoriated such persons. Its October 30, 1867, issue railed that "they tell us that star schools are good enough for us." It thus cast separate schools together with the indignity of the despised and defeated black star streetcars. It sarcastically quipped that "we must not imagine that they will ever send THEIR children to school with negro children."

The 1868 constitution anticipated a variety of schemes to skirt its public school plan, so it left no ambivalence about its mandate. "There shall be no separate schools or institutions of learning established exclusively for any-one race by the State of Louisiana," it reiterated. Moreover, it prohibited local government exceptions. "No municipal corporation shall make any rules or regulations contrary to the spirit and intention of article one hundred and thirty-five (135)," it specified.

The constitution settled the law. Putting legal principle into local practice was another thing. Violent opposition to the constitution signaled recalcitrance. The New Orleans *Bee* at the time of the ratification vote had signaled the antagonism to follow. The newspaper's April 17, 1868, issue urged the document's defeat in stark racial terms. The vote was not about philosophies of government or republican ideology; the vote was about protecting a traditional ideology of whiteness, the *Bee* announced in inflammatory language. It spoke not of manhood, but rather of protecting womanhood. "If you don't want your mothers and sisters, and wives and daughters insulted by insolent and depraved negro vagabonds," the *Bee* told readers, vote *no*. "If you are opposed to amalgamation and miscegenation," it implored, "vote against the new constitution."

Enforcing antidiscrimination law became the challenge. The colored vote had carried the constitution and elected its first slate of state officers. That power at the polls failed, however, to turn into control of the governor or the legislature. The vote seated 16 colored men among the 36 state senate slots. It put 45 among the 101 house seats. The governor's chair went to the 26-year-old, Illinois-born Henry Clay Warmoth. A so-called carpetbagger, the lawyer came from Missouri to Louisiana as a U.S. Army officer during the war. He served as a judge in the Provost Court of the Department of the Gulf that encompassed Louisiana. He proved at best a fickle friend to equal rights. His repeated run-ins with the legislature would lead to his being impeached in 1872.

Recognition of ex-slaves' clout in Louisiana came in the second-highest executive seat. Oscar James Dunn became lieutenant governor. The 42-year-old was born a slave in New Orleans in 1826. Contemporaries hailed his political talent. Widely respected, he worked easily with Creoles, but he was no Creole. Various contemporaries described him as "pure African" or "of pure Negro blood." On his inauguration on June 13, 1868, Dunn became the first black elected lieutenant governor in the United States. He died in November 1871 under mysterious circumstances; supporters said he was poisoned.

During his first year in office, Dunn helped guide passage of an equal rights enforcement act. Fixing on public transportation, the 1869 legislation put the bite of law into the streetcar desegregation won in New Orleans in May 1867. The statute reached broadly to all common carriers in Louisiana, prohibiting them from "discrimination on account of race or color" (Louisiana 1869).

The 1869 Common Carrier Act was the antecedent of the 1890 Separate Car Act Homer Plessy challenged. The two statutes were antithetical, however. The first prohibited segregation; the second commanded segregation. Their contrasting positions located the political turns directing the law of common carriers in Louisiana and other southern states during the last third of the 1800s. Also they signaled public transportation's troublesome persistence as a contentious point along the South's colorline.

Increasingly more accessible public transit created new social demands as it created new public spaces requiring rules for sharing. The problem in more than a few minds lay in part in the very definition of common carriers. They were *common*, which suggested they were to carry all persons. Having anyone and everyone together in the same social space, however, struck many as vulgar. The confines of common carriers could put people in uncomfortably close contact. Passengers could be in positions to rub shoulders and more. And the contact's duration could be more than fleeting. Such closeness violated various views of traditional etiquette.

Much of the discussion about standards for common carriers, particularly in the postwar South, spoke of protecting "ladies" from inappropriate contact. Separating the genders by creating "ladies cars" could answer objections to mixed-sex contacts. Such a measure could shield the genteel of the fair sex from the rough and rude. But that was not enough. It failed to quell objections from people who presumed others did not know how to behave or would purposely behave badly, whatever their gender. Such an attitude viewed some people as offensive by nature and to be avoided. Using price could separate passengers, setting them apart in ticket classes. Yet money was not a sufficient separator everywhere. Cost simply clustered whoever could afford the ticket. On streetcars and other carriers with single-fare structures, ticket price worked no distinction.

In the post-abolition South, distinction was a necessity for many whites—at least on the basis of race. Equally, having no racial distinctions was a necessity for many nonwhites. The Baton Rouge *Grand Era* succinctly reiterated the colored point of view in May 1871, insisting on "the right to travel on any public conveyance in accordance with the class of tickets purchased." The newspaper's fellow and larger pro-colored voice, the New Orleans *Republican*, echoed that sentiment in its May 11, 1871, issue.

The standard for segregationists was simply race. They wanted a clear barrier between whites and nonwhites. Preserving the colorline seemed segregationists' sole concern about propriety. They took no account of personal status or standing beyond race. Thus white men aboard the Mississippi steamboat *Bannock City* in March 1871 bodily threw Edward Butler from a cabin they deemed whites only. It made no difference that Butler was a state senator from Plaquemine Parish; he was not white. That was all his assailants needed to know as they pummeled him and threw him out on the deck for his ride on the river between his home and the capital.

The New Orleans *Republican* reported Butler's ordeal on March 23, 1871. It narrated the common nightmare for supporters of equal rights who believed that whoever paid the appropriate fare and behaved correctly should ride on common carriers wherever they pleased. How was it that white ruffians could ride where they pleased and deny an honorable colored person passage in the compartment for which he had paid? Such a situation defied reason, desegregationists declared. They insisted on a simple standard of good behavior to control passage on common carriers, as Louisiana's 1869 act directed.

The command of state law was clear. So was disobedience to it. The assault on State Senator Butler was merely one of epidemic instances of white passengers and proprietors' defying the law. According nonwhites equal rights was flatly unacceptable to them. No less unacceptable to colored people was denial of their equal rights. Robbing colored people on common carriers of what by right was theirs and of what they had paid for outraged them and others who supported equal rights.

Josephine Dubuclet DeCuir exhibited Creoles' outrage at the indignity of having their rights as passengers denied. In fact, she stood as a direct predecessor of Homer Plessy's in opposing transportation segregation in Louisiana. She, too, fought in the U.S. Supreme Court for a landmark ruling. Plessy would later pose the ultimate test of the 1890 Separate Car Act. DeCuir waged the ultimate test of the 1869 Common Carrier Act. As one of Louisiana's wealthiest persons of color, she had the wherewithal for the battle.

Mrs. DeCuir's ordeal started during her July 1872 trip aboard the *Governor Allen*. The river packet plied a regular 250-mile route with various local landings between New Orleans and Vicksburg, Mississippi. DeCuir booked a first-class cabin befitting her status. Price was no issue for her. She was traveling upriver from New Orleans to Hermitage Landing in Pointe Coupée Parish, where her family owned plantations.

The *Governor Allen*'s master and owner denied the Creole woman use of a first-class cabin. The rules of the boat, he maintained, provided first-class cabins for whites only. Mrs. DeCuir sued him in state court as provided in Louisiana's 1869 Common Carrier Act and won a jury award of $1,000 in damages. Louisiana's Supreme Court sustained the award on appeal.

The case then went to the U.S. Supreme Court. There, in January 1878, Chief Justice Morrison R. Waite delivered a blow to Mrs. DeCuir and advocates of desegregated public transit. The Court's unanimous opinion showed little interest in what happened to Mrs. DeCuir aboard the *Governor Allen*. Waite and his fellow justices focused only on the operation of the 1869 Common Carrier Act. DeCuir's treatment became irrelevant. The Court's decision dismissed not only her but the Louisiana law itself.

The Court decided that the state statute lacked legal force on the *Governor Allen*. The carrier operated beyond Louisiana's jurisdiction, Chief Justice Waite explained. He noted that the *Governor Allen* was a federally licensed coasting vessel operating on the Mississippi. The nation's chief inland waterway flowed entirely under federal control. Interstate transit, such as that of the *Governor Allen*, also flowed entirely under federal control. The U.S. Constitution's Commerce Clause put both under Congress's exclusive jurisdiction, so states had no authority to interfere in their operation. No state could legally impose a direct burden on interstate river traffic. The Court had determined that point long before. The 1824 landmark ruling in *Gibbons v. Ogden* settled the issue in striking down a New York statute that restricted traffic on the Hudson River.

The commerce clause existed to keep interstate transport free of the kind of restriction Louisiana's 1869 Common Carrier Act imposed, the Court decided. The chief justice concluded the Court's ruling simply, stating that "this statute, to the extent that it requires those engaged in the transportation of passengers among the States to carry colored passengers in Louisiana in the same cabin with whites, is unconstitutional and void. If the public good requires such legislation," he advised, "it must come from Congress and not from the States" (United States 1878, 400).

Congress had, in fact, decided the public good required legislation such as Louisiana's 1869 Common Carrier Act. The federal Civil Rights Act of 1875 provided that "all persons within the jurisdiction of the United States shall be entitled to the full and equal enjoyment of the accommodations, advantages, facilities, and privileges of inns, public conveyances on land or water, theaters, and other places of public amusement." The federal language mimicked expressions from Louisiana's 1868 constitution. Adopting a similarly broad view of what constituted "public," the act outlawed racial discrimination and more throughout the United States. It made all business customers and common carrier passengers "subject only to the conditions and limitations established by law and applicable alike to citizens of every race and color, regardless of any previous condition of servitude."

Under the 1875 act, what happened to Mrs. DeCuir aboard the *Governor Allen* would have been a federal crime. But her outrage occurred in July 1872, before Congress passed the 1875 act. She had no protection under federal law. For that matter, the 1875 act ended up providing colored people relatively little protection for what it called "their civil and legal rights."

The failure lay not with Congress, nor did it stem from a lack of federal prosecution. The blame lay with the U.S. Supreme Court. It defeated Congress's efforts to shield the victims of white supremacy. At the start of its civil rights push in 1866, Congress had to override the president's veto to create safeguards. In the 1870s and after, Congress saw its efforts failing as the Court repeatedly overrode civil rights legislation.

A case the Court decided in March 1876 portended the federal shortfall in civil rights. It arose in Louisiana; indeed, it was part of what some contemporaries called the "Louisiana outrages." The criminal case tested an 1870 federal civil right act to protect voters from terrorism. Some referred to the legislation as the Voting Rights Act of 1870.

The 1873 Easter massacre in Louisiana's Grant Parish supplied the immediate facts of the case that became *United States v. Cruikshank.* That Sunday, April 13, white militia slaughtered more than 100 colored people in Colfax, the seat of the parish 230 miles northwest of New Orleans. The attack aimed to settle a disputed election days earlier. Tight balloting reflected the parish's narrow population split. The 1870 federal census counted 2,414 colored and 2,078 white persons in Grant Parish. The election count left both the white conservative-backed Democrat/Fusionist slate and the colored-backed Republican slate claiming victory.

The Sunday battle developed over control of the parish courthouse. Colored forces occupied it to start. White militia laid siege and set the building afire. Witnesses testified that William J. Cruikshank and other white militia executed at least 50 colored victims after they surrendered to escape the blaze. The bodies of more than 15 unidentified colored victims were later dredged from the nearby Red River. Three white attackers died in the fighting.

No prospects developed for state punishment of the attackers. White conservatives simply thwarted local prosecutions. They did the same routinely throughout the South. Earlier failures to combat such terrorism gave rise to the 1870 act and three other federal civil rights enforcement acts that shortly followed. The need for such measures had been made clear long before the Easter 1873 events. Terrorism aimed at suppressing black voting had become so bad in South Carolina in 1871 that President Ulysses S. Grant dispatched federal troops to quell the Ku Klux Klan (KKK) and other white vigilantes. The terrorists hailed themselves as fighting to redeem their homelands for white supremacy; the president declared their violence simply "insurrection."

Federal prosecutors throughout the South sought to fill the vacuum southern state inaction created in civil law enforcement. They did so in

Louisiana in response to what some called the Colfax Massacre. Using section 6 of the 1870 act, the U.S. district attorney secured a 32-count indictment against more than 100 white militia and won convictions at trial in the U.S. District Court. Nine of the accused, including Cruikshank, appealed their convictions to the U.S. Circuit Court.

U.S. Supreme Court Justice Joseph P. Bradley covered the circuit and sat with the court that heard the *Cruikshank* appeal. The 61-year-old New York-born jurist developed a portentous theory of the case. He ignored what Cruikshank and other white terrorists did in Colfax. He focused instead on what Congress did in the 1870 act, which he decided was unconstitutional. Such a decision would quash the convictions of Cruikshank and his accomplices. The members of the circuit panel sitting with Bradley could not agree on that result. Their divided opinion sent the case to the U.S. Supreme Court.

Bradley thus sat on the case again in the Court's October 1875 term. On circuit, he had uttered the first strains of what became known as his state action doctrine. Bradley asserted that the U.S. Constitution provided no federal authority to prosecute local crimes. Those were state matters. Bradley insisted that "any outrages, atrocities, or conspiracies, whether against the colored race or the white race ... [that] spring from the ordinary felonious or criminal intent which prompts to such unlawful acts, are not within the jurisdiction of the United States, but within the sole jurisdiction of the states" (United States 1874, 714).

Justice Bradley's pronouncement promised to cut back, if not entirely cut out, essential federal civil rights enforcement. Traditional federalism plainly prohibited federal policing of individual action in the states, he insisted. Federal action could redress or remedy state action. It had done so in the Civil War. Bradley offered no direct comment on whether the postwar amendments to the Constitution had fundamentally altered federalism. He simply resisted what he saw as national regulation of personal relations.

Accepting that Congress had authority to regulate civil rights, Bradley suggested with evident revulsion, meant accepting that "congress may pass an entire body of municipal law for the protection of person and property within the states." Rejecting that proposition, he maintained that "the preservation of the public peace and the fundamental rights of the people," as always, remained exclusively "the prerogative of the states" (United States 1874, 714).

Justice Bradley's colleagues on the U.S. Supreme Court resisted his theory at least in part as they decided the *Cruikshank* case. They accepted his conclusion that the convictions of Cruikshank and his accomplices failed constitutional scrutiny, however. Chief Justice Waite's opinion for the court rested the decision on faulty wording in the indictment. Various counts, he noted, "do not show that it was the intent of the defendants, by their conspiracy, to hinder or prevent the enjoyment of any right granted or secured by the Constitution" (United States 1876, 557).

The nation's high court did endorse Justice Bradley's premise on federalism. Chief Justice Waite's opinion tempered Bradley's language to balance competing values. Waite emphasized on the one hand that "equality of the rights of citizens is a principle of republicanism." On the other hand, he noted, federalism governed national and state power. "Every republican government is in duty bound to protect all its citizens in the enjoyment of this principle [of equality of rights], if within its power. That duty was originally assumed by the States; and it still remains there," the chief justice stated pointedly. "The only obligation resting upon the United States is to see that the States do not deny the right. This the [Fourteenth] amendment guarantees, but no more. The power of the National government is limited to the enforcement of this guaranty," Waite concluded (United States 1876, 556).

The *Cruikshank* decision proved to be the beginning of the end of Congress's efforts to supply and sustain the civil rights for which Plessy's people had so long pushed.

References

Davis, Donald W. 1965. "Ratification of the Constitution of 1868: Record of Votes." *Louisiana History* 6 (3): 301–306.

Du Bois, W. E. B. 1935. *Black Reconstruction in America: An Essay toward a History of the Part Which Black Folk Played in the Attempt to Reconstruct Democracy in America, 1860–1880.* New York: Russell & Russell.

Louisiana. 1868. *Official Journal of the Proceedings of the Convention, for Framing a Constitution for the State of Louisiana.* New Orleans: J. B. Roudanez and Co.

Louisiana. 1869. "An Act to Enforce the Thirteenth Article of the Constitution of This State, and to Regulate the Licenses Mentioned in Said Thirteenth Article" (Common Carrier Act). 1869 La. Acts 37 (February 23, 1869).

Rankin, David C. 1979. "The Politics of Caste: Free, Leadership in New Orleans during the Civil War." In *Louisiana's Black Heritage*, ed. Robert R. Macdonald, John R. Kemp, and Edward F. Haas, 125–138. New Orleans: Louisiana State Museum.

Reid, D. M. May 5, 1867. Letter to Edward Heath. Quoted in "A Pioneer Protest: The New Orleans Street-Car Controversy of 1867" by Roger A. Fisher. *Journal of Negro History* 53, no. 3 (1968): 219–233.

United States. 1867. "An Act to Provide for the More Efficient Government of the Rebel States" (First Reconstruction Act). 14 Stat. 428 (March 2, 1867).

United States. 1874. *United States v. Cruikshank*, 25 F. Cas. 707 (C.C.D. La. 1874) (No. 14,897).

United States. 1876. *United States v. Cruikshank*, 92 U.S. 542 (1876).

United States. 1878. *Hall v. DeCuir*, 95 U.S. 485 (1878).

EIGHT

The Redemption:
Despair for Equal Rights

HOMER PLESSY turned 21 in 1883, the year Justice Joseph P. Bradley's theories supplanted Congress's civil rights measures. The direction away from federal action to enforce equal rights brought Plessy to the U.S. Supreme Court in 1896. Bradley was then dead. Sickness had forced him from the bench weeks after the start of the October 1891 term, but before then a majority of the Court had come to accept Bradley's state action theory and other of his views about the limits of federal reach against racial discrimination. The result for federal civil rights enforcement became fatal in fact, if not in theory, for generations to come. It helped seal Plessy's fate.

The Court's 1883 decision in five cases from around the nation revealed Bradley's influence. None of the cases came from the 10 reconstructed states. Indeed, only one came from an ex-Confederate state—Tennessee. One case came from another state that maintained slavery at the start of the Civil War—Missouri. The other three cases came from California, Kansas, and New York.

All the 1883 cases tested the equal access provision of the Civil Rights Act of 1875. The Kansas and Missouri cases arose from a hotel's or inn's denial of accommodations on the basis of race, color, or previous condition of servitude. The California and New York cases arose from refusals of service at a theater. Maguire's Theatre in San Francisco refused a colored person a seat in its dress circle. In New York, the refusal occurred at the Grand Opera House. The Tennessee case treated the refusal of the Memphis & Charleston Railroad Company to allow the colored Mrs. Richard A. Robinson of Mississippi to ride in a ladies car.

The Court consolidated the five cases to treat them in a single decision, which Justice Bradley delivered. That the opinion came from him signaled its direction. And he wasted no time in pointing the dagger at the heart of the matter. "It is obvious that the primary and important question in all the cases is the constitutionality of the law: for if the law is unconstitutional none of the prosecutions can stand," he opened. His intention was clear. His opinion in the *Cruikshank* case bared the point of his belief that Congress had limited, if any, constitutional authority over civil rights.

Neither the Thirteenth nor the Fourteenth Amendment altered much in traditional, antebellum federalism, in Bradley's view. Moreover, he insisted, the two amendments stood distant from the bans against racial discrimination Congress pronounced in its 1875 Civil Rights Act. "We must not forget that the province and scope of the Thirteenth and Fourteenth amendments are different: the former simply abolished slavery; the latter prohibited the States from abridging the privileges or immunities of citizens of the United States, from depriving them of life, liberty, or property without due process of law, and from denying to any the equal protection of the laws," the justice explained (United States 1883, 23).

The two amendments worked separately, not together, Bradley contended. "The amendments are different, and the powers of Congress under them are different," he emphasized. "What Congress has power to do under one it may not have power to do under the other. Under the Thirteenth Amendment, it has only to do with slavery and its incidents," Bradley instructed. "Under the Fourteenth Amendment, it has power to counteract and render nugatory all State laws and proceedings which have the effect to abridge any of the privileges or immunities of citizens of the United States, or to deprive them of life, liberty or property without due process of law, or to deny to any of them the equal protection of the laws," he repeated (United States 1883, 23).

The Fourteenth Amendment could not reach the acts of discrimination in the cases at hand, Justice Bradley said. Indeed, the amendment failed to sustain the equal rights provisions Congress enacted in the 1875 Civil Rights Act, according to Bradley. The amendment allowed Congress to reach only instances when "the denial of the right has some State sanction or authority," he stated. In his view, "an individual . . . without any sanction or support from any State law or regulation" could not violate the amendment or fall within the scope of its section 1 prohibitions (United States 1883, 23–24). Private persons had a right to discriminate as they pleased in regard to their property. According to Bradley, proprietors had the right to refuse to admit or service anyone in their businesses without federal interference. Thus the justice concluded that the 1875 federal act could not be constitutional if the Fourteenth Amendment was its basis.

Nor could the Thirteenth Amendment support the act's prohibition and reach, Bradley held. Rejecting any necessary connection between the amendment's subject matter and racial discrimination, Bradley declared that "an act of refusal has nothing to do with slavery or involuntary servitude." Such discrimination was not a federal matter, in any case; he insisted that "if it is violative of any right . . . redress is to be sought under the laws of the State." He persisted in distinguishing discrimination and slavery. "The Thirteenth Amendment has respect not to distinctions of race or class or color, but to slavery," he emphasized (United States 1883, 23–24).

Justice Bradley's constitutional analysis suggested no sympathy for ex-slaves. Slavery was over and done, in his view. The nation had solved that problem. He seemed to want to hear no more about it. "It would be running the slavery argument into the ground to make it apply to every act of discrimination which a person may see fit to make," he huffed. What were colored people complaining about, anyway? They were protesting treatment they earlier had accepted, Bradley claimed. "[B]efore the abolition of slavery . . . no one at that time thought that it was any invasion of his personal status as a freeman because he was not admitted to all the privileges enjoyed by white citizens, or because he was subjected to discriminations," Bradley asserted. "Mere discriminations on account of race or color were not regarded as badges of slavery," he said (United States 1883, 25).

Colored people had no grounds to complain about slavery any longer, at least not to the federal government, Bradley judged. Abolition obligated the nation to do nothing for ex-slaves. It created no special relation between them and the federal government. It freed slaves to become ordinary citizens. That made them in law like everyone else. They had the same legal protections as everyone else. They needed to acknowledge and accept that fact. They should not seek or get special attention or treatment in handling their problems. They should work out their problems in the same ways as anyone else, Bradley instructed.

"When a man has emerged from slavery, and, by the aid of beneficent legislation, has shaken off the inseparable concomitants of that state, there must be some stage in the progress of his elevation when he takes the rank of a mere citizen and ceases to be the special favorite of the laws, and when his rights as a citizen or a man are to be protected in the ordinary modes by which other men's rights are protected," Bradley lectured (United States 1883, 25). Colored people needed to face facts, Justice Bradley suggested. They were not whites, and they had no right to be treated as whites. No law was going to change that. The Thirteenth Amendment had not provided for that, and the Fourteenth Amendment was not designed to do that, Bradley insisted.

Among Bradley's colleagues on the Court, only Justice John Marshall Harlan disagreed. The Kentucky-born scion of a slaveholding family strongly dissented in the *Civil Rights Cases*, calling Bradley's opinion "too narrow and artificial." It misunderstood American Negro slavery and it misconstrued the U.S. Constitution. "I cannot resist the conclusion that the substance and spirit of the recent amendments of the Constitution have been sacrificed by a subtle and ingenious verbal criticism," Justice Harlan protested (United States 1883, 26).

The Court, not colored people, needed to face facts, Justice Harlan argued. Racial discrimination was a fact, and its essential connection with slavery was a fact. It was also a fact, Harlan emphasized, that it was "scarcely just to say that the colored race has been the special favorite of the laws." Federal civil rights protections existed "for the benefit of citizens of every race and color," Justice Harlan observed. The facts were that what he called "class tyranny" persisted in denying colored people equal rights the Constitution conferred. "The difficulty has been to compel a recognition of the legal right of the black race to take the rank of citizens, and to secure the enjoyment of privileges belonging, under the law, to them as a component part of the people for whose welfare and happiness government is ordained," Justice Harlan explained (United States 1883, 61).

In Justice Harlan's view, the Civil Rights Act of 1875 and Congress's other equal rights measures simply executed the Constitution's commands. The Thirteenth, Fourteenth, and Fifteenth Amendments had, in fact, changed federalism. They had changed the nation's fundamental law to make it so that "there cannot be, in this republic, any class of human beings in practical subjection to another class with power in the latter to dole out to the former just such privileges as they may choose to grant," Harlan explained. "The supreme law of the land has decreed that no authority shall be exercised in this country upon the basis of discrimination, in respect of civil rights, against freemen and citizens because of their race, color, or previous condition of servitude," he concluded (United States 1883, 62).

Justice Harlan dissented alone. "Congress has been invested with express power" to enforce the Constitution's decree of "equal protection of the laws," he insisted. The majority on the Court and in the country seemed uninterested in correct constitutional or legal theory; they appeared more interested in comfortable politics and practices for the white majority. The resolution of the disputed presidential election of 1876 had earlier reconfirmed that stubborn fact of American life.

The so-called compromise of 1877 that installed Republican Rutherford B. Hayes in the White House that March spelled the end of national interest in southern reconstruction. As his part in the bargain, Hayes promised to withdraw federal occupation troops from the South. They had been necessary in Louisiana to maintain even a modicum of momentum for equal rights. Their withdrawal stripped protection from colored people and civil rights in the Pelican State and elsewhere.

The end of federal Reconstruction left conservative whites to complete their Redemption. They controlled most places in the South. They had already thwarted many of the 1868 Louisiana constitution's bans on segregation. For instance, they reorganized the Orleans Parish schools in 1877 to segregate them. Creoles led loud protests that availed nothing from state or federal officials. "If you believe there has been a violation of the constitution, the courts are open and there lies your redress," Democrat Governor Francis T. Nicholls told a protest delegation, according to the June 27, 1877, New Orleans *Daily Picayune.*

Politics supplied little leverage for colored protest. Colored voters' registration margins had never materialized sufficiently to permit them to control Louisiana public policies. Creoles understood early their lack of direct political power; it persisted as a constant for them. Their hope lay in persuasion. That had been the point of *L'Union* and the *Tribune,* as it was later for the *Crusader,* published from 1889 to 1896. The newspapers promoted Creoles' ideas for public policy in the court of public opinion. Creoles banked also on the force of law. They used the courts with relative frequency before the Civil War to secure what they could. As Reconstruction ebbed, Creoles increasingly returned to the courts. They did so in 1877 when Orleans Parish moved to segregate its public schools.

Paul Trevigne sued in September 1877 to enjoin the school board's segregation plan. No stranger to controversy, he had endured death threats in the 1860s while chief editor of *L'Union.* He insisted that Article 135 of the state constitution indisputably prohibited "separate schools or institutions of learning established exclusively for any one race by the State of Louisiana." He pointed also to Article 136, which declared that "No municipal Corporation shall make any rules and regulations contrary to the spirit and intention of article one hundred and thirty-five."

The constitution's language appeared incontrovertible on prohibiting Orleans Parish or any other public entity in the Pelican State from racially segregating its schools. Perhaps for that reason Louisiana's Sixth District Court, where Trevigne sued, sidestepped the constitutional issue.

Judge N. H. Rightor dismissed Trevigne's petition on procedural grounds. He ruled that Trevigne had waited too late to sue. The school year had already begun when he filed for the injunction. School assignments could not be reversed in late September without indefensibly disrupting schools and disturbing students. Moreover, the judge ruled, Trevigne had no standing to sue the school board. He lacked a direct or sufficient personal interest in the school reorganization. He was not a student, teacher, or parent of a student. His son and namesake, born in 1862, was apparently not enrolled in any affected school. Thus Trevigne was liable to suffer no personal injury from the school reorganization, Judge Rightor ruled on October 23, 1877.

Trevigne appealed to the Louisiana Supreme Court. Writing seemed, however, to fail the former newspaper editor. His petition against the parish school board and public schools superintendent William O. Rogers appeared hastily done. At least, its arguments against "dividing said schools into schools for exclusively the white children and schools for exclusively the colored children" failed close legal scrutiny (Louisiana 1879b, 105). State Justice Alcibiade de Blanc found the petition rife with procedural errors in January 1879 when the court dismissed the matter.

Before the Trevigne matter met its end, another Creole leader was in court to stop New Orleans's public school segregation. Unlike Trevigne, Arnold Bertonneau had children in New Orleans public school. He sued the school board and principal George H. Gordon when the Fillmore School refused to admit his children. It was their nearest public school. The normal, pre-reorganization policy assigned them to Fillmore as their neighborhood school; the new segregation policy sent them elsewhere.

Bertonneau took a different tack than Trevigne by suing in federal court. He challenged the school board's reorganization and segregation policies for violating not only the state constitution's Article 135 but also the federal Fourteenth Amendment. He sued on behalf of his sons John Arnold and Francis, whose personal interest and injury in being wrongfully refused admission to the Fillmore School were manifest. Bertonneau sued also on the basis of his own personal injury as a parent of children wrongfully denied admission to the public school.

Ohio-born U.S. Fifth Circuit Court Judge William Burnham Woods heard the case of *Bertonneau v. Board of Directors of City Schools* during his November 1878 term in the District of Louisiana. The Yale-educated former U.S. Army Major-General had sat also on the *Cruikshank* case in the April 1874 term with Supreme Court Justice Bradley. He had heard the developing Fourteenth Amendment arguments. He contributed to them and would himself sit on the U.S. Supreme Court from December 1880 to May 1887, when he died. He voted with Justice Bradley in the *Civil Rights Cases* in 1883.

Judge Woods's opinion in the *Bertonneau* case foreshadowed the outcome of Homer Plessy's case in the nation's high court in 1896. The judge's legal reasoning focused on whether the Bertonneau children had, in fact, been refused admission to public school. Woods opened by noting that Bertonneau had not complained that his "children are excluded from the public schools." He emphasized the fact that public schools were open to them—that the matter was not exclusion, but assignment. Woods noted further that Bertonneau had not complained that the schools open to his children were "in any respect whatever inferior to the schools where the children of the white race are educated" (United States 1879, 295).

Woods distilled Bertonneau's complaint to a single point: his "children, being of African descent, are not allowed to attend the same public schools as those in which children of white parents are educated." That raised a crucial legal question in the judge's view: "Is this a deprivation of a right granted by the constitution of the United States?" To consider the question, Judge Woods reviewed what he saw as the asserted rights and the alleged facts in the case.

Bertonneau argued that the actions of the directors of the city schools and their subordinates had deprived him and his children of equal protection of the laws in violation of the Fourteenth Amendment. Woods countered with a question: "Is there any denial of equal rights...?" He answered *no*, and in doing so set out a theory later immortalized as the "separate but equal" doctrine. He emphasized the lack of exclusion and the lack of any claim that provisions were not substantially equal

The school board had injured no one in segregating white and colored students in public schools, Judge Woods ruled. "Both races are treated precisely alike," he reasoned. "White children and colored children are compelled to attend different schools. That is all," he emphasized. Further, he endorsed the state's right to adopt and implement whatever policy it considered best to promote and protect what it deemed to be the best interests of its people. The school segregation policy lay within that realm of state discretion, according to Woods. "The state, while conceding equal privileges and advantages to both races, had the right to manage its schools in the manner which, in its judgment, will best promote the interest of all," the judge decided.

Woods expounded on the state's right to provide separate facilities. For illustration, he likened separate schools for whites and nonwhites to separate schools for girls and boys. "The state may be of opinion that it is better to educate the sexes separately, and therefore establishes schools in which the children of different sexes are educated apart. By such a policy," Woods asked rhetorically, "can it be said that the equal rights of either sex are invaded?" He noted that the supreme court of his native Ohio in 1871 upheld racially segregated public schools. So had other states such as Nevada in 1871 and Michigan in 1869, reaching back to Massachusetts in the oft-cited 1849 case of *Roberts v. Boston*. Woods pointed also to state-enforced separation of the races in so-called anti-miscegenation statutes.

Woods concluded that segregation did not necessarily violate equal protection of the laws or equal rights provisions. Enforced separation did not destroy legal equality, in his view. That was certainly true in regard to schools, he insisted. "Equality of right does not involve the necessity of educating children of both sexes, or children without regard to their attainments or age in the same school," he said. Separate classifications were natural and proper; so students or people in general need not be treated in exactly the same place for them to have the same privileges or rights, he asserted. "Any classification which preserves substantially equal school advantages does not impair any right, and is not prohibited by the constitution of the United States," Woods concluded. "Equality of right does not necessarily imply identity of rights," the future U.S. Supreme Court justice emphasized (United States 1879, 296).

Judge Woods's February 19, 1879, decision dismissed Bertonneau's complaint. Moreover, his theory advanced the groundwork for state law to separate the races. His propositions removed the U.S. Constitution as a restraint on segregation. As for violations of the state constitution, Woods offered no opinion. "This court does not sit to supervise the conduct of state officers unless it impairs some right granted by the constitution of the United States, or unless the citizenship of the parties to the suit gives the court jurisdiction," he noted (United States 1879, 296). In this case, he found no federal right being impaired or any grounds for federal jurisdiction—so he dismissed the case.

Neither federal nor state courts, then, appeared likely to offer support against segregation in Louisiana. Indeed, the courts appeared to be against desegregation. The state court rulings against Trevigne in October 1877 and January 1878 showed their hardly surprising stance against any push for equal rights. The U.S. Supreme Court showed its inclination in its January 1879 ruling in the *DeCuir* case, which drained the force from Louisiana's equal accommodation laws. Judge Woods's February 1879 dismissal of the *Bertonneau* complaint showed local federal courts no more willing to stem the segregationist tide.

Conservative whites in Louisiana viewed Judge Woods's opinion in *Bertonneau* as vindicating their own views. They saw clear openings in his constitutional interpretation of the law for what they called their "Redemption." They aimed to retrench white supremacy in a fresh law of segregation. The *Bertonneau* ruling, and before it the *Cruikshank* decision, showed the way. The New Orleans *Daily Picayune* nearly chortled in hailing the *Bertonneau* ruling. "Judge Woods has swept away every obstacle to the successful workings of our school system that political and social theorizers have attempted to set up," the conservative voice exalted on February 21, 1879, two days after the ruling.

Federal law was the only real concern for Redeemers in Louisiana and elsewhere in the South as the 1870s closed. White conservatives had captured most of the state apparatus through terrorism and shrewd political maneuvering. Louisiana's 1877 elections put Democrat Governor Francis T. Nicholls in office along with a predominantly Democrat legislature, so conservatives could reshape state law as they pleased. They adopted a fresh state constitution in July 1879 to supplant the 1868 document they decried as radical and unreasonable.

Louisiana ratified white conservatives' wishes in December 1879 along with a new constitution that shift away from the equal rights push of Reconstruction. It sought to distance the state from its early postwar direction. The new constitution's Article 150 boldly removed the state capital from New Orleans to Baton Rouge. Conservatives wished to be away from the increasingly polyglot, raucous, and relatively liberal-leaning city then ranked as the tenth most populous in the nation. Many thought New Orleans, with its population of 216,000, had grown too big and exercised too much power. Almost one in four (23.0 percent) Louisiana residents lived in the city in 1879. Moreover, Orleans Parish then had by far the largest number of colored persons (57,617) in the state. The next largest parishes in colored population were west-central St. Landry (19,399) and extreme northwest Caddo (19,368) (University of Virginia, 2004, 1880).

Louisiana's new constitution (Louisiana 1879a) eliminated equal rights provisions such as the 1868 Article 13 on public access and accommodations. The 1879 Article 224 maintained a system of free public schools but eliminated bans on racially segregated schools. On the crucial subject of suffrage, the new constitution moved stealthily in light of the Fifteenth Amendment. Article 185 maintained adult male suffrage. Article 188 even provided that "No qualification of any kind for suffrage or office, nor any restraint upon the same, on account of race, color or previous condition shall be made by law." But the 1879 provisions added a series of qualifications to whittle down the electorate. Among the most ominous provisions was Article 208, levying an annual poll tax between $1.00 and $1.50. The issue of voter qualifications would loom large in coming years and perennially emerged in U.S. history. Should a person need to have or pay some amount of money to vote? All such questions returned to a simple concern over who should have the vote on what basis.

Creoles persisted in fighting Louisiana's segregationist tide. They fought not only because segregation denied them rights to which they thought themselves entitled, but also because segregation denied their identity as neither black nor white. That argument endeared them to neither blacks nor whites. It furthered factionalism among colored people. Yet Creoles clung to their self-selected image. Even amid the dismantling of their long past privileged position among nonwhites, they held fast to elements of their heritage as sacred articles of faith. The fresh Creole journal *Le Carillon* trumpeted such notes from postwar heydays. "French is the language of civilization," *Le Carillon* boomed in October 1869 in elitist tones. "We must love our nationality as our fathers loved it. We must prove by our acts that we are not hybrid creatures, that we are a united whole!" That cry sounded something of a Creole anthem.

Homer Plessy grew up amid those Creole strains. He heard them from family and friends. His stepfather, Victor Martial Dupart, especially impressed his heritage on the boy. The man became young Homer's guide. He did not displace Homer's natural father, Joseph Adolphe Plessy, who died in January 1869. Homer kept his early images of his father, but Dupart became the flesh-and-blood man at hand to whom Homer looked for guidance. His mother had in December 1871 married the recently widowed son of a shoemaker, left with six children ranging in age from 1 to 13 years of age. She had somehow to make a full home for herself, Homer, and his two sisters, Ida and Rosa.

Copying Dupart perhaps moved Homer to restyle himself as Homère Adolphe Plessy. Dupart carried his own father's middle name, Martial, as his middle name. Homer changed Patris, his middle name at birth, to his birth-father's middle name. The Anglicized version dropped the final *e* from both his first and middle names. Thus emerged Homer Adolph Plessy as he explored the character that distinguished his people in language, custom, and community.

Homer learned about political activism from Dupart, who worked in the post office and rallied for equal rights during Reconstruction. Dupart was a persistent voter and joined in Louisiana's short-lived Unification Movement of 1873. The interracial coalition pushed for guaranteed civil and political rights without regard to race or color. Creoles in New Orleans like Dupart promoted the movement as a means to save the state from frightful violence. Race war loomed as a threat in the countryside, presaging horrendous events such as would occur in the April 1874 Colfax Massacre. Such violence would also shake the city. The so-called Battle of Liberty Place on September 14, 1874, saw 3,500 armed White Leaguers take to New Orleans's streets to oust Republican Governor William Pitt Kellogg. They shouted for a "white man's government" and called for ousting "the insolent and barbarous African." During their rampage, the White Leaguers seized control of the statehouse, city hall, and arsenal. Only federal troops restored order. The toll was 38 killed and 79 wounded.

Unification proceeded as a reform party seeking to distance itself from the excesses of both conservative Democrats and radical Republicans. Improving race relations headed the movement's agenda. A letter to the editor in the April 22, 1873, New Orleans *Times* sounded a keynote. "Unless the two races adopt some platform on which they can stand on friendly terms," the writer predicted, "Louisiana has nothing to look forward to but debt, dissension, anarchy."

Creoles such as Dupart saw mostly deteriorating conditions amid fading federal Reconstruction for their hopes to recognize and bolster their unique community. Rather than being embraced, they found their community being besieged. Neither blacks nor whites whom they courted as allies defended what Creoles embraced as sacred and indispensable. For example, the much-heralded 1868 constitution had excluded French as a language of instruction in public schools. Also the constitution ended publication of the state's laws and official proceedings in both English and French. Thus died the official bilingualism that existed in Louisiana since the U.S. takeover in 1803. Losing official recognition of their native tongue signaled Creoles' decline, and more importantly, it signaled their being increasingly dismissed as a singularly identified people.

Entering the post-abolition era, Creoles had hoped to escape the black/white dichotomy of slavery. Instead, they found themselves plunged more deeply than ever into the division. They found themselves simply classified with blacks—a fact that grated on many of these mixed-race people. For most, if they had to choose a side in the racial divide, their choice was simple. *Le Carillon* pronounced that choice in its July 13, 1873, issue as it appeared to toll the knell of racial ambiguity among Creoles. "We must be either White or Black," it proclaimed to its fellow Creoles. Its choice in that world went almost without saying. "The *Carillon* flies the flag of the whites, with the profound conviction that only within its folds can Louisiana be saved." To be clear, it was not the state that *Le Carillon* was most interested in saving, but rather its own distinctive people.

Creoles found themselves being personally swamped and smothered as a community as the Civil War and Reconstruction faded to memories.

Approaching a new century and a so-called New South, Creole craftsmen such as shoemakers saw themselves slipping in status and scratching for their livelihoods. More and more, for example, such men found mechanization debasing their crafts. Skillful hand-sewing and stitching were becoming increasingly pointless or too expensive for many customers. Large-scale, machine-produced, low-cost boots and shoes slashed prices and sales of custom craftsmen. Increasingly, the craft seemed less shoemaking and more shoe-mending. Even so, Homer Plessy would later work to make a living at it.

Amid their sense of slipping status, Creoles found themselves publicly rended and ridiculed. Their shunning of others of mixed ancestry, to say nothing of blacks, appeared as contempt or narrow-minded snobbery. They kept distant even so prominent a person as the fair mulatto Pinckney Benton Stewart Pinchback. Creoles willingly allied with him as a champion against segregated schools, when Pinchback wrote and directed inclusion of Article 135 in the 1868 constitution. But he was what contemporaries called a "carpetbagger"; he was not a local or long-time Louisianan. Pinchback was not one of them, and Creoles did not embrace him socially.

Their seemingly closed community endeared Creoles to few. In fact and fiction, their image suffered. The New Orleans-born Confederate veteran George Washington Cable scathingly portrayed Creoles in his various writings. As a writer for the New Orleans *Daily Picayune* from 1865 to 1879, Cable went against the grain of his newspaper and former fellow rebels in supporting civil rights and opposing reactionary white supremacist retrenchment. In condemning racist practices, Cable held Creoles to the fire. His 1879 short story collection *Old Creole Days*, his 1880 novel *The Grandissimes*, and his 1884 *The Creoles of Louisiana* entombed the community in a moribund, prideful past.

Criticism of Creoles as arrogant, hypocritical, and prejudiced stung and further stigmatized the community. It sullied their identity. Many cringed at hearing the truth of their descent from "such wives as could be gathered haphazard from the ranks of Indian allies, African slave cargoes, and the inmates of French houses of correction," as Cable wrote in his 1884 *Encyclopaedia Britannica* essay on New Orleans. Creoles were clearly not being depicted as they wanted to be seen, as the distinguished people whom they held themselves to be.

Creoles' prewar days seemed to some old-timers preferable to their postwar realities. They partook with conservative whites at times in romanticizing the Old South. Heritage and history shaped so as to project a glorious past became a solace for dim prospects. Creoles maturing in the 1880s, like

Homer Plessy, stood burdened with heroic tales of their community's forebears and encouraged to claim their community's distinctive and rightful
rank. To carry them forward, some re-echoed *Le Carillon*'s 1873 call to
"the flag of the whites." The Creole Association of Louisiana (CAL) organized the like-minded in 1886 to promote what its 19-page charter described
as "knowledge concerning the true origin and real character . . . of the Creole race of Louisiana." Tellingly, the association limited its membership to
"white persons of age and good standing" (CAL 1886, 4, 14).

At the same time, Creoles continued to share common cause with colored people and other civil rights advocates. They persisted in fighting
against segregated schools. Young Homer Plessy exercised his activism
there. He joined the New Orleans Justice, Protective, Educational, and
Social Club (JPESC), which advanced an extensive program, but focused
primarily on public schools. "We will promote education by all the limited
means in our power," club members pledged. The group's 1887 pamphlet,
To All Who May Be Concerned, decried inequities in the city's segregated
public school system. "Our population of school children exceeds twenty
(20) thousand in the Districts. And of the eighteen (18) Public Schools we
cannot claim five (5) for one class, of which the accommodations are
good," the pamphlet complained. It called upon "all honest, intelligent and
just men" to join in "insuring good teachers, a full term and all the necessary articles for the maintenance of schools." The club dedicated itself to
"make lawful demand to the Government for our share of public education"
(JPESC 1887).

The club's public announcement of its principles joined a common genre
of its generation. On such issues reaching back to Reconstruction, various
self-styled groups had similarly made their views known to the public. The
People's Association to Resist Unconstitutional Taxation's similarly titled
1873 pamphlet, *To All Whom It May Concern*, illustrated this type of work.
Such publications served as multipurpose devices. To recruit members and
to solicit funding, they issued announcements and invitations. They drew
attention to their cause, and they confirmed their members' commitments.
Publicly subscribing their names constituted a pledge to the group for
members such as Plessy.

Homer was no silent member of club. He served as vice president in
1887, and his fellow members saw him as committed and reliable. He was
no hothead or rabble-rouser. A relative later described Plessy simply as a
"relatively quiet, ordinary citizen who got involved" (Medley 2003, 16). He
saw the urgent need to correct an ongoing injustice, a community problem
that needed fixing. New Orleans's conservative white regime was denying

colored children an education. Old-line Louisiana whites basically rejected the concept of public education. They resisted being taxed to pay for schools for everyone's children. They loathed paying to school colored children. They were willing enough, however, to pay to school their own. Orleans Parish in 1883 had 205 private schools, yet lack of funding that year pushed the parish school superintendent to close all public schools for almost a semester. That put most colored children on the streets, and it promised to consign them there beyond their school years. That gloomy prospect drew Plessy to action.

In attacking the festering school issue, Plessy and his fellows focused more on immediate consequences than on causes. They did not attack the principle of segregated schools, but rather focused on the resulting lack of schooling. The situation they opposed resembled exclusion. They fought against essentially having no public schooling. They saw their community being left out and responded by demanding "our share." They refused to be excluded from public services. They perhaps acquiesced to separate schools as too settled a practice and policy to budge, yet they insisted on quality public education. They saw themselves not so much prodding to change the system but rather pushing to make the system work for them, which from their perspective would be to work for all. They sought an urgent remedy. They showed no patience for eventual change. Without change now, "our young men and women will grow up in ignorance and immorality, thereby crumbling our societies," Plessy protested with his club (JPESC 1887).

Plessy and his fellows could feel and see the rising tide of segregation surrounding them. Working in the Justice, Protective, Educational, and Social Club, Plessy showed himself willing to do his part to improve what he could publicly. He had private work also to do as a maturing man. He left his stepfather to make a living on his own. Had his birth father lived, Homer probably would have followed him as a carpenter, just as his father had followed his own father. Family and lineage controlled many life-choices from generation to generation in New Orleans's tight-knit Creole community. Joseph Adolph Plessy had not lived to teach his son carpentry, however; Homer learned shoemaking instead. In 1888, he earned wages with French Quarter shoemaker Patricio Brito on Dumaine Street. And he took another major step in maturity—he married.

Plessy wed Louise Bordenave in July 1888. He had turned 25 in March of that year; Louise was nineteen. It was a Creole marriage—the bride was the daughter of Oscar Bordenave and Madonna neé Labranche. The new couple shared an old-line heritage and married in St. Augustine Catholic

Church. Founded in 1842 a block from what developed as the intersection of Esplanade Avenue and North Rampart Street, the church stood from antebellum times as a sacred institution for New Orleans's free people of color. The French-born parish pastor, Père Joseph Subileau—noted for his majestic white beard and his love of cigars—officiated at the ceremony. The newlyweds set up home a few blocks to the northeast at 1108 N. Claiborne Avenue in Faubourg Tremé.

Homer Plessy looked forward to making a life for himself and his family. He and his wife Louise faced the decisions and hopes of any young couple. They had commitments, and among those they assumed together was a commitment to their people. They were born-and-bred Creoles. They felt for and with their community—a community that felt itself being increasingly crushed as 1890 approached. That became a signal year in the chronology that fixed Homer Plessy's name in U.S. history. It carried the siren call that drew him to act on his commitment to his Creole contemporaries and forbears and end up in the U.S. Supreme Court.

References

Creole Association of Louisiana (CAL). 1886. *Charter, By-Laws & Rules of the Creole Association of Louisiana.* New Orleans: Crescent Steam Print.

Justice, Protective, Educational, and Social Club (JPESC). 1887. "To All Who May Be Concerned." In *Crescent City Schools: Public Education in New Orleans, 1841-1991,* ed. Donald E. DeVore and Joseph Logsdon, 115. Lafayette: Center for Louisiana Studies, University of Southwestern Louisiana, 1891.

Louisiana. 1879a. *Constitution of the State of Louisiana, Adopted in Convention at the City of New Orleans, the Twenty-Third Day of July, a.d. 1879.* New Orleans: Printed by J. H. Cosgrove.

Louisiana. 1879b. *Trevigne v. School Board,* 31 La. Ann. 105 (1879).

Medley, Keith Weldon. 2003. *We as Freemen*: Plessy v. Ferguson. Gretna, LA: Pelican.

United States. 1879. *Bertonneau v. Board of Directors of City Schools,* 3 F. Cas. 294 (CC D. La. 1879) (No. 1,361).

United States. 1883. *Civil Rights Cases,* 109 U.S. 3 (1883).

United States. 1896. *Plessy v. Ferguson,* 163 U.S. 537 (1896).

University of Virginia. 2004. *Geospatial and Statistical Data Center, Historical Census Browser.* Charlottesville: University of Virginia.

NINE

The Beginning of the End:
Surging Segregation

HOMER PLESSY landed in court in the continuing struggle over segregated public transit. He enlisted in the fight when the recurring battle over public policy on common carriers returned to Louisiana in 1890. The state's opening postwar salvo had sounded in 1867 with the defeat of the black star car system in New Orleans. The state's 1868 constitution confirmed the victory in its Article 13 provision that "all persons shall enjoy equal rights and privileges upon any conveyance of a public character" in Louisiana. The state's 1869 Common Carrier Act put the principle into effect. That early outcome marked Louisiana as different from its neighbors. It early embraced the principle of desegregated public transit, but by 1890 it had backtracked. Plessy stepped forward to hold the line for his people against the fresh rush to fix segregated transit in law.

Mississippi acted first among the ex-Confederate states to mandate segregated rail transit. It made the provision part of its immediate postwar Black Code. The Mississippi law pronounced it "unlawful for any officer, station agent, conductor, or employee on any railroad in this State, to allow any freedman, negro, or mulatto, to ride in any first-class passenger cars, set apart, or used by, and for white persons." The November 1865 provision exempted colored nurses "traveling with their mistresses." Violators were liable for fines ranging from $50 to $500 (Mississippi 1865, 231).

Florida in January 1866 directly targeted "any negro, mulatto, or other person of color [who] shall intrude himself into . . . any railroad car or other public vehicle set apart for the exclusive accommodation of white people." It made such a violation a misdemeanor. The punishment was "to stand in pillory for one hour, or be whipped, not exceeding thirty-nine stripes, or both." In a nod to evenhandedness, the statute applied the same penalties "for any white person to intrude himself into any railroad car or other public vehicle set apart for the exclusive accommodation of persons of color"

(Florida 1866, 25). The statute implied the running of separate cars, but it did not mandate separate cars. That left the possibility of no cars for people of color; thus they could be wholly excluded from rail travel.

Texas joined in with legislation in November 1866. It mandated separate cars, requiring railway companies "to attach to each passenger train . . . one part for the special accommodation of Freedmen" (Texas 1866, 97). The Lone Star State repealed this provision in 1871 in accord with a new constitution that incorporated congressional Reconstruction civil rights mandates. Texas then prohibited common carriers "from making any distinctions in the carrying of passengers" on account of race, color, or previous condition. Violations carried a fine of $100 to $500 or imprisonment for 30 to 90 days, or both (Texas 1871, 16).

While Reconstruction pushed its neighbors away from mandating segregation on common carriers, Louisiana shifted away from desegregated public transit. The U.S. Supreme Court's 1878 decision in *Hall v. DeCuir* declared Louisiana's 1869 Common Carrier Act unenforceable against interstate carriers. The 1879 state constitution removed the 1868 constitution's mandate that "all persons shall enjoy equal rights and privileges upon any conveyance of a public character." Louisiana then returned to letting practice prevail— and in practice, whites characteristically refused to ride in cars with colored passengers, often forcibly ejecting them from cars deemed de facto whites-only carriages. That practice prevailed beyond Louisiana.

Neither the practice nor the problem of segregated public transit were peculiar to the South. States such as Massachusetts, Pennsylvania, California, Illinois, Iowa, and Michigan had their postwar street car and railway incidents over whites' refusal to ride with colored people in the same undivided carriage. Massachusetts and Pennsylvania illustrated developments outside the South.

The Old Bay State had railroad cars set apart for colored people as early as 1841. It was there, in fact, that the term *Jim Crow* first designated such segregated cars. The state shifted its public position in 1866, when the legislature pronounced it unlawful "to exclude persons from or restrict them in . . . any public conveyance . . . except for good cause" (Massachusetts 1866, 242). That law tacitly made good behavior the standard for riding any public conveyance in the state.

Pennsylvania in March 1867 prohibited railroads from excluding passengers or segregating them in public railcars on account of color or race. The need for state action became clear in light of state law and common practice. Pennsylvanians had voted in 1838, after all, to expressly designate colored people as inhabitants but not citizens of the state. Common carriers in

Pennsylvania such as the West Chester & Philadelphia Railway Company made segregation the policy on their vehicles even after the Civil War, as the 1867 case of Mary E. Miles exposed.

The colored woman, then in her 30s, refused segregated seating on a West Chester & Philadelphia Railway coach on its 50-mile run west to Oxford, Pennsylvania, from Philadelphia, where she lived. In line with company policy, a conductor ejected Miles. She sued in the Philadelphia Court of Common Pleas, and a jury found in her favor with a verdict awarding her $5 in damages. Defending its policy, the railway appealed.

Public outrage over the case moved the Pennsylvania legislature to enact an antidiscrimination measure in March 1867. It made railways liable for $500 in damages for any violation. It made railway employees also liable individually for taking part in any violation: They faced fines of $100 to $500 and sentences from 30 days to 3 months in prison for any transgression (Pennsylvania 1867a, 38). But that got Ms. Miles nothing.

The Supreme Court of Pennsylvania heard the railway's appeal in April 1867. The facts of the case occurred before the March statute, so it had no affect on the outcome. The state's attorney general put the case simply in stating that "a regulation which prohibits a well-behaved colored person from taking a vacant seat in a car simply because she is colored, is not a regulation which the law allows" (Pennsylvania 1867b, 209).

The railway defended its right of private property to separate passengers in the public interest. The carrier imposed segregated seating, its attorneys argued, "so as to preserve order and decorum and prevent contacts and collisions arising from natural and well-known repugnancies, which are liable to breed disturbances by promiscuous sitting." Further, the company insisted that "the seat which the plaintiff was directed to take, was in all respects a comfortable, safe and convenient seat, not inferior in any respect to the one she was directed to leave" (Pennsylvania 1867b, 209).

The court accepted the company's argument. Its members voted 5–1 to reverse the lower court verdict for Miles. Pennsylvania Justice Daniel Agnew's opinion for the court explained that the rule of decision in the case turned on whether the rail company separated passengers on the basis of "clear and reasonable difference." The separation, he noted, "cannot be justified by mere prejudice." He left murky, however, the standard for determining what was "mere prejudice" and what was "clear and reasonable difference." Also, he left as a question of fact for a jury to decide in a new case whether the seat to which the railroad directed Ms. Miles was "in all respects a comfortable, safe and convenient seat, not inferior in any respect" (Pennsylvania 1867b, 209).

"It is not an unreasonable regulation to seat passengers so as to preserve order and decorum, and to prevent contacts and collisions arising from natural or well-known customary repugnancies, which are likely to breed disturbances by a promiscuous sitting," Justice Agnew stated. Making such a regulation was, he explained, "a proper use of the right of private property, because it tends to protect the interests of the carrier as well as the interests of those he carries" (Pennsylvania 1867b, 212).

As for Ms. Miles, as a passenger she had only the right "of being carried safely, and with a due regard to [her] personal comfort and convenience, which are promoted by a sound and well-regulated separation of passengers," Justice Agnew stated. He concluded for the court that "at the time of the alleged injury, there was that natural, legal and customary difference between the white and black races in this state which made their separation as passengers in a public conveyance the subject of a sound regulation to secure order, promote comfort, preserve the peace and maintain the rights both of carriers and passengers" (Pennsylvania 1867b, 215).

The Pennsylvania high court's 1867 reasoning and wording would echo in Plessy's case. Its emphasis resounded in 1879 in federal Circuit Court Judge William Burnham Woods's decision in *Bertonneau v. Board of Directors*. The school segregation case in New Orleans repeated exclusion as the law's keynote. That line of thought let courts accept racial discrimination as natural or reasonable, and typically left such discrimination beyond the scope of legal remedy. The thinking targeted exclusion, however, as something law could and would remedy—at least within the realm of public law.

Tennessee showed how exclusion fit with segregation in the law of common carriers. The state in April 1881 passed legislation titled "An act to prevent discriminations by railroad companies among passengers who are charged and paying first-class passage." The law exhibited the miserable response offered colored protests against segregation. The statute's preamble noted "the practice of railroad companies located and operated in the State of Tennessee to charge and collect from colored passengers traveling over their roads first-class passage fare, and compel said passengers to occupy second-class cars where smoking is allowed, and no restrictions enforced to prevent vulgar or obscene language" (Tennessee 1881, 211).

The Tennessee law hardly remedied discrimination. Instead, it accepted discrimination in fact and moved only to prevent exclusion. It simply segregated colored passengers. It directed that "all railroad companies located and operated in this State shall furnish separate cars, or portions of cars cut off by partition walls, in which all colored passengers who pay first-class passenger rates of fare, may have the privilege to enter and occupy." The statute provided further that "such apartments shall be kept in good repair, and with the same conveniences, and subject to the same rules governing other first-class cars, preventing smoking and obscene language" (Tennessee 1881, 211).

Tennessee's legislation demonstrated the direction of white conservative racial policy for public spaces. It skirted federal restrictions on exclusion by admitting nonwhites to public services but relegating them to the margins. It made a place for colored people and directed them to stay in that separate space. It maintained the racial divide, subordinating nonwhites and privileging whites. The law left whites to do as they pleased in their private relations and transactions. That typically made racial mingling verboten—at least in regard to colored persons' entering white facilities or functions. Taboos made it so without the force of law. Popular practice made it so that colored persons could go only where whites let them, while whites could go wherever they chose, unless the law intruded, as it did with anti-miscegenation statutes, for example. The 1881 act put the principle into practice on public transit.

The Tennessee statute illustrated how the South's post-Reconstruction law of segregation developed, like prewar practices in the North, to replace the law of slavery in ordering race relations. Before abolition, few southern places required public accommodations to meet free colored people's demands. Restraints on slaves had sufficed to maintain the racial order. Only New Orleans and a few other southern places had sufficiently large antebellum free colored populations to require separate accommodations. Elsewhere, slavery had sufficed to maintain the white/nonwhite divide from birth to death. The South's newly fashioned law of segregation sought to publicly re-enforce traditional racial separation.

The immediate postwar battles in New Orleans over segregation on common carriers revealed the intensity of the contending postwar forces on the issue. Increasing demand for public transportation challenged conservative whites' sense of social order. Sharing public space created new experiences in an expanding realm of personal contacts. Also it created more anonymous encounters. Who knew who was who any longer? Deference from immediately recognized personal identity faded. Surrounded by strangers on common carriers, what immediately stood out for many people was the colorline. If passengers knew nothing else about those riding with them, they knew—or at least thought they knew—who was who based on race which constituted a primal identity for many. White conservatives pushed to entrench the colorline in extending their old white/nonwhite divide.

Tennessee showed the way on railroads. Its 1881 law purported to "prevent discriminations," though it did no such thing. Instead, it initiated a fresh round of discrimination that legally entrenched behavior already practiced in fact. Yet the law introduced an important difference: It prohibited exclusion of colored passengers. Other Southern states followed the example, beginning in 1887 with Florida. Mississippi followed suit in 1888, then Texas in 1889. Louisiana stepped in line in 1890, and that was where Homer Plessy also stepped in.

Ascension Parish Representative Joseph Saint Amant introduced the future Separate Car Act in the Louisiana legislature on May 14, 1890, as House Bill No. 42, setting in motion the immediate controversy that led to Plessy's arrest in June 1892. Civil rights proponents vigorously protested the measure. Prominent Creoles led the opposition. They joined with others in the American Citizens' Equal Rights Association (ACERA) to petition the Louisiana General Assembly to dismiss the bill and all other "class legislation." Their printed protest dated May 24, 1890, invoked constitutional, legal, moral, policy, and religious arguments against legally mandated segregation. "Citizenship is national and has no color," they insisted (ACERA 1890, 128).

White conservatives countered protests with appeals of their own when the Louisiana General Assembly finally took the bill under serious consideration in July. The New Orleans *Times-Democrat* strongly endorsed the measure. In an editorial on July 9, 1890, it urged passage as a measure "against that commingling of the races inevitable in a 'mixed car'." The weekly partisan voice of the state Democratic Party insisted that on railroads and elsewhere, "the white race should be kept pure from African taint."

The bill became law on July 10, 1890. It required that "all railway companies carrying passengers in their coaches in this State, shall provide equal but separate accommodations for the white, and colored races, by providing two or more passenger coaches for each passenger train, or by dividing the passenger coaches by a partition so as to secure separate accommodations." The statute required railroad officials "to assign each passenger to the coach or compartment used for the race to which such passenger belongs." It imposed a $25 fine or not more than 20 days in the parish prison on "any passenger insisting on going into a coach or compartment to which by race he does not belong" (Louisiana 1890a, 152).

Interestingly, and inconsistently in many eyes, the act exempted street railroads. The framers perhaps wanted no reprise of the 1867 black star car uprising in New Orleans streets. The more than 64,000 colored people in New Orleans posed a potentially formidable and physical opposition to such a measure. Few on either side of the question wanted to see a round of massive confrontations in the streets like those that occurred in 1867. No other place in the state had a city rail system or population that posed anything near the potential for trouble as that in the Crescent City. Thus the 1890 street railroad exception stood essentially as an exemption for New Orleans local traffic. The act fully covered passengers traveling beyond the city's confines and so beyond the limited reach of its street railways.

Another exemption also rankled some, as the act included a provision like that for common carriers in the old Mississippi Black Code of November 1865 allowing colored nurses or attendants to ride in otherwise whites-only cars. St. Martin Parish Representative Victor Rochon raised the point during debate on the measure in the Louisiana House of Representatives. In rhetorical style, he challenged white representatives on "the idea that you and family would not be offended in traveling hundreds of miles with a dozen or perhaps more negro servants. But would be insulted to travel any distance with me and my family on account of our color" (Louisiana 1890b, 203).

Having lost in the legislature, opponents of the Separate Car Act turned their eyes to the courts. The 18 colored members in Louisiana's lower house in 1890 were too few to change the legislative outcome. Hope existed, however, that the act would fall under constitutional challenge. The Louisiana statute had modeled itself, after all, on the 1888 Mississippi statute. The U.S. Supreme Court, in its March 1890 ruling in *Louisville, N. O. & T. Ry. Co. v. Mississippi*, upheld the act but only in part. Opponents in Louisiana figured they could also get their state's statute struck down at least in part, if not in whole.

Thinking the courts would save them appeared odd. Reaching back to the 1870s, federal courts frequently had proved to be no friend of colored people or federal protection of civil rights. Transportation cases provided no exception. Colored people in Louisiana had direct evidence of that fact. The key court decision allowing racial segregation on common carriers had arisen from Louisiana. The U.S. Supreme Court in *Hall v. DeCuir* struck down Louisiana's Reconstruction attempt to outlaw racial discrimination on common carriers, at least in regard to those in interstate commerce. Fully revealing its pro-segregationist leaning, the Court in 1890 brushed aside the substance of its 1878 restrictions on state power to further allow segregated transit.

In *Hall v. DeCuir*, the Court concluded that the U.S. Constitution's Commerce Clause barred states from prohibiting segregation on common carriers. In *Louisville, N. O. & T. Ry. Co. v. Mississippi*, the Court decided that the Commerce Clause did not bar states from requiring segregation on common carriers. Each ruling noted state authority to regulate intrastate commerce. Indeed, a crucial point in the 1890 decision turned on the fact that the Supreme Court of Mississippi in 1889 found the statute to have "no application save to those traveling wholly within the state" (Mississippi 1889, 675).

The distinction between interstate and intrastate transportation buoyed opponents' hopes of having Louisiana's Separate Car Act limited at least to intrastate application. The two dissents on the nation's high court in *Louisville, N. O. & T. Ry. Co. v. Mississippi* also buoyed hopes. Civil rights nemesis Justice Joseph P. Bradley announced his view that the Mississippi statute was "void as a regulation of interstate commerce" (United States 1890, 595). Civil rights champion Justice John Marshall Harlan went further in finding the statute void.

In Justice Harlan's view, the rule established in *Hall v. DeCuir*, limiting the 1869 Louisiana statute, directed the same result for the 1888 Mississippi statute. "It is difficult to understand how a state enactment, requiring the separation of the white and black races on interstate carriers of passengers, is not a regulation of commerce among the States, while a similar enactment forbidding such separation is not a regulation of that character," Harlan complained (United States 1890, 594). That Bradley and Harlan agreed on the constitutional infirmity of the Mississippi Separate Car Act could do no less than encourage opponents of Louisiana's Separate Car Act.

Factionalism that persistently flared in Louisiana among colored people and civil rights proponents since the Civil War slowed court challenges to the 1890 act. Many who agreed the legislation was bad law sometimes disagreed on exactly on why. They agreed on the constitutional principle of equal protection of the laws. They shared discomfort over the act's interference with the right to travel. They understood the growing invasion of segregationist law. To some, however, the Separate Car Act loomed more as a symbol than as substance. To others, it was a more dire sign; they viewed the act as the beginning of the end.

The New Orleans *Crusader* arrayed the arguments against laws based on race and decreeing that people be separated by race on railcars or anywhere else. Creole attorney Louis A. Martinet founded the newspaper in 1889 at 411 Exchange Alley in French Quarter to carry on the attack against segregation's spread. The weekly, published on Saturday, devoted itself to "justice and equal rights." It promoted the idea of taking the Separate Car

Act to court. It pushed ACERA to raise funds for a test case. Talk proved cheaper than action, however, as money dribbled in to fund the litigation. More than a year passed before serious action occurred. By then, Martinet and many of his Creole frères had decided on their own separate action. They organized the *Comité de Citoyens* to press their case. To reach the broader public, the group translated it full name into English as "the Committee to Test the Constitutionality of the Separate Car Law."

Two cases developed against the 1890 act. Creoles such as Martinet and Rodolphe L. Desdunes supported both, but the second case was their own. Both cases revealed interesting allies in the protest. More than colored folk and civil rights advocates resisted the Separate Car Act. Railroad officials also opposed the Louisiana statute, as they worried about their liability under its provisions. Two sets of penalties faced railroads and their workers under the act. Train officials, such as conductors, who failed to comply with the act faced fines of $25 to $50. The railroads themselves, along with their corporate officers and directors, faced fines from $100 to $500 for any failure to comply with the law.

Railroad officials balked at the cost of complying with the act more than at the penalties for not complying. Compliance demanded both capital and operating outlays. Louisiana State Senator Joseph Henry noted the costs during debate. "This bill would compel the alteration of about 250 coaches, at an average expense of $75 per coach," Henry stated. But that $18,750 marked merely the start of the railroads' expenditures. Apparently privy to the railroads' own estimates, the senator noted further that "if two extra coaches are put on each passenger train it would entail an additional expense of fifteen cents per miles for hauling the same, or in the aggregate for all roads of $1450 per day" (Louisiana 1890c, 437–438). Such an ongoing outlay would cost the railroads about $500,000 per year.

With profits at stake and legal talent at hand, the railroads moved first against Louisiana's Separate Car Act. Their case to protect their interests mirrored the Mississippi suit the U.S. Supreme Court had decided in March 1890. In that case, the Louisville, New Orleans & Texas Railway Company had sued the state. The case in Louisiana, which proceeded under the title *Abbott v. Hicks*, was much the same. The effective forces in bringing the case were the Pullman Palace Car Company and the Texas & Pacific Railway. They set up to defend W. C. Abbott, a Pullman car conductor on the Texas & Pacific line arrested for failing to separate a colored passenger as Louisiana's Separate Car Act directed.

The company-provided attorneys for Abbott argued that the selected colored man the conductor admitted to a rail car was an interstate passenger and, therefore, beyond the reach of the state statute. Judge A. W. O. Hicks heard the case in Louisiana's First Judicial Court of Caddo Parish on the state's northwest border with Texas. What happened then mapped the procedural path Homer Plessy would later follow: The constitutional challenge to the statute went to the Louisiana Supreme Court for decision.

While *Abbott v. Hicks* worked its way to resolution, Creoles in New Orleans arranged their own test case. Their pockets were not so deep as the railroads' and their action was not as quick. Martinet spearheaded the action from the start of the Comité in September 1891. He and his fellows planned to create a case that could carry their cause to the U.S. Supreme Court. They wanted more than a Commerce Clause ruling. Legal distinctions between interstate and intrastate traffic might serve their tactics, but their strategy focused on legal distinctions between people based on race.

Martinet and other prominent Creoles such as Aristide May and Rodolphe Desdunes focused on identity as the core issue at stake. Segregation ignored who they were—that was their essential complaint. Segregation dismissed and distorted their ancestry and heritage. It plunged Creoles into the black/white abyss from which they had struggled to scramble since the 1700s. It cast them back beyond slavery. It retrenched the infernal dichotomy essential to white supremacy. It dictated that Creoles in no way differed from blacks, an ignominy leading Creoles refused to abide.

Segregation took no account of personal achievements, earnings, education, occupation, or refinements. It collapsed personal status into the singular notion of race. And what was race, after all? Creoles such as Martinet and Desdunes, like many of their people before them, hammered such questions. Was race a hypothetical? Was it merely an assumption, a presumption, a theory, an image someone had conjured? Or was race real, existing independently as an actual, unalterable, physical fact? And if it existed in fact, was it not complex—so much so as to be veritably indefinable or at least indeterminate among some people, such as Creoles?

Martinet and his frères wanted what many of their ancestors had long craved—a public pronouncement that they were, in fact and in law, who they wanted to be. They desired official recognition of their distinction as neither black nor white. They wished their self-identity confirmed. They wanted the law to verify their capacity to declare who they were. They wanted to do away with any claim of state government or anyone else to determine their identity. They claimed the power to identify oneself inhered in the person himself or herself. How to get the nation's high court to rule on their claim became their present problem.

The Comité needed one or more capable and receptive attorneys to raise their questions and make their argument. The members wished also to retain the foremost legal counsel. Money was a problem there. No small gap yawned between what they wanted and what they could afford. Martinet made the rounds. He found the best-known, most likely attorneys in New Orleans beyond the Comité's price range. He did not consider himself a candidate, nor did he consider other local colored attorneys. Most of them worked routine cases in the police courts. The Comité needed more than that. It needed a lawyer who could shepherd the case not only through the local criminal process but also through the constitutional and jurisprudential issues the Comité hoped to raise ultimately in the U.S. Supreme Court.

Martinet settled on local lawyer James Campbell Walker to handle issues in the Louisiana courts. Martinet spoke well of the fiftyish, Louisiana-born son of Scottish immigrants, describing him as "a conscientious & painstaking lawyer" and as one who "will give us solid work" (Lofgren 1987, 30). But Walker was not the lawyer to make the ultimate arguments. The Comité required a more experienced and renowned attorney to ready and argue the case in the nation's highest tribunal. That attorney, too, would be white. The U.S. Supreme Court in 1865 had admitted its first colored lawyer to practice—John Swett Rock, a Massachusetts resident born in 1825 in New Jersey. But no colored lawyer had yet argued a case before the Court. The first would come only in 1910, when University of Michigan Law School graduate James Alexander Chiles argued his own railroad segregation case before the Court in *Chiles v. Chesapeake & Ohio Railway Co.*

Martinet secured the Comité's lead lawyer and legal strategist, when Albion Winegar Tourgée signed on to the cause in January 1892. The Ohio-born Civil War veteran stood as one of the nation's most noted legal minds. An outspoken critic of white supremacist segregation and racial caste, he served during Reconstruction as a state judge in North Carolina. He later moved to New York and developed a national reputation as a commentator and lecturer on the nation's straying from the equal rights principles established by the Civil War.

With the legal team settled, the case preparation began in earnest. The strategy called for arranging the arrest of a racially ambiguous Creole man for violating the Separate Car Act. Rodolphe Desdunes volunteered his eldest son, 22-year-old Daniel F. Desdunes to become the defendant in the case. Young Desdunes dutifully acted his part. On February 24, 1892, he purchased a first-class ticket on a Louisville & Nashville (L & N) Railroad train from New Orleans to Mobile, Alabama. He was not going to make 150-mile trip. As carefully scripted, Desdunes entered a whites-only car, and by prior arrangement, the conductor challenged him and called for his arrest for not being in the proper place according to Louisiana's Separate Car Act.

The action went as planned. It called for collaboration. The L & N and other lines opposing the Separate Car Act cooperated. The conductor challenging Desdunes had his orders, as did the arresting officers, selected for being favorably disposed. (A small financial incentive no doubt helped their disposition.) After the arrest, the plan relied on anticipating legal procedure. But what the prosecutors decided to do and what the judges in the case decided to do lay beyond the plan's control.

The Orleans Parish District Attorney's Office proceeded as Walker advised the Comité to expect. Prosecutors filed an information on March 14, laying out the accusation against Desdunes and forwarding it to the Orleans Parish Criminal District Court, Section A. It set Desdunes's arraignment for March 21. Walker planned then to challenge the legitimacy of the Separate Car Act. Legal form directed him to file a plea to jurisdiction. It requested the court examine and judge the legal basis to hear the case being presented to it. And, in fact, the plan required that the court deny the plea and accept the case so as to allow an appeal that could work its way to the U.S. Supreme Court.

The plan went awry on May 25, 1892, when the Louisiana Supreme Court handed down its ruling in *Abbott v. Hicks*. The court there took notice of the 1890 U.S. Supreme Court ruling in *Louisville, New Orleans & Texas Railway v. Mississippi*. The Louisiana court especially noted how its Mississippi counterpart had saved that state's 1888 separate car act by limiting its application to intrastate passengers. It adopted the same reasoning, as the rail lines behind the *Abbott* case expected. But the Louisiana high court's ruling derailed the line Walker, Tourgée, and Martinet had laid out for Desdunes's case. It could no longer get them where they wanted to go: At best it would stop in the Louisiana Supreme Court, not the U.S. Supreme Court.

Desdunes's February 24 L & N ticket designated him as an interstate passenger. The result in the *Abbott* case meant Louisiana's Separate Car Act had no legal force against Desdunes. It would be only a matter of time before newly seated Section A Judge John H. Ferguson accepted Walker's jurisdictional plea and dismissed the case—an outcome recorded on July 9.

As soon as Martinet and Walker read the *Abbott* decision that last week in May, they knew they needed a new case, and they scrambled to set up one. They needed another racially ambiguous Creole man to stand as a defendant under Louisiana's Separate Car Act. Desdunes would not do, as his case remained pending. Homer Plessy answered the call for the role, and on Tuesday, June 7, 1892, he took his fateful ride.

References

American Citizens' Equal Rights Association (ACERA). 1890. "Memorial . . . Protest of the American Citizens' Equal Rights Association of Louisiana against Class Legislation." In *Official Journal of the House of Representatives of the State of Louisiana*. Baton Rouge: *The Advocate*.

Florida. 1866. "An Act Prescribing Additional Penalties for the Commission of Offenses against the State." 1866 Fla. Laws 25 (January 15, 1866).

Lofgren, Charles A. 1987. *The Plessy Case: A Legal Historical Interpretation*. New York: Oxford University Press.

Louisiana. 1890a. "An Act to Promote the Comfort of Passengers on Railway Trains." 1890 La. Acts 152 (July 10, 1890).

Louisiana. 1890b. *Official Journal of the Proceedings of the House of Representatives of the State of Louisiana*. Baton Rouge: The State Printer.

Louisiana. 1890c. *Official Journal of the Proceedings of the Senate of the State of Louisiana*. Baton Rouge: The State Printer.

Massachusetts. 1866. "An Act in Relation to Public Places of Amusement." 1866 Mass. Acts 242 (May 23, 1866).

Mississippi. 1865. "An Act in Relation to Railroads, and for Other Purposes." 1865 Miss. Laws 229 (November 21, 1865).

Mississippi. 1888. "An Act to Promote the Comfort of Passengers on Railroad Trains." 1888 Miss. Laws 48 (March 2, 1888).

Mississippi. 1889. *Louisville, N. O. & T. Ry. Co. v. State*, 66 Miss. 662 (1889).

Pennsylvania. 1867a. "An Act Making It an Offence for Railroad Corporations, Within This Commonwealth, to Make Any Distinction with Their Passengers, on Account of Race or Color, and Punishing Said Corporations, and Their Agents and Employees, for the Commission of Such Offence." 1867 Pa. Laws 38 (March 23, 1867).

Pennsylvania. 1867b. *West Chester and Philadelphia Railroad Company v. Miles*, 55 Pa. 209 (1867).

Tennessee. 1881. "An Act to Prevent Discriminations by Railroad Companies among Passengers Who Are Charged and Paying First-Class Passage, and Fixing Penalty for the Violation of Same." 1881 Tenn. Pub. Acts 211 (April 7, 1881).

Texas. 1866. "An Act Requiring Railroads Companies to Provide Convenient Accommodations for Freedmen." 1866 Tex. Gen. Laws 97 (November 6, 1866).

Texas. 1871. "An Act to Enforce Section XXI, Article I., of the Constitution." 1871 Tex. Gen. Laws 16 (October 28, 1871).

United States. 1890. *Louisville, N. O. & T. Ry. Co. v. Mississippi*, 133 U.S. 587 (1890).

TEN

The Case: From Start to Finish

Homer Plessy followed his script, eager enough to play his part for his people. Like Daniel Desdunes, Plessy was not a principal member of the Comité de Citoyens who were mostly graybeards. At age 30 in 1892, Plessy stood between the younger Desdunes at age 22 and the older Rodolphe Desdunes and Louis Martinet, both age 43. Plessy had made his reputation for the Creole cause with his work in the Justice, Protective, Educational, and Social Club. He stood as a man on whom the Comité could count.

Plessy had little to do, actually. The script called for him to appear only briefly. He had few lines; his was almost a walk-on part. He was directed to buy a ticket to ride an intrastate rail carrier. He did just that and boarded an East Louisiana Railroad (ELR) train scheduled to run from New Orleans around Lake Pontchartrain to Covington, Louisiana. The Comité carefully arranged the collaboration that played out. It wanted no surprises. It enlisted ELR conductor John J. Dowling to identify and confront Plessy and Detective Chris C. Cain to arrest Plessy and take him to New Orleans's Fifth Precinct station on charges of violating the Separate Car Act.

The performance went smoothly. The New Orleans *Daily Picayune* on June 9, 1892, noted the opening acts. "On Tuesday evening, a negro named Plessy was arrested by Private Detective Cain on the East Louisiana train and locked up for violating section 2 of act 111 of 1890, relative to separate coaches," the newspaper reported. It noted further that Plessy waived examination before Judge A. R. Moulin in recorder's court on June 8 and was released on $500 bond for trial in criminal court. When New Orleans Assistant District Attorney Lionel Adams filed a formal information against Plessy on July 20, the Comité again had its test case on track.

The action unfolded bit by bit. The Comité hurried no part. The case appeared a final recourse. It loomed as the ultimate battle of the Creole cohorts that had matured since the 1870s. Their forebears and parents had fought other fights; this battle was theirs. They had glimpsed but lost the prizes of congressional Reconstruction. Resurgent white supremacy dominated their growing reality. They built Plessy's case with the care of a people who saw it as all that might stand between them and the utter destruction of their community.

Fifteen weeks passed before the Plessy case's first arguments in court. Plessy appeared with his local attorney James C. Walker on October 28 before Criminal Court Judge John H. Ferguson. Plessy hardly spoke; he simply pleaded "not guilty." Walker's oral argument offered a plea to jurisdiction and attacked the Separate Car Act for violating equal protection of the laws and due process, in depriving Plessy of rights and remedies the state or federal constitution guaranteed him. District Attorney Adams argued simply that the statute was a reasonable regulation in line with federal and state court precedents and in light of well-known interracial discomfort. Three more weeks elapsed before Judge Ferguson on November 18 overruled Plessy's plea to jurisdiction, and the case went forward.

Following the model of *Abbott v. Hicks*, Walker moved to stay the criminal court proceedings. He filed petitions for writs of certiorari and prohibition to move Plessy's case to the Louisiana Supreme Court. The goal, after all, was not to get a mere trial court verdict but to get the case to the U.S. Supreme Court. Francis T. Nicholls granted provisional writs on November 22. Nicholls acted then as Louisiana chief justice; he had been the governor who in 1890 signed Louisiana's Separate Car Act into law.

The Louisiana Supreme Court in December 1892 acted quickly on the case it titled *Ex parte Plessy*. Justice Charles Erastus Fenner reduced Walker and Tourgée's arguments for Plessy to 83 words he quoted from their brief. He noted that the argument alleged that "the statute in question establishes an insidious distinction and discrimination between citizens of the United States based on race." The argument for Plessy objected to such discrimination as "obnoxious to the fundamental principles of national citizenship." Also it contended that the act "perpetuates involuntary servitude as regards citizens of the colored race." The act had no legitimate purpose and operated "under the merest pretense of promoting the comforts of passengers on railway trains." In sum, Walker and Tourgée argued that the separate car act "abridges the privileges and immunities of citizens of the United States and the rights secured by the thirteenth and fourteenth amendments of the federal constitution," Fenner recapped (Louisiana 1893, 83).

The Louisiana justice made short work of Walker and Tourgée's arguments. His own sympathies were perhaps clear from the fact that ex-Confederate president Jefferson Davis died in Fenner's New Orleans home in December 1889. Writing for a unanimous court, Fenner denied that the Separate Car Act itself or segregation in general had anything to do with slavery; thus, he ruled, the Thirteenth Amendment had no role in the case. The U.S. Supreme Court's 1883 decision in the *Civil Rights Cases* had held as much, he noticed.

As for the Fourteenth Amendment, Fenner repeated the equal application doctrine developed in state and federal courts since the 1870s. Railroad segregation, like segregation in general, "impairs no right of passengers of either race, who are secured that equality of accommodation which satisfies every reasonable claim," Fenner stated. He capped his opinion with what was becoming an oft-repeated refrain. "To hold that the requirement of separate, though equal, accommodations in public conveyances, violates the Fourteenth Amendment, would, on the same principles, necessarily entail the nullity of statutes establishing separate schools, and of others, existing in many states, prohibiting intermarriage between the races" (Louisiana 1893, 87). Segregation was all of a piece in Justice Fenner's view, and Creoles and other colored persons agreed. That was why they were fighting its pieces.

Justice Fenner gave even shorter shrift to identity issues. He claimed it did not matter whether Plessy was white or not. He noted that "the record brought up for our inspection does not disclose whether the person prosecuted is a white or a colored man." He listed that as evidence that the "statute applies to the two races with such perfect fairness and equality" (Louisiana 1893, 87).

Fenner similarly shrugged off arguments that "the statute vests the officers of the [railroad] company with a judicial power to determine the race to which the passenger belongs." The statute vested "only that necessary discretion attending every imposition of a duty, to determine whether the occasion exists which calls for its exercise," he said. The law required an exercise of judgment, as any law did when requiring a person to act. And as with other such laws, the separate car statute left railroad officials liable for their errors in judgment, Fenner explained. If Plessy proved he had not "insist[ed] on going into a coach to which he did not belong," then he would not be guilty of the charged violation, and he could sue the conductor and the railway in an action for damages, Fenner indicated (Louisiana 1893, 87–88).

Fenner ignored the substance of the arguments Walker and Tourgée presented. He hardly nodded at the fact that while the arrest affidavit asserted Plessy was "a passenger of the colored race," Plessy had refused to announce any racial identity. Fenner pretended no interest in who Plessy was. He persisted with the presumption that identity was not an issue. But for Plessy's people identity was exactly the issue. To emphasize that point, on January 2, 1893, Plessy's attorneys asked for a rehearing on the issue, but the court denied their request. Yet they got from Justice Fenner the decision they expected.

The Comité had in hand what it had planned for and requested. The highest state court in Louisiana had delivered a decision appealable to the U.S. Supreme Court.

Without delay, Walker applied for and received permission to send Plessy's case to the nation's high court. He and Tourgée finished the necessary filings with the Supreme Court in Washington, D.C., in February 1893. Tourgée enlisted his friend Samuel F. Phillips to join the Plessy legal team. The former U.S. solicitor general had argued the losing side in the 1883 *Civil Rights Cases*. A longtime Washington insider, Phillips stood among the preeminent experts on the nation's Supreme Court. His inclusion lifted the team's stature, but the question was whether he could help win where he had lost in 1883. The Court then sat no more favorably disposed toward civil rights than it had earlier. Even so, the Comité had gotten its case where it wanted the case to go. The question was whether the case would get them what they wanted.

The high court's scheduling calendared Plessy's case for the October 1895 term. The Court heard oral arguments in the case on Monday, April 13, 1896. The title of the case identified Plessy as the plaintiff in error. The defendant in error was Criminal Court Judge John H. Ferguson, who sat over Plessy's trial and awaited a decision on the legitimacy of the Separate Car Act to conclude the case. Washington attorney Alexander Porter Morse, a native Louisianan, appeared for Ferguson. Actually, he appeared on behalf of the state to defend the statute. Louisiana Attorney General Milton J. Cunningham considered the case not worth his appearance. His name appeared on the state's brief with New Orleans Assistant District Attorney Lionel Adams, who did much of the basic work. Tourgée and Phillips argued Plessy's case to the Court. They had filed two briefs with the Court. Walker was on one with Tourgée; Phillips was on the other with his law partner F. D. McKenney from their Washington, D.C., firm of Phillips, Zachry, & McKenney.

The argument for Judge Ferguson to uphold the Louisiana Separate Car Act was uncomplicated. Justice Fenner put the legal point succinctly in his decision in *Ex parte Plessy*: "The statute here in question is an exercise of the police power and expresses the conviction of the legislative department of the State that the separation of the races in public conveyances, with proper sanctions enforcing the substantial equality of the accommodations supplied to each, is in the interest of public order, peace and comfort" (Louisiana 1893, 87). In simple language, the Louisiana law rested on its being a reasonable way to relieve popular discomforts, on its excluding no one, and on its providing all with "substantial equality."

Tourgée and Phillips attacked the Separate Car Act for violating the U.S. Constitution's Thirteenth and Fourteenth Amendments. Their points sounded old, standard, and stale. They repeated much of what Phillips had argued in 1883. The Court's personnel had changed since then. Only Justices Stephen J. Field, Horace Gray, and John M. Harlan sat on the Court when it heard both the *Civil Rights Cases* in 1883 and *Plessy v. Ferguson* in 1896. But the newcomers—Chief Justice Melville Fuller and Associate Justices David J. Brewer, Henry B. Brown, George Shiras Jr., Edward D. White, and Rufus W. Peckham—had repeatedly heard and seen Tourgée and Phillips's well-worn constitutional arguments and their repeated rejection. Justice Harlan alone had shown himself sympathetic. Justice Brewer took no part in the case.

The fresh points for Plessy came in Tourgée's arguments on race and identity. The Comité's hopes for its distinctive community rested there. The issue of racial identity encompassed both the long history of their people and the prospects of their future. It invited no easy argument; it never had. Challenging prevailing ideas of race ran headlong into entrenched beliefs and privileged self-images among ruling whites. Moreover, Creoles' prolonged attack on the black/white divide had repeatedly yielded to self-aggrandizing temptations that weakened it. Leading Creoles persistently claimed to be neither black nor white. Yet with equal persistence they claimed to be entitled to white privilege. They resisted arguing to tear down privilege. Despite Civil War and early Reconstruction rhetoric, many Creoles never fully embraced equal rights arguments that called for all people to have equal privileges; they persisted in demanding distance from blacks. That position proved more than a rhetorical problem; it exposed a profound liability. It weakened the Creoles' political alliance with the bulk of colored people.

At the U.S. Supreme Court in 1896, Creoles' stance on who they were— or at least on who they saw themselves as being—butted up against long, legally entrenched perspectives on race. Their age-old problem remained getting others to see them as they saw themselves. Such a shift required that others also see themselves differently. To recognize Creoles as distinct, as neither black nor white, required many blacks and whites to recognize themselves as something other than who they saw themselves as being. Insisting on standing outside the black/white paradigm, Creoles challenged elements of basic identity in U.S. history and law. Their challenge reached back to the historical development of the Atlantic world. They were battling centuries of cultural biases, beliefs, inferences, and self-justifications.

Tourgée shouldered a heavy load as he stood before the Court to argue the fallacies of race. His point was simple: Race offered no valid basis for law "to make a distinction . . . in the enjoyment of chartered privileges within the state" (Tourgée & Walker 1896, 3–80). Tourgée had to mount a steep peak to get where he wanted to reach. As a base marker, he noted that Louisiana had no statute defining race. The state had no set standards to identify "the white, and colored races," which its 1890 Car Act required to be identified and separated (Louisiana 1890). Tourgée hardly wanted to make too much of that point, as it could undercut his argument that no law could, in fact, adequately define race. He wanted to issue no invitation for Louisiana to pass a statute defining race, as its neighbor Mississippi and other states did long before.

Tourgée might have rested there. He might have argued that due to its lack of any statutory standard, the Separate Car Act was void for vagueness, as the legal argument came to be known. If Louisiana law never said who was *white* or who was *colored*, it fixed no clear and precise direction to give people adequate notice of what they could or should do to avoid criminal penalty for behaving as white or colored. Prosecuting a person in the face of a lack of such direction violated one of the U.S. Constitution's most fundamental principles—due process.

A long history of Anglo-American jurisprudence led to a guarantee that no person should face prosecution without having notice of his or her crime. The Fifth and Fourteenth Amendments enshrined the rule in U.S. law. Had his argument aimed simply to keep Plessy from criminal punishment, Tourgée might indeed have stopped there. But the case was not about Plessy's escaping a penalty; it was about Plessy's people securing their long elusive legal right to be legally recognized as themselves, as they saw it.

Tourgée moved on to the issue of race itself. Before attacking the summit, he paused to note how prominent race stood in American life and society. Racial identity had become a form of property, Tourgée noted. "[T]he reputation of belonging to the dominant race, in this instance the white race, is *property*," he emphasized. "How much would it be *worth* to a young man entering upon the practice of law, to be regarded as a *white* man rather than a colored one?" Tourgée asked rhetorically. "Probably most white persons, if given a choice, would prefer death to life in the United States *as colored persons*," he continued. "Under these conditions, is it possible to conclude that the *reputation of being white* is not property? Indeed," he insisted, "is it not the most valuable sort of property, being the master-key that unlocks the golden door of opportunity?"

Tourgée edged along a precipice in recognizing the power of race. His basic argument denied race any power in law. He argued in part that race was not real. But arguing race was imaginary on the one hand, while holding up its power on the other hand, appeared at least contradictory. Dangerous inconsistencies lurked in his strategy. Getting people to deny what they saw, or at least thought they saw, required overcoming the confidence of personal experience. Race was something Americans lived. It wrapped the nation at birth. Even whites in America who lived in homogenous, insular communities lived with an idea of race. They may never have seen any American Indian or anyone of African or Asian ancestry, yet they carried concepts of such persons. Images of various nonwhites as *Others* formed the substance and suspicions that structured the supremacy whites popularly accepted as their privilege.

Having race *be* and *not be* at the same time complicated Tourgée's argument. It made his point easy to mistake. As he spoke indirectly about Creoles' origins, for example, Tourgée spoke of race as a physical fact. He spoke of "race-intermixture." He called attention to a blending of race— the creation of "a great number of citizens in whom the preponderance of the blood of one race or another, is impossible of ascertainment, except by careful scrutiny of the pedigree."

Such an argument explained something of Creoles' appearance and lineage, yet it hardly advanced the argument that race was not real. His line of reasoning reduced Tourgée to arguing about where persons should be placed within racial categories. If anything, such a line called simply for expanding the categories beyond the commonly accepted dichotomy, because black and white failed to cover the spectrum of possibilities. Tourgée summarized the point rhetorically in asking, "[E]ven if it were possible to determine predominance of blood and so determine racial character in certain cases, what should be said of those cases in which the race admixture is equal. Are they white or colored?"

Tourgée attacked notions of racial purity. He especially targeted the ideology of pure whiteness. What supported conceptions of unmixed ancestry? He asked how anyone could see ancestry with certainty in everyday interactions. Was appearance an appropriate marker? If looks could tell, Tourgée suggested, then persons such as Plessy who looked white were white. And if blood were the measure, he asked, "why not count every one as white in whom is visible any trace of white blood?" Popular American custom and practice used hypodescent, instead, to mark as non-white anyone with any trace of nonwhite blood. Why was that?

Tourgée's answer reached back to Thirteenth and Fourteenth Amendment arguments against segregation as an extension of slavery. He probed two rhetorical questions to summarize his point. "Is not a statutory assortment of the people of a state on the line of race, such a perpetuation of the essential features of slavery as to come within the inhibition of the XIIIth Amendment?" Tourgée stressed the colorline as an undeniable feature of slavery. And that being so, he asked, "Is it not the establishment of a statutory difference between the white and colored races in the enjoyment of chartered privileges, a badge of servitude which is prohibited by that amendment?"

The racial discrimination of segregation and slavery were parts of the same whole cloth of American racial dominance and subordination, Tourgée argued. "Slavery not only introduced the role of caste but prescribed its conditions," he explained. "The trace of color raised the presumption of bondage and was a bar to citizenship," he noted. Louisiana's Separate Car Act extended that colorline. "The law in question is an attempt to apply this rule to the establishment of legalized caste-distinction *among citizens*," Tourgée emphasized. It violated due process. It violated the equal protection of the laws, he insisted. It violated personal liberty.

"A law assorting the citizens of a State in the enjoyment of a public franchise on the basis of race is obnoxious to the spirit of republican institutions because it is a legalization of caste," Tourgée continued. Turning back to his argument on identity, he further probed the basis of America's color castes. He addressed those who refused to accept race as an illusion. Accepting for argument's sake that race was something that now you could see and then you could not see, he posed a query to the Court: "Is not the question of race, scientifically considered, very often impossible of determination?"

If appearances could be deceptive and science itself struggled to determine who was who in regard to race, how could law depend on race? Tourgée questioned both the essential substance of race and its use in Louisiana's Separate Car Act. He ridiculed the statute's inconsistency. How could the law reasonably declare separating white people and colored people so necessary as to invoke criminal penalty and at the same time permit colored persons acting as nurses not to be separated from whites? More outrageous, he declared, was the statute's directing railroad officers, such as conductors, to decide passengers' identity by assigning them a race, which they did in assigning them to one of the separate cars designated by race. How could it be reasonable for a law to require a conductor to do such a job? And to do such a job in the absence of any statutory definition of race went beyond being unreasonable, Tourgée insisted. Such a policy was arbitrary and, therefore, violated due process.

Tourgée made his argument clearly about more than flawed phrasing or logical inconsistencies in the 1890 Separate Car Act. He laid siege to the very foundations of race in American law and life. The Louisiana statute failed because it rested on an unsupportable basis—the fiction of race. It violated the promise of America expressed in the resounding phrases of the nation's founding document, the 1776 Declaration of Independence. "All men are created equal and endowed with certain inalienable rights, among which are life, liberty and the pursuit of happiness," Tourgée quoted. In moving to make segregation the law, he said, "the statute is a violation of the fundamental principles of all free government and the Fourteenth Amendment."

Beyond all else, government segregation such as that inherent in Louisiana's Separate Car Act usurped the most basic of liberties in imposing identities on persons. That was the bottom line in the arguments for Plessy. His case was not about where he could ride, or about the quality of accommodations. Whether one coach was better than another coach was certainly not Plessy's point. Louisiana's illegitimate exercise of power to classify and divide people on the basis of images it imposed was the point. "The gist of our case is the unconstitutionality of the assortment; *not* the question of equal accommodation," Tourgée explained. "The question is not as to the *equality* of the privileges enjoyed, but *the right of the State to label one citizen as white and another as colored*," he emphasized.

The case for Plessy rested on who he was. It invoked his ancestors to identify their Creole son. It invited them to testify to their intermixture in him. They stood to prove he was neither black nor white. He looked white. The Comité had picked him for that reason. The ELR conductor who confronted him had to have Plessy pointed out to identify him as not white. The record showed that "the mixture of colored blood was not discernible in him." Yet Plessy never said he was white, nor had he said he was colored. He stood mute on that point in Judge Ferguson's criminal court. Plessy admitted to the U.S. Supreme Court that he was "seven eighths Caucasian and one eighth African" (United States 1896, 541). What did that make him? Could any law say?

Tourgée hammered home the point that Louisiana had no right to designate who Plessy was by race. Plessy's attorneys persistently denied "the right of the State to label one citizen as white and another as colored." Tourgée and Walker steadfastly advanced the Comité's challenge of the state's authority to dismiss or disregard Plessy's ancestors—and by extension those of Creoles at large. Their argument denied the state's authority to count some ancestors and discount others. It rejected the idea that the state could legitimately recognize only part of Plessy's identity and prohibit him from fully determining and expressing his own identity.

The case for Plessy charged Louisiana with acting to usurp his identity. The Separate Car Act disregarded Plessy's Creole heritage, his attorneys insisted. It dismissed his ancestry and, in doing so, disrespected Creoles at large. It ignored what distinguished them as a community and as individuals. It simply entrenched the historical black/white divide Creoles had fought since the 1700s.

Plessy's case had brought Creoles' fight to the Supreme Court of the United States. It laid out Louisiana's (mis)construction of racial identity, particularly as it related to issues of citizenship. It assailed the culture and politics of white supremacy that marginalized Creoles and others deemed "colored." It denounced the state for its restricted recognition of its people's multicultural, multiethnic, and multiracial heritages.

The argument for Plessy emphasized what the law should be, rather than what the law was. It invited the Court to change positions taken since the 1870s. Indeed, the briefs for Plessy reviewed several lines of cases. They particularly revisited *Cruikshank* and the 1883 *Civil Rights Cases*. Their rehearsal raised arguments lost in the past. To reach the present and change the future, they needed something to change minds on the Court. They aimed for the identity issues developed in Plessy's case to make a difference.

Justice Henry Billings Brown suggested at the outset of his opinion that the Court saw little different or special about Plessy's case. The justices viewed the case as a simple challenge to the constitutionality of a state statute. Writing for the Court majority, Justice Brown opened his opinion by summarizing the charges against Plessy and quoting Louisiana's Separate Car Act. "The constitutionality of this act is attacked upon the ground that it conflicts with the Thirteenth Amendment of the Constitution, abolishing slavery, and the Fourteenth Amendment, which prohibits certain restrictive legislation on the part of the States," he explained (United States 1896, 543). As the Court had done in prior civil rights cases, Justice Brown dismissed out of hand the Thirteenth Amendment claims. The Louisiana statute involved nothing related to slavery or involuntary servitude, he asserted. He refused to link slavery and segregation and repeated Justice Joseph Bradley's comment from the *Civil Rights Cases* that "It would be running the slavery argument into the ground to make it apply to every act of discrimination" (United States 1896, 543).

Writing for a seven-member majority, Justice Brown declared that "A statute which implies merely a legal distinction between the white and colored races—a distinction which is founded in the color of the two races, and which must always exist so long as white men are distinguished from the other race by color—has no tendency to destroy the legal equality of the two races, or reestablish a state of involuntary servitude" (United States 1896, 543).

Plessy's case presented a single issue in Justice Brown's view. "[T]he case reduces itself to the question whether the statute of Louisiana is a reasonable regulation," he explained. Such a standard accorded large discretion to the legislature. The Court would not second-guess legislators. It would accept at face value whatever the lawmakers claimed as advancing the state's legitimate interest in its people's health and safety. The official title of the 1890 act reflected Louisiana lawmakers' understanding of the doctrine, as they had titled the measure "An act to promote the comfort of passengers on railway trains."

The unstated part of the reasonable basis test Justice Brown announced put the burden of proof on whoever challenged the statute. The state needed to prove nothing; Plessy had to prove the Louisiana act lacked any rational basis—a burden Tourgée tried to carry by attacking the rationality of race.

Justice Brown turned aside the attack on state authority to segregate. Nothing in U.S. law abolished "distinctions based upon color," he asserted (United States 1896, 544). Pointing to commonly accepted separate schools and to bans on intermarriage, Brown listed examples of states validly exercising their legislative power to segregate people on the basis of race or color. He identified the high court in his own native Massachusetts as among the earliest to sanction public school segregation. Courts in California, Indiana, Kentucky, Louisiana, Ohio, Missouri, and New York had followed Massachusetts's lead. He observed that Congress, too, had provided racially separate schools in the District of Columbia. Thus nothing in principle or practice invalidated segregation statutes, Brown reasoned. "Laws permitting, and even requiring . . . separation [of the two races] in places where they are liable to be brought into contact do not necessarily imply the inferiority of either race to the other, and have been generally, if not universally, recognized as within the competency of the state legislatures in the exercise of their police power," he stated (United States 1896, 544).

The Court in 1890 had recognized that "the State has the power to require that railroad trains within her limits shall have separate accommodations for the two races," Justice Brown noted. That decision in *Louisville, New Orleans & Texas Railway v. Mississippi* matched Plessy's case, Brown explained. In *Abbott v. Hicks*, the Louisiana Supreme Court in May 1892 had followed the Court's 1890 ruling and the April 1889 Mississippi Supreme Court in also confining its state separate car act to apply only to passengers traveling exclusively within the state. Plessy was such a passenger. The East Louisiana Railway ran, Justice Brown noticed, as "purely a local line, with both its termini within the State of Louisiana." So no interstate commerce strictures applied to it, as they had in the 1878 case of *Hall v. DeCuir*. That made the case easy for the Court to decide (United States 1896, 548).

Justice Brown delivered the core of the Court's decision in a 252-word paragraph. He flicked away the carefully crafted arguments for Plessy, starting with segregation. For himself and others in the majority, he wrote that "we think the enforced separation of the races, as applied to the internal commerce of the State, neither abridges the privileges or immunities of the colored man, deprives him of his property without due process of law, nor denies him the equal protection of the laws, within the meaning of the Fourteenth Amendment" (United States 1896, 548). The rule Brown announced would haunt America for generations: It withdrew the Constitution as a protection against segregation.

Justice Brown's opinion barely touched identity issues. Creoles had pushed such issues as fundamental. The leading members of the Comité viewed identity as the crucial point in case, but no one on the Court shared their view. Justice Brown indicated that the Plessy case brought only one issue to the Court—that of the constitutionality of the Separate Car Act. The role and liability of railway conductors and the railways themselves were not issues properly before the Court, Brown stated. If the question were whether Plessy was white or colored, the justice suggested Plessy go to court to settle the issue. That was not a matter for the U.S. Supreme Court, he said. State courts handled such matters.

True enough, Justice Brown noted, no single standard in America determined who was who in regard to race. "[T]he question of the proportion of colored blood necessary to constitute a colored person, as distinguished from a white person, is one upon which there is a difference of opinion in the different States," he admitted. "But these are questions to be determined under the laws of each State and are not properly put in issue in this case," he insisted (United States 1896, 552). If he and his brethren heard Creoles' *cri de coeur* to be saved from the black/white abyss, they offered no solace. They left Creoles' cry for recognition to become a whimper.

Brown's majority opinion closed with a quick lecture on race relations, attitudes, and the law. "We consider the underlying fallacy of the plaintiff's argument to consist in the assumption that the enforced separation of the two races stamps the colored race with a badge of inferiority," Brown wrote with evident exasperation. Nothing in law marked either side of the black/white divide as superior or inferior, he insisted. Such thinking merely reflected mistaken attitudes. Moreover, such thinking reflected misunderstanding of the power and purpose of law, he asserted. "The argument also assumes that social prejudices may be overcome by legislation, and that equal rights cannot be secured to the negro except by an enforced commingling of the two races," Brown stated. "We cannot accept this proposition," he wrote. "Legislation is powerless to eradicate racial instincts or to abolish distinctions based upon physical differences, and the attempt to do so can only result in accentuating the difficulties of the present situation," he declared. "If one race be inferior to the other socially, the Constitution of the United States cannot put them upon the same plane," Justice Brown concluded (United States 1896, 551–552).

The decision was not what Creoles hoped to hear. Even Justice John Marshall Harlan's magnificent dissent could lift their spirits little. Harlan regretted and rejected the Court's "conclusion that it is competent for a State to regulate the enjoyment by citizens of their civil rights solely upon the basis of race" (United States 1896, 559). Yet he was unable to see or understand the arguments for Plessy against the black/white racial dichotomy. He accepted Tourgée's argument that the law should be color-blind. He could not, however, accept arguments that race was indeterminate. Harlan believed race was a physical, differentiating reality. Indeed, he harbored his own strong biases. His own ugly racism spilled over against the Chinese, whom he described as "a race so different from our own that we do not permit those belonging to it to become citizens of the United States" (United States 1896, 561).

Neither Justice Harlan nor the Court majority grappled with the racial identity questions raised in the arguments for Plessy. The members of the Court accepted the state's authority not only to identify persons by race but also to impose racial identity on persons by whatever standards the state chose. The justices focused their attention only on what, under the U.S. Constitution, the state could and could not do in regard to personal rights on the basis of race. Like most Americans at the time, the members of the Court accepted what they thought of as the science of race and the popular stereotypes it projected. They sat unable or unwilling to treat identities that crossed traditional boundaries. The black/white dichotomy worked for them, just as it worked for the majority of Americans. Accepting race as an artificial construct lay far in the future, as did the idea that individuals, like Creoles, interwove in their persons multiple cultures, ethnicities, and heritages.

The identity battle at the center of Plessy's case was immediately lost in popular views. Newspapers praised or pilloried the Supreme Court decision solely in terms of black/white segregation. None discussed identity. The Creoles' underlying arguments went begging. In the press, Plessy simply became "colored" or "negro." Generations much later would mark him simply as "black" or "African American."

Plessy's case took on a life of its own—but it never really was *his* case. He was a stand-in, a proxy for his Creole people. Their complex history charted a path along America's perilous colorline. They had struggled to balance themselves between black and white. They feared falling, and they resisted being pushed, from the line they toed, for only one fate awaited them—landing among blacks. Such a vision long filled many Creoles with horror. It carried them back to their ancestors' slavery. It marked them as African in an America that disdained Africans and made black nothing to embrace and everything to avoid.

In his dissent, Justice Harlan predicted that "the judgment this day rendered will, in time, prove to be quite as pernicious as the decision made by this tribunal in the Dred Scott case." U.S. Chief Justice Roger B. Taney declared in the 1857 case that descendents of Africa never were and never could be U.S. citizens or "claim any of the rights and privileges . . . secured to citizens of the United States," Harlan fumed. "We boast of the freedom enjoyed by our people above all other peoples. But it is difficult to reconcile that boast with a state of the law which, practically, puts the brand of servitude and degradation upon a large class of our fellow-citizens, our equals before the law," he railed. "The thin disguise of 'equal' accommodations for passengers in railroad coaches will not mislead any one, nor atone for the wrong this day done," he declared (United States 1896, 559, 562).

Justice Harlan was right about the *Plessy* decision. It became a catchphrase to legitimate inequities in public access and accountability. *Plessy's* "separate but equal" doctrine became the sanction for de jure segregation.

It sealed in law what was in fact a long-standing American principle of separating people by race. Its strictures for equal accommodations went begging. The overwhelming differences in public education funding and facilities in the South became the prime example of separate meaning unequal.

Segregationists seized the ruling as a banner in their march to subjugate nonwhites. In short order, Louisiana launched its official campaign to isolate colored people. It drafted a new constitution in 1898 and with its provisions struck more than 120,000 mostly colored voters from the rolls. Governor Murphy Foster could boast to the Louisiana General Assembly in 1898 that "the White supremacy for which we have so long struggled . . . is now crystallized into the constitution" (Medley 2003, 209). And so it was. The legislature in 1902 ordered New Orleans to re-segregate streetcars, reversing the result of the 1867 black star car protests. Further extending the colorline, the legislature in 1908 mandated separate water fountains for white and colored people in public spaces. Nothing seemed too small for the segregationists' minds to reach.

Louisiana was hardly alone. Segregation surged far beyond the state. It covered the nation. Indeed, it reached throughout the world. Europe's fresh end-of-the-century colonial push to take up "the White Man's burden," as the English writer Rudyard Kipling put it in 1899, created separate racial compounds in Africa and Asia and doled out rights and privileges on the basis of race. Racial separation expanded as part of the world order and became part of a global culture. National identities embraced it. Modernizing America grasped whiteness as essential to U.S. culture. White supremacy was the rule of the day at home and abroad.

The decision in *Plessy v. Ferguson* helped to entrench segregation as an essential part of U.S. law and order. It replaced slavery there. It put the force of law alongside terrorist lynchers and other vigilantes who insisted on separating and subordinating nonwhites. The decision came as no surprise. It extended a line of judicial decisions reaching back to the 1870s that repudiated the civil rights promises of Reconstruction. It initiated its own line of cases, however. It became often cited in arguments treating transportation law, state's rights and the police power doctrine, race and equal protection, and the scope of federal constitutional protections of civil rights.

The "separate but equal" doctrine became segregation's bedrock. In that sense, the decision in *Plessy v. Ferguson* represented a low point in the long struggle for equal rights in America as it contributed a sanction from the nation's highest court. Vigilante and mob violence added a popular sanction. Both carried the same message of keeping nonwhites in their place. Both also generated staunch opposition. Fresh organizers and organizations came together to defend and advance the principle of equal protection of the law. Voices such as that of the eminent intellectual and civil rights advocate William Edward Burghardt Du Bois rose in groups such as the Niagara Movement in 1905 and the National Association for the Advancement of Colored People (NAACP), organized in 1909–1910.

In New Orleans, another generation of Creoles arose to fight the good fight. The lawyer Alexander Pierre Tureaud, Sr., stood as a prime example. He battled segregation across the board. He fought for voting rights. He fought to equalize educational opportunity, as illustrated in his 1941 victory in *McKelpin v. Orleans Parish School Board* and his launching of *Bush v. Orleans Parish School Board* in 1949. Tureaud marched in the long line of Creoles who did battle for civil rights, yet he stepped away from old Creole narrow-mindedness on the black/white divide. He embraced his black ancestry, standing tall as an Afro-Creole.

In solidifying the black/white divide, the *Plessy* decision set the stage for A. P. Tureaud and his generation. Born in New Orleans in 1899, Tureaud fought segregation all his adult life. Joining NAACP lawyers such as Thurgood Marshall, Tureaud worked to chip away at the *Plessy* doctrine. He pushed first for the "equal" side of the "separate but equal" formula, then he attacked the "separate" side. The grudging results of decades-long campaigns trickled slowly from the arena where Plessy's Comité had thought best to do battle but lost.

The U.S. Supreme Court slowly shifted its position on the *Plessy* doctrine. It started by holding states to account on the "separate but equal" formula. If states provided separate accommodations, then they had to provide equal accommodations. And in the absence of equal accommodations, they had to admit colored persons to the existing accommodations, for not to do so would amount to unconstitutional exclusion. A series of colored plaintiffs hammered that proposition.

Missouri ex rel. Gaines v. Canada in 1938 provided the first blush of success. The U.S. Supreme Court directed the law school at the University of Missouri to admit Lloyd Gaines, as the state provided no similar separate institution for such colored applicants. The Court extended that ruling in 1948 in *Sipuel v. Oklahoma Board of Regents* and again in 1950 in *Sweatt v. Painter* and *McClaurin v. Oklahoma State Regents*. Suits in lower federal courts, such as *Mendez v. Westminster School District* in California in 1946, also chipped away at segregation in public schools. The high court moved further against racial segregation on interstate buses in *Morgan v.*

Commonwealth of Virginia in 1946 and against residential segregation in *Shelley v. Kraemer* in 1948, outlawing enforcement of racially restrictive housing covenants. As in the 1867 New Orleans black star car episode, protests against segregation would take to the streets in the 1950s and 1960s to force change.

The Court's momentous blow came in its May 1954 ruling in *Brown v. Board of Education*. U.S. Chief Justice Earl Warren's decision for a unanimous Court rejected the *Plessy* doctrine. "We conclude that, in the field of public education, the doctrine of 'separate but equal' has no place," Warren declared. "Separate educational facilities are inherently unequal" (United States 1954, 495). The ruling reached only public education. It did not overturn *Plessy* everywhere. The law banning segregated public access and accommodations came finally with the Civil Rights Act of 1964. The Court's rulings that year in *Heart of Atlanta Motel v. United States* and *Katzenbach v. McClung* upheld the 1964 federal act, which in large part provided what the 1875 Civil Rights Act had offered.

Only in 1967 did the U.S. Supreme Court finally and fully repudiate *Plessy*'s "separate but equal" doctrine and outlaw state action to segregate people on the basis of race. In *Loving v. Virginia*, a unanimous Court in an opinion by Chief Justice Warren declared "we reject the notion that the mere 'equal application' of a statute containing racial classifications is enough to remove the classifications from the Fourteenth Amendment's proscription of all invidious racial discriminations." The Court there struck down anti-miscegenation statutes. "There is patently no legitimate overriding purpose independent of invidious racial discrimination which justifies this classification," the chief justice wrote. "The fact that Virginia prohibits only interracial marriages involving white persons demonstrates that the racial classifications must stand on their own justification, as measures designed to maintain White Supremacy" (United States 1967, 8, 12).

De jure segregation thus died a lingering death. The *Plessy* case had become attached to it alone. The identity theme that brought Homer Plessy to the Supreme Court of the United States was early lost along the way. The late twentieth-century clamor over diversity and multiculturalism made no connections to *Plessy*, yet those themes resonated in his arguments to the Court.

Even amid twenty-first-century announcements of a postracial America, race appeared profoundly fixed as a category in U.S. law and life. Few could accept race as artificial, as merely a social construct. Its position had changed little over time. Racial classifications had simply multiplied, even as the colorline remained fixed. The black/white division gave way to a broader spectrum, yet the colorline continued to relegate people of color on one side and whites on the other. The ideology of white supremacy refused to die. Nevertheless, it lost ground. Homer Plessy and his people contributed significantly to that.

Plessy saw the sad results of spreading segregation. It crushed his Creole people's dream of being recognized as a distinct community, as personally being neither black nor white. He might have wondered how his case might have ended differently or whether his people could or would ever be saved in the way they wanted. He had done what he could.

The Supreme Court decision left Plessy to finish up the particulars of the trial on which he embarked in June 1892. He had to head back to court. On January 11, 1897, he returned to the Orleans Parish Criminal Court, Section A. Attorney James C. Walker accompanied him. Judge Ferguson was gone; his term had expired. Judge Joshua Baker now presided. With the court's consent, Plessy withdrew his July 1892 "not guilty" plea. Instead, he pleaded guilty. Following the provisions of the validated Separate Car Act, Judge Baker sentenced Plessy to pay a $25 fine or spend 20 days in Orleans Parish prison. Plessy paid the fine and got on with the rest of his life. He had done his part in what became Creoles' last hurrah for official recognition of their distinct identity.

Plessy lived until March 1, 1925, dying 16 days short of his 63rd birthday. His wife, Louise Bordenave, survived him and attended his burial in New Orleans's St. Louis Cemetery #1. He had not gone far on his fateful ride, but he had opened the way for others. And that, after all, was his aim—to do his part to make a case for his people.

References

Louisiana. 1890. "An Act to Promote the Comfort of Passengers on Railway Trains." 1890 La. Acts 152 (July 10, 1890).

Louisiana. 1893. *Ex parte Plessy*. 45 La. Ann. 80 (1893).

Medley, Keith Weldon. 2003. *We as Freemen*: Plessy v. Ferguson. Gretna, LA: Pelican.

Tourgée, Albion W., and James C. Walker. 1896. "Brief for the Plaintiff in Error." In *Landmark Briefs and Arguments of the Supreme Court of the United States: Constitutional Law*, ed. Phillip B. Kurland and Gerhard Casper. Washington, DC: University Publications of America, 1975.

United States. 1896. *Plessy v. Ferguson*, 163 U.S. 537 (1896).

United States. 1954. *Brown v. Board of Education of Topeka*, 347 U.S. 483 (1954).

United States. 1967. *Loving v. Virginia*, 388 U.S. 1 (1967).

Biographies of Key Figures

Henry Billings Brown (1836–1913)

Justice Henry Billings Brown wrote the 1896 U.S. Supreme Court decision in *Plessy v. Ferguson*. Republican President Benjamin Harrison nominated the 54-year-old Brown to succeed 74-year-old Justice Samuel Freeman Miller, who died in October 1890. Confirmed and seated in December 1890, Brown served until the end of the Court's term in May 1906, retiring due largely to failing eyesight. He had come to the nation's high court after 15 years as a judge on the U.S. District Court for the Eastern District of Michigan, where he had settled in 1859 to practice law in Detroit.

A scion of a Massachusetts merchant family, Brown graduated from Yale College in 1856. After a year traveling in Europe, he studied at the law schools at Yale and Harvard but took no degree. He read enough, however, to pass the bar in Michigan in 1860. An ambitious man, Brown made good connections. Almost immediately he became a lecturer in law at the University of Michigan. Within a year of starting practice as a lawyer, he became a deputy U.S. marshal for Detroit. Within three years, he became an assistant U.S. attorney for the District of Michigan. To escape the Civil War draft begun in July 1863, Brown paid a substitute $850 to take his place. He married well in 1864; his wife Caroline Pitts came from a prominent Detroit family. Brown became a Wayne County Circuit Court judge in 1868, and in 1875 he rose to the federal bench.

The *Plessy* decision was one of more than 450 opinions Brown wrote for the Supreme Court from 1890 to 1906. The transportation features of the case fit him for *Plessy*, as Brown was an authority on transport law. His special area was water, however—not land. Brown had established himself as an expert in admiralty law, treating shipping, which was a hot area when he became a lawyer. Shipping had begun booming in the 1850s on the Great Lakes, which served as America's principal inland waterway. Interregional traffic in grain, ore, and passengers had begun then to build thriving port cities. Buffalo, Chicago, Cleveland, and Detroit, for example, together in

1850 had only 110,277 residents. By 1880, they had 924,526 residents, an almost ninefold increase. Henry Brown rode that growth and the law it demanded for accidents, contracts, liability, and regulation.

A conservative wedded to free market competition and protection of private property, Justice Brown generally disapproved of state regulation of commerce. Instead, he approved laissez-faire principles. He objected particularly to state laws imposing duties on railroads—at least in economic areas. On property issues, he consistently championed strict equal protection restraints on states under the Fourteenth Amendment.

Brown's opinion in *Plessy* showed none of the concern for racial discrimination that he demonstrated for economic discrimination against corporations as he saw it. He saw no violation of equal protection in Louisiana's mandating racial segregation, yet he fretted about state economic regulations' oppressing business. He joined the Court in denouncing what it described in *Lochner v. New York* (1905) as "meddlesome interferences with the rights of the individual." Brown saw nothing unnatural or undesirable, however, about state regulations segregating nonwhites from whites, "permitting, and even requiring, their separation in places where they are liable to be brought into contact."

Looking down from his privileged position as a white man of wealth, Justice Brown subscribed to social Darwinism, accepting as fact the idea of inherent differences naturally and necessarily distinguishing and distancing groups and individuals from one another in society. He thought simply that what he called "natural affinities" and "racial instincts" should prevail for whites to prefer to be with whites and for nonwhites to prefer to be with nonwhites. He saw such affinities and instincts as social matters, not as matters of civil rights. Brown accepted segregation as following "the general sentiment of the community." It was that simple for him—so he saw nothing wrong with Louisiana expressing in law what he viewed as a simple fact of American life.

John Howard Ferguson (1838–1915)

John Howard Ferguson was the other person in the duo named in the case title *Plessy v. Ferguson*. Attention to the case in the growing struggle against segregation made Homer Plessy's name a fixture in U.S. history. Ferguson became at most a footnote. Yet he was more than incidental to the case the U.S. Supreme Court decided in May 1896: Ferguson was the first judge to hear Plessy's case.

Sitting in the Criminal District Court of Louisiana's Parish of Orleans, Judge John H. Ferguson in October 1892 presided at Plessy's arraignment for violating the state's segregationist 1890 Separate Car Act. Ferguson took Plessy's elaborate 14-point plea, heard oral arguments 15 days later, and in November issued his written opinion ruling on the case then titled *State v. Plessy*, no. 19,117.

Judge Ferguson understood what its proponents hoped to achieve with Plessy's case. More than that, he showed apparent sympathy for their aims and objectives. One of Plessy's attorneys referred to him as "my friend Judge Ferguson," in describing his help to expedite the case. Ferguson smoothed the way for the *Plessy* case to reach the U.S. Supreme Court.

Ferguson was no diehard southern white conservative. He understood the struggle of Plessy's people. In many ways he was himself a striver. He had scrambled to big-city judicial respectability from the Outer Lands, as New Englanders called the island group off their southern coast.

Ferguson was born in June 1838 on Martha's Vineyard when the Massachusetts island had fewer than 13,000 residents. His birthplace—the little town of Chilmark in Duke County—sat at the island's least inhabited end in Massachusetts's least populous county, with a bit fewer than 4,000 residents, including 20 blacks. Whaling was the primary industry. It occupied Ferguson's father, a shipmaster, after whom he was named. A life at sea held no attraction for the younger Ferguson. At age 21, he went off to read law in the shadow of Boston's City Hall.

Ferguson made good connections. He studied with Benjamin Franklin Hallett, then in his sixties, who mentored him as perhaps something of a kindred spirit. Hallett's father, too, had been a shipmaster like Ferguson's. Hallett had risen to stand as a grand pillar in many areas. Renowned as a lawyer and one-time U.S. attorney for the District of Massachusetts, he was also a leading journalist and a local and national Democratic Party leader. He early advocated emancipation, pushing the state Democratic Party in Massachusetts to adopt in its 1848 platform a plank declaring, "We are opposed to slavery in every form and color, and in favor of freedom and free soil wherever man lives throughout God's heritage." Hallett taught the young Ferguson the ins and outs of law and public life before dying in September 1862.

Ferguson learned well enough. He passed the Massachusetts bar in 1863. With his mentor dead and his own family in Chilmark also gone, the 25-year-old Ferguson had nothing holding him in the Bay State. Opportunities elsewhere beckoned, and one especially caught his ear. He heard much from returning Civil War veterans about the lush panoramas of the South. Ferguson heard particularly about New Orleans, which Massachusetts regiments had helped capture in May 1862. What he heard led him to envision favorable prospects for an ambitious, loyal man—so he set sail south.

Ferguson arrived in the Crescent City not merely as a stranger or even an outsider, but as a Yankee. To many New Orleans residents, he was and would long continue to be the enemy. They scorned him and others like him as carpetbaggers, moving in from the North with the war and its aftermath. They generally spurned such men as opportunists, occupiers, extortionists, colonizers, and worse.

Not everyone shunned him. Ferguson found some welcome among New Orleans's Unionists. They had lived in the South before the war and opposed secession. Many had also opposed slavery. One such man was Thomas Jefferson Earhart. Born in Pennsylvania, he had settled in New Orleans in the 1840s with his Washington, D.C.-born wife, Elizabeth, and their four children. Earhart's daughter Virginia, born in Arkansas in 1842, became Ferguson's wife in July 1866 and in time bore him three sons—Walter, Milo, and Donald.

Ferguson's Democratic Party connections from Hallett helped at least with introductions in his new home. He got himself attached to a Louisiana faction former Confederate Brigadier General Francis T. Nicholls led. That got Ferguson a brief seat as a representative of four uptown New Orleans wards in the Louisiana General Assembly in 1877, when Nicholls claimed the governorship. In 1892, it got him tapped to replace the failing 73-year-old Robert H. Marr as judge of the Criminal District Court for the Parish of Orleans. By then Ferguson had more than 25 years of legal practice in the city.

Ferguson handled mostly civil matters but gained a splash of notice on the criminal side from his work on the edge of another New Orleans *cause célèbre*. He represented one of the immigrant Italians accused of murdering New Orleans Police Chief David C. Hennessy on October 15, 1890. His client never went to trial and so escaped the horrible fate of the nine who did. The trial jury in March 1891 found six of the nine defendants not guilty but reached no verdict on the other three. A mob outraged at the acquittal stormed the parish prison shouting, "We want the Dagoes!" The mob lynched 11 Italian Americans at the prison—the three on whom the jury reached no verdict, three whom the jury had found not guilty, and five who had not been on trial. The savagery drew international notoriety to New Orleans.

Sworn in on July 5, 1892, Ferguson sat as judge of Section A in Orleans Parish's two criminal courts. Public notice shortly attached to his directing a grand jury and the police chief to root out gambling in the city infamous for being a place where chance paid little attention to the law. Few at the time focused on Ferguson's sitting for an arraignment on October 13, 1892, although it would fix Ferguson's name in history long after November 1915, when he died quietly in New Orleans.

John Marshall Harlan (1833–1911)

Justice John Marshall Harlan alone on the U.S. Supreme Court dissented from its 1896 decision in *Plessy v. Ferguson*. More than any other justice, Harlan saw black-white segregation as violating fundamental rights the U.S. Constitution guaranteed all Americans. He denounced racial segregation as a denial of basic liberty and as an extension of slavery.

Harlan knew slavery firsthand. He was the Kentucky-born and -bred scion of a prominent slaveholding family. Only one other justice on the Supreme Court in 1896 had similar direct experience with slavery: Justice Edward Douglass White was born into a slaveholding family on a sugar cane plantation in Lafourche Parish in south Louisiana. White defended slavery and segregation, while Harlan opposed both and distinguished himself on the Court as a champion of reversing slavery's legacy.

Harlan opposed secession and fought for the Union in the Civil War. He resigned as a colonel in the 10th Kentucky Volunteer Infantry in February 1863 on the death of his father, James Harlan, and went home to attend his family in Frankfort, Kentucky's capital. He had earlier practiced law there, joining his father's firm on passing the bar in 1853. Also following in his father's footsteps, Harlan was early active in politics and served from 1854 to 1858 as Frankfort's city attorney.

Harlan stood against old-line, traditional Democrats, but his party attachments continually shifted. He started as a Whig, like his father. When that party dissolved in 1856, Harlan joined the Native American Party, popularly known as the Know-Nothings, and in 1858 won election as Franklin County judge. In 1859, he stood unsuccessfully as a candidate for Congress, after joining the Opposition Party cobbled together from former Whigs, Know-Nothings, and others opposed to pro-slavery Democrat fire-eaters preaching secession.

Harlan supported Constitutional Union candidate John Bell for president in 1860 and campaigned in 1864 for antiwar Democrat candidate George B.

McClellan, the U.S. Army major-general whom Republican President Abraham Lincoln had dismissed as Union field commander. Harlan won election as Kentucky's attorney general in 1863, running as a moderate Democrat, but he lost his reelection bid in 1867. In 1868, he joined the Republican Party. He ran unsuccessful campaigns to be Kentucky governor in 1871 and 1875. In 1876, Harlan ended up backing and campaigning for Republican Rutherford B. Hayes, who as president nominated Harlan to the U.S. Supreme Court in October 1877.

Justice Harlan embraced the expansive meaning of freedom he saw embodied in the Thirteenth Amendment and the fundamental rights he saw guaranteed in the Fourteenth Amendment. "These two amendments, if enforced according to their true intent and meaning, will protect all the civil rights that pertain to freedom and citizenship," he insisted in his *Plessy* dissent. He consistently espoused that view in his opinions on the Court.

Justice Harlan early showed his firm support for federal power to enforce the freedom and civil rights he recognized in the U.S. Constitution. His most famous stand prior to the *Plessy* case came in the Court's 1883 decision in the *Civil Rights Cases*, in which he again dissented alone. The majority opinion in 1883 held that Congress overreached its authority in the Civil Rights Act of 1875 in mandating that "all persons within the jurisdiction of the United States shall be entitled to the full and equal enjoyment of the accommodations, advantages, facilities, and privileges of inns, public conveyances on land or water, theaters, and other places of public amusement; subject only to the conditions and limitations established by law, and applicable alike to citizens of every race and color, regardless of any previous condition of servitude." Justice Harlan disagreed with his eight fellow justices, who in 1883 recognized nothing in the U.S. Constitution to allow Congress to regulate, punish, or outlaw racial discrimination by private persons. Harlan insisted that discrimination in "the accommodations, advantages, facilities, and privileges of inns, public conveyances on land or water, theaters, and other places of public amusement" was not private action. It was public action; the discrimination occurred in places operating public functions. Moreover, even if it were private action, the Constitution authorized Congress to reach such behavior through "appropriate legislation" under the Thirteenth and Fourteenth Amendments, Justice Harlan explained.

The grand effect of the Thirteenth Amendment was "to secure to all citizens of every race and color ... those fundamental rights which are the essence of civil freedom," Justice Harlan declared in his dissent in the *Civil Rights Cases*. The Fourteenth Amendment further guaranteed "the fundamental rights of American citizenship," he insisted. Racial discrimination and segregation violated those rights, and the United States could not permit such violations. No state could impose such violations, in Justice Harlan's view.

Consistently refusing to agree with his colleagues on the high court earned Justice Harlan the title "the great dissenter." He was willing to stand up alone for his view of America and its Constitution as resting on "the broad and sure foundation of the equality of all men before the law," as he wrote in his *Plessy* dissent.

Louis André Martinet (1849–1917)

Louis André Martinet was an energizer who continually pumped life into the crusade in Louisiana for equal rights that in 1896 carried *Plessy v. Ferguson* to the U.S. Supreme Court. A man who got things done, he appeared a tireless worker. His Belgian-born father, Hippolyte Martinet, early instilled the attribute. The elder Martinet trained his sons to work hard, well, and with pride. He was a master carpenter, and he taught his sons the trade. The second child and son among four boys and four girls born to Hippolyte and the Louisiana-born woman of color Marie Louise Benoit de la St. Claire Martinet, Louis learned to plan carefully and to build with patience and persistence. He earned respect enough for being smart and solid so that the freshly enfranchised voters of color around his family environs in St. Martinsville elected him to serve as a state representative from Louisiana's St. Martin Parish from 1872 to 1875. He was just 22 years old when he set off to the big capital city, New Orleans, about 140 miles southeast of his home. Martinet rose as a political star and worked to prepare himself better to do the job at hand. He had become a lawmaker, so he read law and passed the bar, becoming a lawyer in December 1875.

Even as Martinet's star was rising, the darkness of what conservative whites called "redemption" began to sink early Reconstruction reforms in Louisiana. Martinet marched in the front ranks in fighting white supremacy and spreading segregation. In February 1889, he began publishing a weekly newspaper aptly titled *The Crusader*. It became a civil rights record, tracking attacks on persons of color and advocating public equality. The newspaper went daily in 1891 in further efforts to stem the onslaught of segregation signaled in Louisiana in July 1890 when the legislature passed the Separate Car Act.

Martinet had joined in opposing the separate car mandate when it was first introduced as a bill in May 1890. When it became law, he immediately called to challenge its constitutionality in a test case. He envisioned a case focusing on not only segregated transportation but also on the constitutionality of a state's determining people's identity by race and segregating them on that basis. Martinet helped to assemble the ablest legal team available, and he helped plot strategy to get his envisioned test case heard in the nation's highest court.

Martinet worked mostly with others like him of mixed French, Spanish, and African ancestry. Such individuals were generally known as "people of color" (*gens de couleur*), and many of them, like Martinet, grew up in a Creole version of French language and culture. The inner circle of Martinet's action group reflected its Creole heritage in calling itself the *Comité des Citoyens*. The full English name of the group organized in September 1891 was the "Citizens' Committee to Test the Constitutionality of the Separate Car Law." Like Martinet, many of the group's members had white forebears and demanded recognition of their right to their distinct multicultural heritage and personal identity.

Martinet gave his all for the cause, but his public efforts appeared not to help his business and private life. Having published since February 1889, *The Crusader* folded within months of the U.S. Supreme Court's fateful decision in *Plessy* in May 1896. Within years, Martinet and his wife divorced. He had in September 1882 married the New Orleans native and school teacher Leonora Jeanne Miller. Their firstborn, Marie Divonne, died three weeks after birth in July 1884. Their only other child, Leslie Louise, came in 1886 and eventually went off to live with her husband Edward J. Condlon in New York City.

The loss in *Plessy* signaled the political tide sweeping against the civil rights for which Martinet had pushed his whole adult life. Perhaps deciding finally to go with the flow, Martinet appeared to busy himself with practicing as a medical doctor—he had found time even while the *Plessy* case was afoot to earn a degree from Flint Medical College in New Orleans. He died quietly at home in New Orleans in June 1917. Recognizing his contributions to the cause of civil rights, lawyers in several of Louisiana's minority bar associations in 1957 founded the Louis A. Martinet Legal Society, dedicated to pursuing the goal of ending racial segregation.

Homer Plessy (1862–1925)

Homer Plessy's ancestors did most to cast him for the role that fixed his name in U.S. history. Their pooled genes, more than anything else, made him a model for the landmark 1896 *Plessy v. Ferguson* U.S. Supreme

Court case. They blended his features beyond simple black-and-white. Plessy looked white, but he did not claim to be white. He was who he was—and that was exactly what made him an ideal example of the demonstrably false basis and illogic of laws categorizing people according to a racial dichotomy and segregating them as either white or nonwhite. In Plessy's time and place, the legal terms for these categories were "white" and "colored." Plessy opposed government's asserting authority to force him into one or the other category and to segregate him on that basis. He asserted his own separate identity, individuality, and equality under law.

The first Plessys in Homer's line in Louisiana were Germain and his brother Dominique. They arrived in New Orleans from the then war-torn French Caribbean colony of Saint-Domingue. The pair fled the 1790s revolution to end slavery and establish independence in the place that in 1804 became the *République d'Haïti*, the second independent nation in the Americas. Germain was Homer Plessy's paternal grandfather.

Germain was French, born about 1777 in France's southwest city of Bordeaux. He migrated to the Americas in an effort to improve his life—and improve it he did. Germain prospered in New Orleans as a master carpenter, operating Plessy & Co. He married Catherina Mathieu, daughter of a Frenchman and a free woman of color. Catherina bore Germain four sons and four daughters. The last of the sons and second-to-last child was Joseph Adolphe.

Born in 1822, Adolphe (as he was usually called) in time married Rosa Debergue, a free woman of color 13 years his junior. The couple's second of three children and first son was born on March 17, 1862: His birth certificate gave his name as Homère Patris Plessy. *Homère* reached back to the ancient Greek poet who authored the epics the *Iliad* and the *Odyssey*, perhaps expressing the parents' ambitions for their newborn son. *Patris* derived from the same source as *Patrick*, and Homère's parents perhaps gave him that name because he was born on the Roman Catholic St. Patrick's feast day.

Homère later adopted *Adolphe* to replace Patris as his middle name, so as to honor his father, who died in January 1869. Homère's mother, left a widow who had to care for both Homère and his two sisters, Ida and Rosa, married Victor Martial Dupart in May 1871. The recently widowed son of a shoemaker, Dupart carried his own father's middle name as his own middle name. That perhaps persuaded the young boy to style himself later as Homère Adolphe Plessy. The Anglicized version dropped the final "e" from both his first and middle names.

Plessy's stepfather engaged in immediate post–Civil War politics. He paid his poll tax to vote in 1869 and 1870. He joined in Louisiana's short-lived Unification Movement of 1873. The interracial coalition pushed for guaranteed civil and political rights. Many of its leaders came, like Dupart, from the "colored" class free long before the Civil War. Indeed, in 1860 members of this class collectively owned property valued then at more than $2 million. They stood apart from black slaves. They had never been illiterate field hands. Instead, they dominated the ranks of skilled craftsmen such as bricklayers, carpenters, cigar makers, and shoemakers. Most had styled themselves in antebellum times as *gens de colour libres*— free people of color. As their chosen self-reference suggested, they reveled in their French heritage and persisted in its language. Their number included men such as Louis C. Roudanez, who in 1864 founded the *New Orleans Tribune* newspaper that trumpeted equal rights under the law. A physician by training, Roudanez held degrees from Dartmouth College and the University of Paris.

His stepfather's activism was not lost on Homer. He followed Dupart's politics, just as he also followed Dupart's trade as a shoemaker. More and more, however, mechanization was debasing the craft by eliminating the skillful work of hand-sewing. Large-scale, machine-produced, low-cost shoes slashed both the prices and the sales of custom-crafted shoes. Indeed, the craft increasingly became less shoemaking and more shoe-mending.

More than a shifting marketplace threatened the likes of Dupart and Plessy in the 1880s. Reactionary white politicians increasingly pushed to return Louisiana to the race-based rules that existed in slavery. Such conservatives insisted on segregation. Idealizing a society segregated as white and nonwhite, their early battle lines attacked schools and transportation. Plessy enlisted to fight such racist reactionaries.

Plessy took his first noted public stand on schools. In 1887, he served as vice president of the Justice, Protective, Educational, and Social Club in New Orleans. The club insisted on enforcement of the 1868 Louisiana Constitution's Article 135 provision that "there shall be no separate school or institution of learning established exclusively for any race by the State of Louisiana." From that principle Plessy and his fellow club members worked to advance "lawful demands to the Government for our share of public education."

Plessy and his fellows opposed segregation as the practice allowed whites to hoard privileges. It served whites a lion's share of public goods and services and left all nonwhites to scramble for leftovers; many got nothing, in fact. Moreover, for Plessy and many of his fellows, segregation's white/nonwhite dichotomy not merely ignored, but disregarded, the identity of their Creole heritage. The practice labeled them as other than who they felt they were.

Like Plessy, many Creoles saw themselves as neither nonwhite nor white. They denounced such a dichotomy as simply wrong. Who was to say who they were, other than they themselves? If identity simply was to follow appearance, then many like Plessy who appeared "white" would have that identity. But who, after all, was "white"? Who was to decide? And how? Was such an identity something the law could routinely recognize? Did a state's requiring separate public access and services on the basis of such identity deprive any person of life, liberty, or property without due process of law? Did it provide all "person within its jurisdiction the equal protection of the laws," as the Fourteenth Amendment to the U.S. Constitution required?

Plessy took his most noted public stand to raise questions about the state's power over the personal identity segregation imposed. He boarded a train at the New Orleans Press Street Depot on Tuesday, June 7, 1892, to challenge the constitutionality of Louisiana's Separate Car Act of 1890. He hoped his arrest would lead to stopping spreading segregation. The plan, in which he played his part, was to fight all the way to the U.S. Supreme Court. His case made it there but lost against a surging tide of white supremacy.

Plessy became no public hero in his day. He died in New Orleans in March 1925, long before the tide turned against racial discrimination. But it did turn in time to sink segregation by law and fix his case and name in U.S. history.

Albion Winegar Tourgée (1838–1905)

Albion Winegar Tourgée became the lead lawyer and principal strategist in the challenge to racial segregation in the 1896 U.S. Supreme Court case, *Plessy v. Ferguson*. His arguments laced with metaphorical phrases about color-blind justice became oft-repeated in time. "Justice is pictured as blind and her daughter the Law, ought at least to be color-blind," he wrote on behalf of Homer Plessy in his brief to the Court.

Tourgée was multitalented. He did many things in many places. Born on a farm in northeast Ohio in 1838, he died in 1905 in a château in Bordeaux, France, where he was serving as a U.S. consul. Along the way, he occupied himself as a school teacher, poet, lawyer, horticulturalist, real estate broker, lecturer, judge, propagandists, novelist, newspaper editor and publisher, and diplomat. He was also a soldier.

Shot in the spine at the first Battle of Bull Run on July 4, 1861, Tourgée never fully recovered from wounds in his back, legs, and arms.

He stubbornly refused to let even his lost left eye keep him from rejoining the war. In May 1862, he reenlisted as a first lieutenant, only to again suffer hip wounds in October 1862 at the Battle of Perryville in central Kentucky. Hospitalized until December 1862, he rejoined his ranks only to be captured near Murfreesboro, Tennessee, in January 1863. He sat as a prisoner of war in Libby Prison in Richmond, Virginia, until being exchanged for Confederate prisoners of war in May 1863. He resigned his commission in December 1863, still not completely well.

Tourgée returned to Ohio, where his new bride awaited him. Within days after being released as a prisoner of war in May 1863, he had married Emma Lodoiska Kilbourne in Columbus. She was his high school sweetheart; Tourgée said he fell in love with her at first sight at Kingsville Academy. Tourgée resumed reading law at Sherman & Farmer in Ashtabula, a course of study he had begun while convalescing from his first wounds. He passed the bar in May 1864 but taught school until early in 1865 at Erie Academy in northwest Pennsylvania. Looking for better prospects and a climate easier on his war wounds, he explored relocating.

Tourgée toured the southern Atlantic coast, lingering in Georgia, but after working as counsel in a court-martial in Raleigh, North Carolina, he decided on residence in Greensboro, North Carolina. He and Emma set up house there in October 1865. Not all of their new neighbors welcomed them. Bitter white southerners reviled Albion as a "carpetbagger"—a term deriding northerners who moved to the South after the Civil War. It labeled people like Tourgée as colonizers, opportunists, exploiters, and agitators. In short, it branded them as public enemies.

Tourgée did little to ingratiate himself with old-line white southerners. A man of uncompromising convictions, he characteristically said what he thought and walked the way he talked. He saw the Civil War as a grand crusade. He loathed the southern aristocratic conception of society expressed in slavery. Any caste system such as racism ran afoul of what he held to be America's democratic commitment and promise. He held an unshakable belief in egalitarianism.

Tourgée practiced his principles. He embraced blacks politically and socially. He lived in a racially integrated neighborhood. As a slap in the face of the conventions of the time and place, he and his wife had blacks into their home for dinner and other social occasions. Such practices made him notorious. Yet it was his pronouncements that made him anathema to many of his southern neighbors. He minced no words in denouncing what he scorned as the "poor, misguided and mismanaged South" and its "slough of ignorance and prejudice."

Tourgée became a hated target. The terrorist Ku Klux Klan (KKK) marked him, increasingly threatening his life, home, and family as he grew as a political figure. Tourgée served in the North Carolina state constitutional convention in January 1867 and also became a judge on North Carolina's Superior Court for its eight-county Seventh Judicial District.

As so-called white conservatives regained power in North Carolina and purged opponents from the state's political ranks, Tourgée's position became more and more untenable. His safety was repeatedly in question. After his daughter Aimée's birth in November 1870, the sharpening threats worried him more and more. But he was loath to quit a job undone. He held on to serve as a delegate at North Carolina's 1875 constitutional convention. After losing a run for Congress in 1878, he left the Tar Heel State.

Tourgee remained forever bitter that the Civil War stopped short of rooting out the underlying evils of slavery. In *A Fool's Errand, by One of the Fools*, published in 1879, he penned his view of his and his fellow Radical Reconstructionists' efforts to reform the South. The novel became a sensational best-seller, as did the 1880 sequel, *Bricks without Straw*. Their success settled Tourgée's finances and made him a sought-after commentator and lecturer. Moving back not far from his boyhood home along Lake Erie, Tourgée in 1881 settled with his wife and daughter in Mayville, New York, near the Chautauqua Institution noted for its public adult education programs

Judge Tourgée, as he was popularly known from his syndicated newspaper column "A Bystander's Notes," opposed Louisiana's Separate Car Act from the moment of its passage in July 1890. His national reputation as an outspoken critic of white supremacist segregation and racial caste and his acknowledged legal acumen made him the prime candidate to be the lead lawyer for the Citizens Committee to Test the Constitutionality of the Separate Car Law after it organized in New Orleans in September 1891.

Tourgée did not disappoint in *Plessy v. Ferguson*. He argued hauntingly to the Supreme Court and to the nation for an America free of the lasting harm of racial classes and segregation mandated by law.

Primary Documents

Protest against the Separate Car Bill (1890)

Introduction in the legislature of what became Louisiana's 1890 Separate Car Act provoked immediate protest. Prominent Creoles led the opposition. They joined with others in the American Citizens' Equal Rights Association (ACERA), which petitioned the Louisiana General Assembly to dismiss the bill and all other "class legislation." Their protest dated May 24, 1890, invoked constitutional, legal, moral, policy, and religious arguments against de jure segregation.

We, the undersigned American citizens, and citizens of the State of Louisiana, do most respectfully but earnestly protest against the passage of any class legislation now pending before the General Assembly, or which may hereafter come before the honorable body, for the following reasons:

That such legislation is unconstitutional, un-American, unjust, dangerous and against sound public policy.

There is no warrant in this Constitution of the State of Louisiana for the passage of any law establishing discrimination *per se* against any class of American citizens, while, on the contrary, that instrument, in letter and spirit, seems to protect, with a jealous care, all the essentials of equality.

The boast of the American people is that this government is based upon the self-evident truth, that all men are created equal and has for some of its objects the establishment of justice and the insuring of domestic tranquility. It is then difficult to conceive how any caste legislation can maintain the sacredness of these truly American principles; we are rather inclined to the belief that any measure lacking the essential of justice is an unfortunate blow at those high conceptions which adorn the preambles of the Federal and State Constitutions and the Immortal Declaration of Independence.

We ground our protest further upon the high moral precept, that men should not do unto others what they do not wish should be done unto them.

We say that it is unjust, unchristian, to inflict upon any portion of the people the gratuitous indignities which take their motive and their bitterness from the dictates of an unreasonable prejudice. . . . We do not think that citizens of a darker hue should be treated by law on different lines than those of a lighter complexion. Citizenship is national and has no color. We hold that any attempt to abridge it on account of color is simply a surrender of wisdom to the appeals of passion. . . .

It is hardly necessary to remark that such legislation is against good public policy, as it is in direct contradiction with the well recognized principle that every act of the government must rest upon the authority that it is intended for the common good. . . .

In the name of God and the Constitution, Federal and State, in the name of justice, reason and equity, in the name of peace, in the name of an enlightened and Christian civilization, we humbly trust that our protest may be heeded by the loyal hearts of our legislators, and that the chalice of political bitterness may be snatched from the grasp of intolerant persecution and made to melt into the sacred fires of patriotic mercy!

Source: "Memorial . . . Protest of the American Citizens' Equal Rights Association of Louisiana Against Class Legislation," in *Official Journal of the House of Representatives of the State of Louisiana* (Baton Rouge: *The Advocate*, 1890), 127–128.

An Appeal for the Separate Car Act (1890)

The leading organ of Louisiana's white conservatives exhorted the state legislature to enact the Separate Car bill. The New Orleans Times-Democrat *pushed segregation across the board. The newspaper advocated what it viewed as racial pride and purity; it flatly rejected "mixed" society as abhorrent social equality. Begun in 1881 as a partisan voice of Louisiana's Democratic Party, the weekly decried a failed vote on July 8, 1890, to pass the separate car bill in the Louisiana Senate. Such a failure put the state at odds with the Jim Crow tide rolling across the South, the editorial noted. It sought to pressure senators who voted "nay" to reconsider. Passage required only three more "yea" votes. The editorial cast any white senator who voted against passage as a traitor to his race. It cast segregation itself as something of a black/white tug-of-war, if not an outright race war. Yet it insisted that a separate car law was not an act of hostility against nonwhites. Such an act would take away no rights, the paper insisted. It suggested that the U.S. Supreme Court agreed with this position, pointing to Mississippi and its March 1888 separate car act, which the nation's highest court upheld against challenge in its March 1890 decision in* Louisville, New Orleans & Texas Railway Co. v. Mississippi. *Further, the* Times-Democrat *argued, a separate car act protected decency.*

In making this argument, it conjured up images of disgusting contact between colored men and white women. The depth of opposition in the editorial foreshadowed much in generations to come.

The bill providing separate cars for white and colored peopled failed to pass the Senate yesterday in consequence of a lack of three votes. This is greatly to be regretted because it places Louisiana in opposition to the other Southern States; and because the failure will be misunderstood by the negroes and produce unpleasant results. Neighboring States have passed a law of this kind. It has, in the case of Mississippi, been pronounced legal; it is in actual operation and wherever it has been tried, it has given satisfaction.

The Southern whites, in no spirit of hostility to the negroes, have insisted that the two races shall live separate and distinct from each other in all things, with separate schools, separate hotels and separate cars. They would rise to-morrow against the proposition to educate the white and black together; and they resist any intercourse in theatre, hotel or elsewhere that will bring the race into anything like social intercourse. The quarter of a century that has passed since the war has not diminished in the slightest degree the determination of the whites to prevent any such dangerous doctrine as social equality, even in the mildest form. They give the negroes schools; but these must be separate; and the cars also should be separate, in order to keep the races as far apart as ever. We cannot afford to surrender anything in this case.

The law—private not public—which prohibits the negroes from occupying the same place in a hotel, restaurant or theatre as the whites, should prevail as to cars also. As a matter of fact, one is thrown in much closer communication in the car with one's traveling companions than in the theatre or restaurant with one's neighbors. Whites and blacks may there be crowded together, squeezed close to each other in the same seats, using the same conveniences, and to all intents and purposes in social intercourse. A man that would be horrified at the idea of his wife or daughter seated by the side of a burly negro in the parlor of a hotel or at a restaurant cannot see her occupying a crowded seat in a car next to a negro without the same feeling of disgust.

The Louisiana Senate ought to step in and prevent this indignity to the white women of Louisiana, as the Legislatures of other Southern States have done.

It is not proposed to refuse the negroes any right to which they are entitled. They are to have the same kind of cars, but separate ones. The man who believes that the white race should be kept pure from African taint will vote against that commingling of the races inevitable in a "mixed car" and which must have bad results.

The matter comes up again before the Senate. Let it consider well over it and do as the Legislatures of Texas, Mississippi and other Southern States have done.

Source: Editorial, *New Orleans Times-Democrat*, July 9, 1890.

Louisiana's Separate Car Act (1890)

Homer A. Plessy's case rested on his challenge to a statute Louisiana's legislature enacted on July 10, 1890. Popularly known as the Separate Car Act, it mandated "separate accommodations for the white, and colored races." The Louisiana legislation followed a trend Tennessee initiated in 1881. Florida followed with similar legislation in 1887, Mississippi in 1888, and Texas in 1889. Such railroad segregation statutes further advanced de jure segregation. They covered an expanding mode of transportation, but even more, they suggested the unrelenting stretch of segregation as a fixed rule that presumed the singular identity of all persons as either white or nonwhite. Further, the Louisiana law authorized and commanded "officers of . . . passenger trains" to decide who was who in regard to passengers' personal identity. Plessy and his people challenged being pigeonholed in the white/nonwhite dichotomy.

"An act to promote the comfort of passengers on railway trains"

Sec. 1. [A]ll railway companies carrying passengers in their coaches in this State, shall provide equal but separate accommodations for the white, and colored races, by providing two or more passenger coaches for each passenger train, or by dividing the passenger coaches by a partition so as to secure separate accommodations: Provided, That this section shall not be construed to apply to street railroads. No person or persons, shall be admitted to occupy seats in coaches, other than, the ones, assigned, to them on account of the race they belong to.

Sec. 2. [T]he officers of such passenger trains shall have power and are hereby required to assign each passenger to the coach or compartment used for the race to which such passenger belongs; any passenger insisting on going into a coach or compartment to which by race he does not belong, shall be liable to a fine of twenty-five dollars, or in lieu thereof to imprisonment for a period of not more than twenty days in the parish prison, and any officer of any railroad insisting on assigning a passenger to a coach or compartment other than the one set aside for the race to which said passenger belongs, shall be liable to a fine of twenty-five dollars, or in lieu thereof to imprisonment for a period of not more than twenty days in the parish prison; and should any passenger refuse to occupy the coach or compartment to which he or she is assigned by the officer of such railway, said officer shall have power to refuse to carry such passenger on his train, and for such refusal neither he nor the railway company which he represents shall be liable for damages in any of the courts of this State.

Source: 1890 La. Acts 152 (July 10, 1890).

Ex parte Plessy (1893)

Creoles of color led the opposition to what in July 1890 became Louisiana's Separate Car Act. Creoles organized the Comité des Citoyens to contest the act's legitimacy; the group's full name in English was the Citizens' Committee to Test the Constitutionality of the Separate Car Law. The Comité mounted a test case in 1892 with Homer Plessy, arguing that the act violated the Thirteenth and Fourteenth Amendments and other parts of the U.S. Constitution. The arguments posed as central the question of Plessy's identity—and by extension that of Creoles generally and other persons of mixed race. The case went to the state's high court. Louisiana Supreme Court Justice Charles Erasmus Fenner (1834–1911) delivered a decision in January 1893, upholding the statute as proper and reasonable and as not intruding on the identity of Plessy, who stood as what the law called a relator— a person in whose interests the case proceeded.

The statute here in question is an exercise of the police power and expresses the conviction of the legislative department of the State that the separation of the races in public conveyances, with proper sanctions enforcing the substantial equality of the accommodations supplied to each, is in the interest of public order, peace and comfort. It undoubtedly imposes a severe burden upon railways; but the Supreme Court of the United States has held that they are bound to bear it. It impairs no right of passengers of either race, who are secured that equality of accommodation which satisfies every reasonable claim.

The regulation of domestic commerce is as exclusively a State function as the regulation of interstate commerce is a federal function. It is as much within the control of State legislation as the public school system or the law of marriage. To hold that the requirement of separate, though equal, accommodations in public conveyances violated the XIVth Amendment would, on the same principles, necessarily entail the nullity of statutes establishing separate schools, and of others existing in many States prohibiting intermarriage between the races. All are regulations based upon difference of race, and if such difference can not furnish a basis for such legislation in one of these cases it can not in any.

The statute applies to the two races with such perfect fairness and equality that the record brought up for our inspection does not disclose whether the person prosecuted is a white or a colored man. . . .

Even were it true that the statute is prompted by prejudice on the part of one race to be thrown in such contact with the other, one would suppose that to be a sufficient reason why the pride and self-respect of the other race should equally prompt it to avoid such contact, if it could be done without the sacrifice of equal accommodations. . . .

We will conclude by noticing some charges made against the statute by relator, based, as we think, on an utterly unwarranted construction. He claims that the statute vests the officers of the company with a judicial power to determine the race to which the passenger belongs; that they may assign the passenger to a coach to which by race he does not belong, and that such an assignment is binding on the passenger, and that, though wrongfully made, the officers and railway companies are exempted from any legal responsibility.

The reading of the statute utterly repels these charges. . . .

The discretion vested in the officer to decide primarily the coach to which each passenger by race belongs is only that necessary discretion attending every imposition of a duty, to determine whether the occasion exists which calls for its exercise. It is a discretion to be exercised at his peril and at the peril of his employer.

It is very certain that if relator shall prove in this prosecution that he did not, as charged, "insist on going into a coach to which he did not belong," an erroneous assignment by the conductor would not stand in the way of his acquittal, or exempt the officer and the railway from action for damages, whatever defences might be open to them based on good faith and probable cause.

Source: *Ex parte Plessy*, 45 La. Ann. 80, 11 So. 74 (La. 1893) (citations omitted).

Plessy's Brief to the U.S. Supreme Court (1895)

Albion W. Tourgée wrote Homer Plessy's main brief to the U.S. Supreme Court. The Ohio-born Civil War veteran was a nationally known legal authority and advocate against racial caste and Jim Crow segregation. The argument he penned for Plessy attacked state power to discriminate on the basis of race. In fact, Tourgée attacked the concept of race itself. He posed a litany of questions for the Court. Was race any more than an artificial construct? Was it something that could be factually determined? Who could determine it? On what basis? Could mere eyeballing discern ancestry? Could railroad conductors unerringly tell passengers' race? Could a mere ocular test carry the force of law? Tourgée hammered the proposition that race was an arbitrary assignment. It could not and should not carry the force of law, he insisted. Its vagary touched and concerned too much. Such an assignment could deprive persons of liberty and property. In determining who and what a person was, state-imposed racial identity determined the possibilities and qualities of life itself in America, Tourgée argued. Moreover, state-imposed racial identity revived the involuntary servitude of slavery. It deprived persons of "the equal protection of the laws" the U.S. Constitution guaranteed, Tourgée noted. Plessy's case was not simply about where persons were to sit on any public conveyance, he contended. "The question is not as to the equality of the privileges enjoyed, but the right of the State to label one citizen as white and another as colored," Tourgée concluded.

Has the State the power under the provisions of the Constitution of the United States, to make a distinction based on color in the enjoyment of chartered privileges within the state?

Has it the power to require the officers of a railroad to assort its citizens by race, before permitting them to enjoy privileges dependent on public charter?

Is the officer of a railroad competent to decide the question of race?

Is it a question that *can* be determined in the absence of statutory definition and without evidence? . . .

Is not the question of race, scientifically considered, very often impossible of determination?

Is not the question of race, legally considered, one impossible to be determined, in the absence of statutory definition? . . .

Is not a statutory assortment of the people of a state on the line of race, such a perpetuation of the essential features of slavery as to come within the inhibition of the XIIIth Amendment?

Is it not the establishment of a statutory difference between the white and colored races in the enjoyment of chartered privileges, a badge of servitude which is prohibited by that amendment? . . .

Points of Plaintiff's Contention

II—We shall . . . contend that, in any mixed community, the reputation of belonging to the dominant race, in this instance the white race, is *property* . . . and that the provisions of the act in question which authorize an officer of a railroad company to assign a person to a car set apart for a particular race, enables such officer to deprive him, to a certain extent at least, of this property—his reputation. . . .

How much would it be *worth* to a young man entering upon the practice of law, to be regarded as a *white* man rather than a colored one?

Six-sevenths of the population are white. Nineteen-twentieths of the property of the country is owned by white people. Ninety-nine hundredths of the business opportunities are in the control of white people. These propositions are rendered even more startling by the intensity of feeling which excludes the colored man from the friendship and companionship of the white man. Probably most white persons, if given a choice, would prefer death to life in the United States *as colored persons*. Under these conditions, is it possible to conclude that the *reputation of being white* is not property? Indeed, is it not the most valuable sort of property, being the master-key that unlocks the golden door of opportunity? . . .

V . . . The Court will take notice of the fact that, in all parts of the country, race-intermixture has proceeded to such an extent that there are a great number of citizens in whom the preponderance of the blood of one race or another, is impossible of ascertainment, except by careful scrutiny of the pedigree. As slavery did not permit the marriage of the slave, in a majority of cases even an approximate determination of this preponderance is an actual impossibility, with the most careful and deliberate weighing of evidence, much less by the casual scrutiny.

But even if it were possible to determine preponderance of blood and so determine racial character in certain cases, what should be said of those cases in which the race admixture is equal. Are they white or colored?

There is no law of the United States, or of the State of Louisiana defining the limits of race—who are white and who are "colored"? By what rule then shall any tribunal be guided in determining racial character? It may be said that all those would be classed as colored in whom appears a visible admixture of colored blood. By what law? With what justice? Why not count every one as white in whom is visible any trace of white blood? There is but one reason—to wit, the domination of the white race. Slavery not only introduced the rule of caste but prescribed its conditions, in the interests of that institution. The trace of color raised the presumption of bondage and was a bar to citizenship. The law in question is an attempt to apply this rule to the establishment of legalized caste-distinction *among citizens*.

It is not consistent with reason that the United States, having granted and bestowed one equal citizenship of the United States and prescribed one equal citizenship in each state, for all, will permit a State to compel a railway conductor to assort them arbitrarily according to his ideas of race, in the enjoyment of chartered privileges.

VI—The Plaintiff in Error, also insists that, even if it be held that such an assortment of citizens by race in the enjoyment of public privileges is not a deprivation of liberty or property without due process of law, it is still such an interference with the personal liberty of the individual as is impossible to be made consistently with his rights as an equal citizen of the United States and of the State in which he resides. . . .

IX—The prime essential of all citizenship is *equality* of personal rights and the *free* and secure enjoyment of all public privileges. These are the very essence of citizenship in all free governments.

A law assorting the citizens of a State in the enjoyment of a public franchise on the basis of race, is obnoxious to the spirit of republican institutions because it is a legalization of caste. Slavery was the very essence of caste; the climax of unequal conditions. The citizen held the highest political rank attainable in the republic; the slave was the lowest grade of existence. ALL rights and privileges attached to the one; the other had *no legal rights*, either of person or property. Between them stood that strange nondescript, the "free person of color," who had such rights only as the white people of the state where he resided saw fit to confer upon him, but he could neither become a citizen of the United States *nor of any State.* The effect of the words of the XIVth Amendment was to put *all* these classes on the *same level of right*, as *citizens*; and to make this Court the final arbiter and custodian of these rights. The effect of a law distinguishing between citizens as to race, in the enjoyment of a public franchise, is to legalize caste and restore, in part at least, the inequality of right which was an essential incident of slavery. . . .

[What does it mean, as the Fourteenth Amendment declares,] that no State shall deprive any person of life, liberty or property, without due process of law, or to deny any person within its jurisdiction, the equal protection of the laws. What is this but declaring that the law in the States shall be the same for the black as for the white; that all persons, whether colored or white, shall stand equal before the laws of the States, and, in regard to the colored race for whose protection the Amendment was primarily designed, that no discrimination shall be made against them by law because of their color? The words of the Amendment are prohibitive but they contain a necessary implication of a most positive immunity or right most valuable to the colored man—the right to exemption from unfriendly legislation against them as colored—exemption from legal discrimination *implying inferiority* in civil society, lessening the enjoyment of the rights which others enjoy, and *discriminations which are steps towards reducing them to the condition of a subject race.*"

In our case, the Plaintiff in Error contends that this is the precise purpose and intended and inevitable effect of the statute in question. It is a "step toward reducing the colored people and those allied with it, to the condition of a *subject race.*" . . .

Because it does this the statute is a violation of the fundamental principles of all free government and the Fourteenth Amendment should be given that construction which will remedy such tendency and which is in plain accord with its words. Legal refinement is out of place when it seeks to find a way both to avoid the plain purport of the terms employed, the fundamental principle of our government and the controlling impulse and tendency of the American people.

Source: Brief for Plaintiff in Error [by Albion W. Tourgée & Jas. C. Walker], *Plessy v. Ferguson* (No. 210, Oct. Term 1895), reprinted in *Landmark Briefs and Arguments of the Supreme Court of the United States*, ed. Philip B. Kurland and Gerald Gunther (Washington, DC: Univ. Publications of America, 1975), 13:33–57.

Plessy v. Ferguson (1896): The Court's Decision

Massachusetts-born Justice Henry Billings Brown wrote the U.S. Supreme Court's 7–1 decision in Plessy v. Ferguson. *His majority opinion rejected Plessy's Thirteenth and Fourteenth Amendment arguments. That Louisiana's Separate Car Act had nothing to do with slavery was, Brown asserted, "too clear for argument." He and the majority refused to recognize any reasonable connection between slavery and racial segregation. Nor did "the equal protection of the laws" prescribed in the Fourteenth Amendment prohibit state-mandated segregation, according to Brown's majority. The justices sharply distinguished legal equality from social equality; U.S. law had no reach regarding social equality, they insisted. As for identity determined by race, Brown said that was not a matter for the Court to consider. Who Homer Plessy was and what rights he had based on his identity depended on who Louisiana said he was. Whatever Plessy's identity, according to Justice Brown, Louisiana's Separate Car Act reasonably accorded him "equal but separate accommodations." The Court determined that was all the U.S. Constitution required.*

This case turns upon the constitutionality of an act of the General Assembly of the State of Louisiana, passed in 1890, providing for separate railway carriages for the white and colored races. . . .

The constitutionality of this act is attacked upon the ground that it conflicts both with the Thirteenth Amendment of the Constitution, abolishing slavery, and the Fourteenth Amendment, which prohibits certain restrictive legislation on the part of the States.

1. That it does not conflict with the Thirteenth Amendment, which abolished slavery and involuntary servitude, except as a punishment for crime, is too clear for argument. Slavery implies involuntary servitude—a state of bondage; the ownership of mankind as a chattel, or at least the control of the labor and services of one man for the benefit of another, and the

absence of a legal right to the disposal of his own person, property and services. . . .

A statute which implies merely a legal distinction between the white and colored races—a distinction which is founded in the color of the two races, and which must always exist so long as white men are distinguished from the other race by color—has no tendency to destroy the legal equality of the two races, or reestablish a state of involuntary servitude. . . .

2. . . . [W]e think the enforced separation of the races, as applied to the internal commerce of the State, neither abridges the privileges or immunities of the colored man, deprives him of his property without due process of law, nor denies him the equal protection of the laws, within the meaning of the Fourteenth Amendment. . . .

So far, then, as a conflict with the Fourteenth Amendment is concerned, the case reduces itself to the question whether the statute of Louisiana is a reasonable regulation, and with respect to this there must necessarily be a large discretion on the part of the legislature. In determining the question of reasonableness it is at liberty to act with reference to the established usages, customs and traditions of the people, and with a view to the promotion of their comfort, and the preservation of the public peace and good order. Gauged by this standard, we cannot say that a law which authorizes or even requires the separation of the two races in public conveyances is unreasonable, or more obnoxious to the Fourteenth Amendment than the acts of Congress requiring separate schools for colored children in the District of Columbia, the constitutionality of which does not seem to have been questioned, or the corresponding acts of state legislatures.

We consider the underlying fallacy of the plaintiff's argument to consist in the assumption that the enforced separation of the two races stamps the colored race with a badge of inferiority. If this be so, it is not by reason of anything found in the act, but solely because the colored race chooses to put that construction upon it. The argument necessarily assumes that if, as has been more than once the case, and is not unlikely to be so again, the colored race should become the dominant power in the state legislature, and should enact a law in precisely similar terms, it would thereby relegate the white race to an inferior position. We imagine that the white race, at least, would not acquiesce in this assumption. The argument also assumes that social prejudices may be overcome by legislation, and that equal rights cannot be secured to the negro except by an enforced commingling of the two races. We cannot accept this proposition.

If the two races are to meet upon terms of social equality, it must be the result of natural affinities, a mutual appreciation of each other's merits and a voluntary consent of individuals. As was said by the Court of Appeals of New York in *People v. Gallagher*, 93 N.Y. 438, 448, "this end can neither be accomplished nor promoted by laws which conflict with the general sentiment of the community upon whom they are designed to operate. When the government, therefore, has secured to each of its citizens equal rights before the law and equal opportunities for improvement and progress, it has accomplished the end for which it was organized and performed all of the functions respecting social advantages with which it is endowed." Legislation is powerless to eradicate racial instincts or to abolish distinctions based upon physical differences, and the attempt to do so can only result in accentuating the difficulties of the present situation. If the civil and political rights of both races be equal, one cannot be inferior to the other civilly or politically. If one race be inferior to the other socially, the Constitution of the United States cannot put them upon the same plane.

It is true that the question of the proportion of colored blood necessary to constitute a colored person, as distinguished from a white person, is one upon which there is a difference of opinion in the different States. . . . But these are questions to be determined under the laws of each State and are not properly put in issue in this case. Under the allegations of his petition it may undoubtedly become a question of importance whether, under the laws of Louisiana, the petitioner belongs to the white or colored race.

Source: *Plessy v. Ferguson*, 163 U.S. 537, 540–552 (1896) (citations omitted).

Plessy v. Ferguson (1896): Harlan's Dissent

Kentucky-born Justice John Marshall Harlan bitterly dissented in the 7–1 U.S. Supreme Court decision in Plessy v. Ferguson. *Contrary to the majority, Harlan accepted the Thirteenth and Fourteenth Amendment and other constitutional arguments against the "separate but equal" doctrine, which he decried as a ruse to "permit the seeds of race hate to be planted under the sanction of law." Such a doctrine arose from and entrenched assumptions that "colored citizens are so inferior and degraded that they cannot be allowed to sit in public coaches occupied by white citizens," Justice Harlan explained. Such sanction of law violated the essence of the U.S. Constitution, which, he noted, allowed "no superior, dominant ruling class of citizens." He recoiled at the horrors he foresaw following from the majority's decision. Jim Crow segregation simply extended "badges of slavery or servitude," he warned. Echoing terms from the arguments from Homer Plessy's lawyers, Justice Harlan insisted that "Our constitution is color-blind, and neither knows nor tolerates classes among citizens."*

[W]e have before us a state enactment that compels, under penalties, the separation of the two races in railroad passenger coaches, and makes it a crime for a citizen of either race to enter a coach that has been assigned to citizens of the other race.

Thus, the state regulates the use of a public highway by citizens of the United States solely upon the basis of race.

However apparent the injustice of such legislation may be, we have only to consider whether it is consistent with the constitution of the United States. . . .

The Thirteenth Amendment does not permit the withholding or the deprivation of any right necessarily inhering in freedom. It not only struck down the institution of slavery as previously existing in the United States, but it prevents the imposition of any burdens or disabilities that constitute badges of slavery or servitude. It decreed universal civil freedom in this country. This Court has so adjudged. But that amendment having been found inadequate to the protection of the rights of those who had been in slavery, it was followed by the Fourteenth Amendment, which added greatly to the dignity and glory of American citizenship, and to the security of personal liberty, by declaring that "all persons born or naturalized in the United States, and subject to the jurisdiction thereof, are citizens of the United States and of the State wherein they reside," and that "no State shall make or enforce any law which shall abridge the privileges or immunities of citizens of the United States; nor shall any State deprive any person of life, liberty or property without due process of law, nor deny to any person within its jurisdiction the equal protection of the laws." These two amendments, if enforced according to their true intent and meaning, will protect all the civil rights that pertain to freedom and citizenship. . . .

It was said in argument that the statute of Louisiana does not discriminate against either race, but prescribes a rule applicable alike to white and colored citizens. But this argument does not meet the difficulty. Every one knows that the statute in question had its origin in the purpose, not so much to exclude white persons from railroad cars occupied by blacks, as to exclude colored people from coaches occupied by or assigned to white persons. Railroad corporations of Louisiana did not make discrimination among whites in the matter of accommodation for travellers. The thing to accomplish was, under the guise of giving equal accommodation for whites and blacks, to compel the latter to keep to themselves. . . . The fundamental objection, therefore, to the statute is that it interferes with the personal freedom of citizens. . . .

The white race deems itself to be the dominant race in this country. And so it is, in prestige, in achievements, in education, in wealth and in power. So, I doubt not, it will continue to be for all time, if it remains true to its great heritage and holds fast to the principles of constitutional liberty. But in view of the Constitution, in the eye of the law, there is in this country no superior, dominant, ruling class of citizens. There is no caste here. Our Constitution is color-blind, and neither knows nor tolerates classes among citizens. In respect of civil rights, all citizens are equal before the law. The humblest is the peer of the most powerful. The law regards man as man, and takes no account of his surroundings or of his color when his civil rights as guaranteed by the supreme law of the land are involved. It is, therefore, to be regretted that this high tribunal, the final expositor of the fundamental law of the land, has reached the conclusion that it is competent for a State to regulate the enjoyment by citizens of their civil rights solely upon the basis of race.

In my opinion, the judgment this day rendered will, in time, prove to be quite as pernicious as the decision made by this tribunal in the Dred Scott case. . . . The recent amendments of the Constitution, it was supposed, had eradicated these principles from our institutions. But it seems that we have yet, in some of the States, a dominant race—a superior class of citizens, which assumes to regulate the enjoyment of civil rights, common to all citizens, upon the basis of race. The present decision, it may well be apprehended, will not only stimulate aggressions, more or less brutal and irritating, upon the admitted rights of colored citizens, but will encourage the belief that it is possible, by means of state enactments, to defeat the beneficent purposes which the people of the United States had in view when they adopted the recent amendments of the Constitution, by one of which the blacks of this country were made citizens of the United States and of the States in which they respectively reside, and whose privileges and immunities, as citizens, the States are forbidden to abridge. Sixty millions of whites are in no danger from the presence here of eight millions of blacks. The destinies of the two races, in this country, are indissolubly linked together, and the interests of both require that the common government of all shall not permit the seeds of race hate to be planted under the sanction of law. What can more certainly arouse race hate, what more certainly create and perpetuate a feeling of distrust between these races, than state enactments, which, in fact, proceed on the ground that colored citizens are so inferior and degraded that they cannot be allowed to sit in public coaches occupied by white citizens? That, as all will admit, is the real meaning of such legislation as was enacted in Louisiana.

The sure guarantee of the peace and security of each race is the clear, distinct, unconditional recognition by our governments, National and State, of every right that inheres in civil freedom, and of the equality before the law of all citizens of the United States without regard to race.

Source: *Plessy v. Ferguson*, 163 U.S. 537, 552–560 (Harlan, J., dissenting) (citations omitted).

The Press on the Plessy Decision

Homer Plessy's case caught the eye of many watching in the 1890s as the South expanded segregation. The partisan New Orleans Times-Democrat *hailed Orleans Parish District Court Judge John H. Ferguson's ruling against Plessy at trial in November 1892. Even casual observers could easily understand that Plessy's trial was not about him but about constitutional principles. The* Times-Democrat *noted the case's probable trajectory. When the U.S. Supreme Court delivered its decision on May 18, 1896, newspapers and magazine across the nation hastened to comment on what the pronounced "separate but equal" doctrine meant for America. One newspaper warned it would "spread like the measles." Publications decried it as "unfortunate," "a sad spectacle," and "a damnable outrage." Others hailed the decision as "needed" and "apparently unavoidable." Beginning with the* Times-Democrat *from November 1892 and then shifting to May 1896, the following excerpts illustrate a range of press responses to the Supreme Court's decision.*

"The Separate Car Law," New Orleans *Times-Democrat*, November 19, 1892

We are glad to see that Judge Ferguson has decided the separate car act constitutional, and thus put a quietus to the efforts of some negro agitators to disobey it and sweep it aside.

The *Times-Democrat* earnestly urged the Legislature to pass the act at the time it first came up, and congratulated the people of the State on its passage. Indeed, we should have liked even more far-reaching legislation, that would tend to separate the two races in the South thoroughly. The law, however, was a move in the right direction, framed in the interest of the traveling public and intended to show the negroes that while they lived side by side with the whites the line of distinction and separation between the races was to be forever kept up.

Some negro agitators did not like the statute, and ever since its passage have sought to excite and arouse the colored people against it. There were no complaints that they did not receive the same accommodation as the whites in the cars, but they insisted on occupying the same car and sitting side by side with them.

Quite a campaign against the law was begun, and the political clubs and negro societies raised subscriptions to attack it in the court. A large sum was collected in this way, and every negro who desired to gain a little notoriety was anxious to rush forward and offer himself as a victim, to try and force his way into the white car, to be expelled from there: and on that basis attack the law in the courts. . . .

Judge Ferguson has added his decision to those already given on this point, and presents some additional strong reasons in favor of the law. It is to be hoped that what he says will have some effect on the silly negroes who are trying to fight this law. The sooner they drop their so-called "crusade" against "the Jim Crow Car," and stop wasting their money in combatting so well-established a principle—the right to separate the races in cars and elsewhere—the better for them.

What the *Times-Democrat* would like to see, and what it hopes to see, is the extension of this principle of keeping the races apart, and the Legislature at its next session could make a good beginning by passing the law pigeon-holed this year—prohibiting intermarriage between the races.

"The Unfortunate Law of the Land," *New York Daily Tribune*, May 19, 1896

The Supreme Court of the United States has decided that the Louisiana law requiring separate cars for white and colored passengers on the railroads of that State is not in contravention of the Federal Constitution, and this ruling must be accepted as the law of the land. There will, however, be widespread sympathy with the strong dissenting opinion of Justice [John Marshall] Harlan, who says there is no more reason for separate cars for whites and negroes than for Catholics and Protestants. It is unfortunate, to say the least, that our highest court has declared itself in opposition to the effort to expunge race lines in State legislation.

"Equality, But Not Socialism," New Orleans *Daily Picayune*, May 19, 1896

The Louisiana Law which requires that the railways operating trains within the limits of the State shall furnish separate but equal facilities for white and negro passengers was passed upon by the Supreme Court of the United States, and was yesterday declared to be constitutional. . . .

As there are similar laws in all the States which abut on Louisiana, and, indeed, in most of the Southern States, this regulation for the separation of the races will operate continuously on all lines of Southern railway. Equality of rights does not mean community of rights. The laws must recognize and uphold this distinction; otherwise, if all rights were common as well as equal, there would be practically no such thing as private property, private life, or social distinctions, but all would belong to everybody who might choose to use it.

This would be absolute socialism, in which the individual would be extinguished in the vast mass of human beings, a condition repugnant to every principle of enlightened democracy.

"A Strange Decision," Rochester (New York) *Democrat and Chronicle*, May 20, 1896

The supreme court of the United States has decided that the law of Louisiana requiring the railroads of that state to provide separate cars for white and colored passengers is constitutional. The majority of the court seems to have reasoned by analogy, assuming that if the laws of congress requiring separate schools for the two races is constitutional, therefore the laws requiring separate cars likewise comes under the protection of the fundamental national law.

Justice Harlan's vigorous dissent denouncing these laws as mischievous comes very much nearer the sentiment of the American people upon that question than the decision of the majority does. Justice Harlan says the entire truth that it would be just as reasonable for the states to pass laws requiring separate cars for Protestants and Catholics or for descendants of those of the Teutonic race and those of the Latin race.

The announcement of this decision will be received by thoughtful and fair-minded people with disapproval and regret. It is not in harmony with the principles of this republic or with the spirit of our time. It is a concession to one of the lowest and meanest prejudices to which the human mind is liable, the prejudice which draws a line between citizens and discriminates against people of a specified race and color. It puts the official stamp of the highest court in the country upon the miserable doctrine that several millions of American citizens are of an inferior race and unfit to mingle with citizens of other races.

The certain consequences of this decision will be to encourage Southern legislatures in passing other laws detrimental to the interests of the colored people of those states. . . .

Discrimination by the laws of any state on account of race, color, alien birth or creed is foreign to the genius of this republic, an anachronism and an outrage on humanity. It is humiliating to learn that the supreme court of the United States which, for many years, has commanded the respect and confidence of the American people, has, for reasons which seem to have weight with the majority of that body, declared that the states have authority to separate citizens into classes. We are glad at least one voice was raised in that august tribunal in warm and earnest protest against this unjust, dangerous and mischievous doctrine.

"According to the Custom," *New York Journal*, May 20, 1896

State laws providing for separate cars for colored persons have been declared constitutional by the United States Supreme Court. The case was one which came from Louisiana on appeal against the decision of the State courts in favor of the East Louisiana Railway for compelling colored persons to ride in "Jim Crow" cars provided especially for their use. The road lies wholly within Louisiana, hence there was no question involving the Interstate Commerce law broached in the case. The court decided simply that the local road can regulate its local traffic, in the matter of separating the two races, according to the custom which prevails in the South. The judgment of the court is that the practice of separate cars is analogous to the laws of Congress and of many States in maintaining separate schools for the two races.

In justification of this law it is urged that while many colored people are less objectionable than many of the white race to first-class passengers, the majority of them are not only objectionable, but their presence in the same cars with the whites is a source of constant disorder. Hence it is simply a police regulation which any State has a perfect right to sanction. Of course, this decision does not interfere with the colored passengers' rights to demand safe and comfortable accommodations, nor prevent them from suing for damages in the event of injury of person or loss of property.

Colored persons are entitled to all the common rights which pertain to any other persons, but they frequently exaggerate a denial of special privileges, not necessary to them, though hurtful to others, into rights. They are getting their rights; soon they will have their own privileges. They ought to deserve both, then there will be no need to appeal to the courts. In this State colored persons have the same rights in public conveyances, halls and hotels that others have, but they find it produces less friction and promotes their welfare not to use them offensively.

"Settled," Providence (Rhode Island) *Journal*, May 20, 1896

The constitutionality of the Louisiana law for separate railroad carriages for whites and blacks has been settled. The Supreme Court of the United States declares that the principle on which the law is based is one which the State Legislatures may adopt at any time, since Congress itself has already passed such discriminative legislation in other forms. One may understand from that, inferentially, that there is no equal rights legislation to force whites to grant equality of social usage to the colored. Everybody, of course, knows that such is the fact, and yet in spite of the absence from the statute books of laws of that character, people do not cease sending inquiries to the Supreme Court regarding the constitutionality of State laws like this lately passed by the Louisiana Legislature.

As was to be expected, Justice Harlan dissented from the view of his colleagues. He took the ground that it was as improper for a State to compel the colored people to separate from the white in cars as it would be for a law to be executed requiring separate coaches for Protestants and Roman Catholics. It must be admitted that that is a suggestive argument. Think of having trains on our railroads made up of some coaches for the members of the A.P.A. [the anti-Catholic American Protective Association] and others for the religious body which they profess to fear and would like to persecute!

"Like the Measles," Springfield (Massachusetts) *Republican*, May 20, 1896

The South ought to be happy now that the United States supreme court has affirmed the constitutionality of the Louisiana law providing separate coaches for negro passengers on the railroads. The law may now be expected to spread like the measles in those commonwealths where white supremacy is thought to be in peril. Did the southerners ever pause to indict the Almighty for allowing negroes to be born on the same earth with white men? We fear it was the one great mistake in creation not to provide every race and every class with its own earth.

"Hardly Expected," Richmond (Virginia) *Dispatch*, May 21, 1896

The Supreme Court of the United States has affirmed the constitutionality of the Louisiana statute providing separate coaches for white and colored passengers on the railroads in that State. This decision was hardly expected. It is none the less a law of the land. We quote an exchange as follows [from the Duluth (Minnesota) *News Tribune* of May 22, 1896]:

> The necessity for such a law exists only in the South, and the statute would never have been enacted but for conditions which made the separation of the races in railroad travel apparently unavoidable, in order to secure the comfort of all concerned. The railroads are required to supply colored passengers with accommodations substantially equal to those with which the whites are furnished, and there is thus no unfair discrimination. The matter of separate coaches has been agitated for several years in the Southern States, and it has been feared that a law to this effect would not stand the test of the courts. Now that the Supreme Court has declared the Louisiana statute constitutional, it is probable that the Legislature of other Southern states will enact similar laws.

Some colored people make themselves so disagreeable on the cars that their conduct leads white men to ponder the question whether such a law as that of Louisiana is not needed in all the Southern States.

"A Damnable Outrage," Parsons (Kansas) *Weekly Blade*, May 30, 1896

The Democratic majority of the Supreme Court of the United States has wantonly disgraced . . . the highest tribunal of this the land that has

proclaimed it the world over that "all men are created equal" by declaring
... the "Jim Crow" car laws of the South to [be] constitutional. When such
an august body stoops so low, then it is time to put an end to the existence
of infernal, infamous bodies. If such an act as the Louisiana "Jim Crow" car
law can be declared constitutional then it is time to make null and void all
that tail end of the constitution; for it is certain that under such circumstances it is of no earthly use. Justice Harlan was the only one on that
bench with grit enough in him to utter a protest against this damnable outrage upon a race that for more than 275 years labored the yoke of bondage,
but in 30 years of partial freedom has reached the very gate of the nation's
most noble.

"Plausible Sophistry," *[African Methodist Episcopal] A.M.E. Church Review (Nashville, Tennessee)*, XIII (1896), 156–162

Briefly stated, the Court virtually takes the position [in its *Plessy* deci-
sion] that any law not involving the rights of the Negro to sit upon juries
and to vote, is constitutional, on the ground that conflicts will arise, if the
prejudices of large numbers of the white race are thwarted.

Justice Harlan takes the ground that the intent and purpose of the
constitution was to wipe out all official knowledge of race among citizens,
by both State and nation, and that greater evils are in store by validating
laws made in hate than can result from standing upon the broad grounds
of right and humanity.

Which is the right position? Let the great American people answer as it
answered once before when plausible sophistry had well-nigh obscured
the plain teachings of Him who inspired the saying, "God is no respecter
of persons;" "Of one blood hath God created all the nations of the earth;"
for in Christ Jesus there is neither Jew nor Greek, bond nor free, Scythian
nor Barbarian.

"A Sad Spectacle," *Donahoe's Magazine* (Boston, Massachusetts), XXXVI (1896), 100–101

It is more than thirty years since Appomattox; time enough assuredly for
race prejudice against the negro to have died from the heart of the white
man under influence of the Constitutional Amendments in his favor. Yet
here is the United States Supreme Court lending its weight and sanction
to-day to what must necessarily tend to prolong and solidify in the republic
the olden antipathy of the white man against his colored brother. The
declared constitutionality of the Louisiana law requiring railroads to provide separate cars for white and colored passengers is a decision from
which the intelligence and heart of the country revolt, and though it
may make such distinctions lawful according to statute, can never render

them just or consonant with the spirit of American liberty, with its equal rights to all.

Events are shaping themselves strangely in this free land of late. With legislation against the negro backed up by the highest tribunal in the country (just as if the Dred Scott decision had not passed into lasting infamy, and as if there had been no Civil War); with Congress passing restrictive immigration laws directed perceptibly and unfairly against special European nationalities with religious prejudices organized into a conspiracy against the expressed pledges of the Constitution to American citizens, the United States presents to the world a sad spectacle of inconsistency and contradiction—a spectacle which reflects most significantly upon our boasted human freedom and brotherhood. Selfishness—individual, class, sectional and racial selfishness—is the great curse and danger of the American republic to-day.

The Real End of Plessy's "Separate but Equal" Doctrine (1967)

Popular notice usually incorrectly cites the 1954 U.S. Supreme Court's Brown v. Board of Education *decision as finally overturning* Plessy v. Ferguson's *1896 "separate but equal" doctrine. In fact, it was the Court's 1967 decision in* Loving v. Virginia *that fully denounced the so-called equal application doctrine and declared that state-imposed racial segregation violated "the equal protection of the laws" the U.S. Constitution guaranteed. That case took on hoary taboos against interracial sex and marriage. The holding declared state anti-miscegenation laws unconstitutional as "invidious racial discriminations."*

[W]e reject the notion that the mere "equal application" of a statute containing racial classifications is enough to remove the classifications from the Fourteenth Amendment's proscription of all invidious racial discriminations. . . .

There can be no question but that Virginia's miscegenation statutes rest solely upon distinctions drawn according to race. The statutes proscribe generally accepted conduct if engaged in by members of different races. Over the years, this Court has consistently repudiated "distinctions between citizens solely because of their ancestry" as being "odious to a free people whose institutions are founded upon the doctrine of equality." At the very least, the Equal Protection Clause demands that racial classifications, especially suspect in criminal statutes, be subjected to the "most rigid scrutiny," and, if they are ever to be upheld, they must be shown to be necessary to the accomplishment of some permissible state objective, independent of the racial discrimination which it was the object of the Fourteenth Amendment to eliminate. . . .

There is patently no legitimate overriding purpose independent of invidious racial discrimination which justifies this classification. The fact that Virginia prohibits only interracial marriages involving white persons demonstrates that the racial classifications must stand on their own justification, as measures designed to maintain White Supremacy. We have consistently denied the constitutionality of measures which restrict the rights of citizens on account of race. There can be no doubt that restricting the freedom to marry solely because of racial classifications violates the central meaning of the Equal Protection Clause.

Source: *Loving v. Virginia*, 388 U.S. 1, 7–9 (1967) (citations omitted).

Glossary

Abolition The ending of slavery, particularly American Negro slavery. The movement for abolition, called *abolitionism*, distinguished itself from antislavery by demanding an immediate end to slavery. Its adherents were called abolitionists.

Affidavit A legal affirmation or sworn statement.

Amalgamation An early term used in the United States to describe interbreeding of persons considered to be of different races or ethnicities, creating so-called mixed offspring. The term *miscegenation* displaced the older term after the 1860s.

Ancien Régime A phrase in French referring specifically to France's aristocratic political and social system preceding the French Revolution of the 1790s; more generally the phrase refers to an outmoded or passé state of affairs.

Antebellum A term used in U.S. history for the years 1820 to 1860 or, generally, the period before the Civil War of the 1860s.

Artisan A worker skilled with hand tools who produces or crafts objects for market.

Black Code A system of laws or pronouncements generally used in the colonial Americas to identify and designate the place of blacks or persons of African descent. Before general emancipation, it often appeared synonymous with *slave code*. More specifically in the United States, it identified laws ex-Confederate states enacted in 1865 and 1866 to suppress colored persons following U.S. abolition of slavery.

Bourbon dynasty   The European royal house that spread its rule from Navarre in northeastern Spain into Italy and over France. Expanding from the 1550s, it largely fell with the French Revolution in the 1790s.

Carpetbagger   A term of derision in U.S. history branding as exploiters and opportunists persons from the North who came South during the Civil War (1861–1865) and Reconstruction (1865–1877), particularly those who took positions or aided in Republican Party control in ex-Confederate states. The term developed later as a label for political office-seekers in a place where they had brief residence or shallow community roots.

Cede (cession)   To give, surrender, or yield territory as, for example, in the 1848 Mexican Cession to the United States.

Citizen(ship)   A person or the status of such a person recognized by law in a political community as owing allegiance and obligation and having full rights and responsibilities, especially rights of political participation such as voting and holding governmental or other public office.

Civil rights   A term that refers generally to legal claims of persons to do something or not to have something done to them by other persons or by government. When such protections constitute restraints on government, the rights often are also called civil liberties. Civil rights may be described in various categories such as cultural, economic, political, or social rights.

Code   A legal term indicating a collection of laws, regulations, or rules.

Code noir   A term for the set of regulations France's King Louis XIV issued in 1685 to govern Africans enslaved or living under French control in the Americas. Literally translated as "black code," the term came to designate any set of laws governing blacks, whether in slavery or not.

Colorline   A term for a dividing line between whites and nonwhites, or between lighter people and darker people, or between Europeans and non-Europeans. The U.S. abolitionist and civil rights advocate Frederick Douglass introduced the term in an 1881 essay. The twentieth-century intellectual W. E. B. Du Bois popularized the term in his writings, such as his 1903 book *The Souls of Black Folk*.

Commerce Clause A part of the U.S. Constitution—article I, section 8, paragraph 3—providing the U.S. Congress with exclusive power "to regulate commerce with foreign nations, and among the several states, and with the Indian tribes."

Common carrier A person, company, or vehicle engaged in public transport of cargo or passengers.

Concubine A woman in a marriage-like relationship with a man she cannot marry for whatever reason of custom or law.

Conveyance An instrument for transferring something, such as title to land or other property or persons or goods, from one person or place to another.

Copperhead A term dating from the U.S. Civil War era for persons in the North, particularly members of the Democratic Party, who opposed the war or sympathized with the South. In derision, the term likened such persons to the North American poisonous snake named copperhead, noted for striking often unseen because of its effective camouflage. So-called Peace Democrats turned the term into an image of Liberty from the copper pennies of the day, which they adopted as badges.

Coterminous Having the same boundaries or scope or ending in same place.

Creole Defined strictly, any person of non-American ancestry, as an African or European, who was born in the Americas. In early Louisiana, the term applied particularly to persons of French heritage and culture. In this work, it applies to persons of mixed African and European ancestry, also referred to as Creoles of color or Afro-Creoles.

Damages A legal term for an award paid to compensate for injury or loss.

Deep South A term used to indicate in the United States the seven states of Alabama, Florida, Georgia, Louisiana, Mississippi, South Carolina, and Texas; also referred to as the Cotton States or Lower South.

Egalitarianism A doctrine or mode of thinking or acting on the basis that all human beings should be treated as equals.

Emancipation   A point or process of freeing or releasing from a restraint such as slavery.

Emigrant   A person who leaves from someplace to settle in another location.

Endogamy   The practice of marrying within a specified group.

Enfranchise   The act or process of enabling a person to vote or to gain the civil right to vote.

Equal application doctrine   An interpretation of the U.S. Constitution's Fourteenth Amendment Equal Protection Clause that let state laws treat races separately as long as the law's provisions applied equally to each race.

fait accompli   French for "accomplished fact," indicating something already done and unlikely to be undone.

Fire-eaters   A term used in U.S. history to identify proslavery extremists who advocated seceding from the Union; more generally the term describes ultra-militants.

Hierarchy   A graded arrangement of persons or things.

Hypodescent   A practice or system of assigning children of mixed parentage to the status of whichever parent is deemed inferior or lower in social rank.

Ideology   A system or the substance of ideas or thinking characterizing an outlook of a specified group.

Impeachment   Generally, to call into question; in U.S. law, the process of calling a public official to account for alleged misbehavior, which may lead to removal from office.

Information   In U.S. law, an official accusation of criminal conduct; it differs from an indictment, which is handed down by a grand jury; an information may be filed by a single competent official or other person.

Interstate   Crossing the border from one state into one or more other states.

Intrastate   Wholly confined within one state, not crossing its border.

Isleños   Spanish meaning "islanders"; in Louisiana history, the term refers specifically to emigrants from the Canary Islands off Africa's northwest coast but loosely refers to emigrants from other islands.

Libres   Spanish for freedpersons or ex-slaves.

Maroons   Runaways from slavery who established their own communities and settlements.

Ménagères   A term used in early Louisiana to identify free women of color classified officially as housekeepers but who were, in fact, the concubines of white householders.

Métis   A French term for a person deemed of mixed race.

Miscegenation   The intimate mixing of persons of different races, as in cohabitation or marriage.

Morenos   A Spanish word for mulattoes.

Mulatto   Specifically, a child of one parent of African descent and one parent of European descent; more generally, any person of mixed African and European ancestry.

Mustee   Specifically, a person with one-eighth African ancestry; an octoroon; the child of a white person and a quadroon; generally, any person of mixed race; sometimes also a person of American Indian and African ancestry.

Octoroon   A person with one-eighth African ancestry, such as Homer Plessy.

Pardos   A Spanish term for mulattoes or mixed race persons of light brown complexion.

Partus sequitur ventrum   A Latin phrase describing the legal doctrine that whoever owned the mother owned the offspring; applied in slavery so that the child born of a slave mother became a slave of the person who held the mother as a slave.

Petit bourgeois, petit bourgeoisie   French terms for the little or lower middle class and persons in that class, often described as shopkeepers.

Pillory   A posted wooden framework with holes for hands and head, in which a person would be placed for public display as punishment for crime.

Plaintiff in error   The person who appeals a decision with a writ of error.

Poll tax   A head tax paid as a prerequisite or requirement to vote.

Postbellum   After the war; in U.S. history, designating the years after the Civil War ended in 1865.

Proprietor   An owner of property; a person who owns and operates a business.

Provost court   A military court operating in occupied territory with jurisdiction over civilians as well as military personnel.

Public law   Law treating relations between government and persons and between elements of the government, as opposed to private law treating relations between and among persons.

Quadroon   A person with one-fourth African ancestry.

Quasi-war   Generally, an undeclared war with limited reach; specifically in U.S. history, the battles mostly at sea between United States and France from 1798 to 1800.

Reconstruction   In U.S. history, the dozen years following the end of the Civil War in 1865, including the process of attempting to reshape the politics and society of the ex-Confederate states.

Redeemers In U.S. history, conservative whites in the ex-Confederate states who sought to reestablish their control of local and state government in the aftermath of the Civil War.

Redemption In U.S. history, the movement or process in the ex-Confederate states to reestablish conservative white control of local and state government; also a movement to subjugate former slaves.

Right In law, a claim, immunity, power, or privilege guaranteed to a person.

Right of deposit In U.S. history, a phrase indicating the right of U.S. residents to store goods for export in New Orleans when it was under French or Spanish control.

Scalawag In U.S. history, a term of derision for Southern-born whites who collaborated with Union Reconstruction of the ex-Confederate states following the Civil War, especially those who worked with or joined the Republican Party.

Segregation In U.S. history, indicates the separation of whites and nonwhites by law (de jure) or by custom and practice (de facto) in some or all areas of public contact.

South, the In U.S. history, refers specifically to the 11 states—Alabama, Arkansas, Florida, Georgia, Louisiana, Mississippi, North Carolina, South Carolina, Tennessee, Texas, and Virginia—that announced their secession from the Union and waged civil war against it from 1861 to 1865; more generally, the 15 states (the 11 listed previously, plus Delaware, Kentucky, Maryland, and Missouri) and the District of Columbia that in 1861 maintained slavery by law.

State action doctrine The theory in U.S. law limiting the application of Fourteenth Amendment restrictions to official state actors or actions, excluding the acts of private persons.

Status The rank or standing of a person in relation to others in his or her society.

Statute   An act of a legislature to permit, prohibit, or provide something by law.

Trespass   In law, an intrusion or interference with a person or with the property of another.

Vigilante   A person or group of persons who appoint themselves to enforce their vision of order without any legal authority.

Will   A document or testament indicating how a person's property should be distributed or used after the person's death.

Writ   In law, a written order a court issues to command one or more persons to do or not do a specified act or acts.

Writ of certiorari   An order from a superior court directing an inferior court to deliver its record of a specified matter for review.

Writ of prohibition   An order from a superior court directing a lower court not to exercise jurisdiction in a specified matter.

Bibliography

Augstein, Hannah Franziska. *Race: The Origins of an Idea, 1760–1850*. Bristol, UK: Thoemmes Press, 1996.

Berlin, Ira. *Slaves without Masters: The Free Negro in the Antebellum South*. New York: Pantheon Books, 1975.

Blassingame, John W. *Black New Orleans, 1860–1880*. Chicago: University of Chicago Press, 1973.

Brasseaux, Carl A., ed. *A Refuge for All Ages: Immigration in Louisiana History*. Lafayette, LA: Center for Louisiana Studies, University of Southwestern Louisiana, 1996.

Brasseaux, Carl A., and Glenn R. Conrad, eds. *The Road to Louisiana: The Saint-Domingue Refugees, 1792–1809*. Lafayette, LA: Center for Louisiana Studies, University of Southwestern Louisiana, 1992.

Clinton, Catherine, and Michele Gillespie, eds. *The Devil's Lane: Sex and Race in the Early South*. New York: Oxford University Press, 1997.

Conniff, Michael L., and Thomas J. Davis. *Africans in the Americas: A History of the Black Diaspora*. New York: St. Martin's Press, 1994.

Davis, Thomas J. "More than Segregation, Racial Identity: The Neglected Question in *Plessy v. Ferguson*." *Washington and Lee Race and Ethnic Ancestry Law Journal* 10, no. 1 (Spring 2004): 1–41.

Davis, Thomas J. "Race, Identity, and the Law: *Plessy v. Ferguson*." In *Race on Trial: Law and Justice in American History*, edited by Annette Gordon-Reed, 61–76. New York: Oxford University Press, 2002.

Davis, Thomas J. *Race Relations in America*. Westport CT: Greenwood Press, 2006.

DeConde, Alexander. *The Quasi-War: The Politics and Diplomacy of the Undeclared War with France 1797–1801*. New York: Scribner, 1966.

Desdunes, Rodolphe Lucien. *Nos Hommes et Notre Historie: Our People and Our History: A Tribute to the Creole People of Color*. Trans. and edited by Sister Dorothea Olga McCants. Baton Rouge: Louisiana State University Press, 1973.

Din, Gilbert C. *Spaniards, Planters, and Slaves: The Spanish Regulation of Slavery in Louisiana, 1763–1803*. College Station: Texas A&M University Press, 1999.

Dollar, Susan E. *"Black, White, or Indifferent": Race, Identity, and Americanization in Creole Louisiana*. Fayetteville, AR: University of Arkansas, 2004.

Dominguez, Virginia. *White by Definition: Social Classification in Creole Louisiana*. New Brunswick, NJ: Rutgers University Press, 1986.

Dormon, James H. *Creoles of Color of the Gulf South*. Knoxville, TN: University of Tennessee Press, 1986.

Du Bois, W. E. B. *Black Reconstruction in America, 1860–1880*. New York: Russell & Russell, 1935.

Elliott, Mark. *Color-Blind Justice: Albion Tourgée and the Quest for Racial Equality*. New York: Oxford University Press, 2006.

Fireside, Harvey. *Separate and Unequal: Homer Plessy and the Supreme Court Decision That Legalized Racism*. New York: Carroll & Graf, 2004.

Fischer, Roger A. *The Segregation Struggle in Louisiana, 1862–77*. Urbana, IL: University of Illinois Press, 1974.

Foner, Eric. *Reconstruction: America's Unfinished Revolution, 1863–1877*. New York: Harper & Row, 1988.

Gaspar, David Barry, and David Patrick Geggus. *A Turbulent Time: The French Revolution and the Greater Caribbean*. Bloomington, IN: Indiana University Press, 1997.

Geggus, David Patrick. *The Impact of the Haitian Revolution in the Atlantic World*. Columbia, SC: University of South Carolina, 2001.

Hall, Gwendolyn Midlo. *Africans in Colonial Louisiana: The Development of Afro-Creole Culture in the Eighteenth Century*. Baton Rouge: Louisiana State University Press, 1992.

Hanger, Kimberly S. *Bounded Lives, Bounded Places: Free Black Society in Colonial New Orleans, 1769–1803*. Durham, NC: Duke University Press, 1997.

Hirsch, Arnold R., and Joseph Logsdon. *Creole New Orleans: Race and Americanization*. Baton Rouge: Louisiana State University Press, 1992.

Horsman, Reginald. *Race and Manifest Destiny: The Origins of American Racial Anglo-Saxonism*. Cambridge, MA: Harvard University Press, 1981.

Houzeau, Jean-Charles. *My Passage at the New Orleans Tribune: A Memoir of the Civil War Era*. Edited by David C. Rankin. Baton Rouge: Louisiana State University Press, 1984.

James, C. L. R. *The Black Jacobins: Toussaint Louverture and the San Domingo Revolution*. New York: Dial Press, 1938.

Johnson, Kevin R. *Mixed Race America and the Law: A Reader*. New York: New York University Press, 2003.

Kein, Sybil. *Creole: The History and Legacy of Louisiana's Free People of Color.* Baton Rouge: Louisiana State University Press, 2000.

Kelley, Blair Murphy. *Right to Ride: Streetcar Boycotts and African American Citizenship in the Era of Plessy v. Ferguson.* Chapel Hill, NC: University of North Carolina Press, 2010.

Klarman, Michael J. *From Jim Crow to Civil Rights: The Supreme Court and the Struggle for Racial Equality.* Oxford, UK: Oxford University Press, 2004.

Lachance, Paul F. "The 1809 Immigration of Saint-Domingue Refugees to New Orleans: Reception, Integration and Impact." *Louisiana History* 29, no. 2 (1988): 109–141.

Lachance, Paul F. "The Formation of a Three-Caste Society: Evidence from Wills in Antebellum New Orleans." *Social Science History* 18, no. 2 (1994): 211–242.

Landers, Jane, ed. *Against the Odds: Free Blacks in the Slave Societies of the Americas.* London: Frank Cass, 1996.

Lemann, Nicholas. *Redemption: The Last Battle of the Civil War.* New York: Farrar, Straus and Giroux, 2006.

Lofgren, Charles A. *The Plessy Case: A Legal-Historical Interpretation.* New York: Oxford University Press, 1987.

Lonn, Ella. *Reconstruction in Louisiana after 1868.* New York: G. P. Putnam's Sons, 1918.

Macdonald, Robert R., John R. Kemp, and Edward F. Haas. *Louisiana's Black Heritage.* New Orleans: Louisiana State Museum, 1979.

Mack, Kenneth W. "Law, Society, Identity, and the Making of the Jim Crow South: Travel and Segregation on Tennessee Railroads, 1875–1905." *Law & Social Inquiry* 24, no. 2 (Spring 1999): 377–409.

McConnell, Roland C. *Negro Troops of Antebellum Louisiana: A History of the Battalion of Free Men of Color.* Baton Rouge: Louisiana State University Press, 1968.

Medley, Keith Weldon. *We as Freemen: Plessy v. Ferguson.* Gretna, LA: Pelican, 2003.

Nieman, Donald G., ed. *Black Freedom/White Violence, 1865–1900.* New York: Garland, 1994.

Nieman, Donald G., ed. *Black Southerners and the Law, 1865–1900.* New York: Garland, 1994.

Olsen, Otto H. *The Thin Disguise: Turning Point in Negro History:* Plessy v. Ferguson: *A Documentary Presentation, 1864–1896.* New York: Humanities Press, 1967.

Painter, Nell Irvin. *Creating Black Americans: African-American History and Its Meanings, 1619 to the Present.* New York: Oxford University Press, 2006.

Painter, Nell Irvin. *The History of White People.* New York: W. W. Norton, 2010.

Pascoe, Peggy. *What Comes Naturally: Miscegenation Law and the Making of Race in America.* New York: Oxford University Press, 2009.

Rankin, David C. *The Forgotten People: Free People of Color in New Orleans, 1850–1870.* Baltimore: Johns Hopkins University, 1976.

Schafer, Judith K. " 'Open and Notorious Concubinage': The Emancipation of Slave Mistresses by Will and the Supreme Court in Antebellum Louisiana." *Louisiana History* 28, no. 2 (1987): 165–182.

Schweninger, Loren B. *Black Property Owners in the South, 1790–1915.* Urbana, IL: University of Illinois Press, 1990.

Scott, Rebecca J. *Degrees of Freedom: Louisiana and Cuba after Slavery.* Cambridge, MA: Belknap Press of Harvard University Press, 2005.

Smith, John David, ed. *Anti-abolition Tracts and Anti-black Stereotypes.* New York: Garland, 1993.

Sterkx, H. E. *The Free Negro in Ante-bellum Louisiana.* Rutherford, NJ: Fairleigh Dickinson University Press, 1972.

Taylor, Joe Gray. *Negro Slavery in Louisiana.* Baton Rouge: Louisiana Historical Association, 1963.

Thomas, Brook. *Plessy v. Ferguson: A Brief History with Documents.* Boston: Bedford Books, 1997.

Thompson, Shirley Elizabeth. *Exiles at Home: The Struggle to Become American in Creole New Orleans.* Cambridge, MA: Harvard University Press, 2009.

Vandal, Gilles. *The New Orleans Riot of 1866: Anatomy of a Tragedy.* Lafayette, LA: Center for Louisiana Studies, University of Southwestern Louisiana, 1983.

Vincent, Charles. *Black Legislators in Louisiana during Reconstruction.* Baton Rouge: Louisiana State University Press, 1976.

Vorenberg, Michael. *Final Freedom: The Civil War, the Abolition of Slavery, and the Thirteenth Amendment.* New York: Cambridge University Press, 2001.

Welke, Barbara Young. *All the Women Are White; All the Blacks Are Men, or Are They: Law and Segregation on Common Carriers, 1855 to 1914.* Chicago: American Bar Foundation, 1992.

Wheeler, Roxann. *The Complexion of Race: Categories of Difference in Eighteenth-Century British Culture.* Philadelphia: University of Pennsylvania Press, 2000.

Wood, Forrest G. *Black Scare: The Racist Response to Emancipation and Reconstruction.* Berkeley: University of California Press, 1968.

Zack, Naomi. *Race and Mixed Race.* Philadelphia: Temple University Press, 1993.

Index

About the Author

THOMAS J. DAVIS, PhD, JD, is a historian and lawyer who teaches U.S. constitutional and legal history at Arizona State University, Tempe. He is the author of *Race Relations in the United States, 1940s–1960* (Greenwood, 2008); *Race Relations in America* (Greenwood, 2006); *Africans in the Americas: A History of the Black Diaspora* (with Michael J. Conniff); and *A Rumor of Revolt: The Great Negro Plot in Colonial New York* (1990), among other works.